CIVILIANS
AT THE
SHARP END

CIVILIANS AT THE SHARP END

First Canadian Army Civil Affairs in Northwest Europe

DAVID A. BORYS

McGill-Queen's University Press
Montreal & Kingston • London • Chicago

© McGill-Queen's University Press 2021

ISBN 978-0-2280-0547-6 (cloth)
ISBN 978-0-2280-0649-7 (paper)
ISBN 978-0-2280-0650-3 (ePDF)
ISBN 978-0-2280-0651-0 (ePUB)

Legal deposit first quarter 2021
Bibliothèque nationale du Québec
Reprinted in 2021

Printed in Canada on acid-free paper that is 100% ancient forest free (100% post-consumer recycled), processed chlorine free

Every effort has been made to contact copyright holders and obtain their permission to reproduce material. The author welcomes any further information so that this material may be credited appropriately in reprints or future editions.

This book has been published with the help of grants from Langara College and the University of British Columbia.

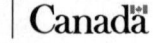

We acknowledge the support of the Canada Council for the Arts.

Nous remercions le Conseil des arts du Canada de son soutien.

Library and Archives Canada Cataloguing in Publication

Title: Civilians at the sharp end : First Canadian Army Civil Affairs in northwest Europe / David A. Borys.
Names: Borys, David A., 1981- author.
Description: Includes bibliographical references and index.
Identifiers: Canadiana (print) 20200353845 | Canadiana (ebook) 20200354108 | ISBN 9780228005476 (cloth) | ISBN 9780228006497 (paper) | ISBN 9780228006503 (ePDF) | ISBN 9780228006510 (ePUB)
Subjects: LCSH: Canada. Canadian Army. Army, First. Civil Affairs. | LCSH: World War, 1939-1945—Regimental histories—Canada. | LCSH: World War, 1939-1945—Civilian relief—Europe, Western.
Classification: LCC D809.C2 B67 2021 | DDC 940.53/145—dc23

This book was designed and typeset by studio oneonone in Minion 11/14

This book is dedicated to William Ponomarenko, who served in the Canadian Corps and fought at Passchendaele; Ernie Little, RCAF; and Eileen Little, WAAF. As well, to my Uncle Duane who, like me, was always interested in Canada's military history.

Contents

Acknowledgments ix

Abbreviations xi

Figures follow page xi

Introduction 3

1 The AMGOT Model 13

2 A Battlefield Classroom – Civil Affairs in Northern France 44

3 Death from Above in Belgium 103

4 To Free or Feed the Netherlands 143

5 From Civil Affairs to Military Government 183

Conclusion 204

Notes 211

Bibliography 239

Index 245

Acknowledgments

This book could not have been completed without the help of a battalion's worth of people. To all those who gave in to my pestering and eventually read and commented on my work: Sean Kennedy, Marc Milner, David Charters, Chris Hyland, Terry Copp, Tim Cook, Michel Ducharme, Mike Bechthold, Julien Vernet and especially to Robert Engen who went above and beyond the call of duty to provide invaluable feedback on one of my many drafts. Thank you to the lovely and talented Rachel Smalls. Thank you to Edward Flint, for giving me full and unfettered access to his dissertation as well as incredibly helpful direction while also buying me a beer and talking me through the nucleus of what became this book. That conversation set me on the path to the manuscript that sits here today. To one of my favourite historians in the west, Christine "Lep-Force" Leppard, thank you for your unending confidence. To my esteemed colleague Russ Benneweiss, may you rest in peace. Thank you Kyla Madden and the McGill-Queen's publishing team for your patience and support. A big thank you to the anonymous reviewers who were brutally and at times crushingly honest, you helped make this book stronger.

As always, it is my family's unconditional love and support that allow me to achieve anything. For that, and for them, I am eternally grateful to Miriam, Gene, Jonathan, Alexandra, Cori, Kelly, and Carl (RIP), and to the new additions Kelsey and little Eileen.

Familia mea, meum fundamentum –
My family, my foundation

Abbreviations

ACC	Allied Control Commission
AFHQ	Allied Forces Headquarters
AMG	Allied Military Government
AMGOT	Allied Military Government Occupied Territories
CA	Civil Affairs
CAID	Civil Affairs inland depot
CAO	Civil Affairs Officers
CATS	Civil Affairs Training Schools
CFLN	Comité Français de Libération Nationale
DCA	Directorate Civil Affairs
FFI	French Forces of the Interior
GPRF	Gouvernement Provisoire de la République Francaise
MBF	Militärbefehlshaber in Frankreich
MG	Military Government
OKW	Oberkommando der Wehrmacht
PLB	Passieve Lucht-Bescherming
SAC	Supreme Allied Commander
SCAEF	Supreme Commander Allied Expeditionary Force
SHAEF	Supreme Headquarters Allied Expeditionary Force
SOMG	School of Military Government

Figure 1 *Top* Canadian engineers at work in the rubble of Caen, August 1944. Source: Mikan no. 3192330, LAC.

Figure 2 *Bottom* The aftermath of the V-2 rocket attack on the Rex Cinema, 16 December 1944.

Figure 3 A Canadian soldier oversees the unloading of a convoy truck by Dutch civilians during Operation Faust, May 1945. Source: Mikan no. 3204053, LAC.

Figure 4 Canadian hygiene team delousing Russian POWs, April 1945. Source: Mikan no. 3229492, LAC.

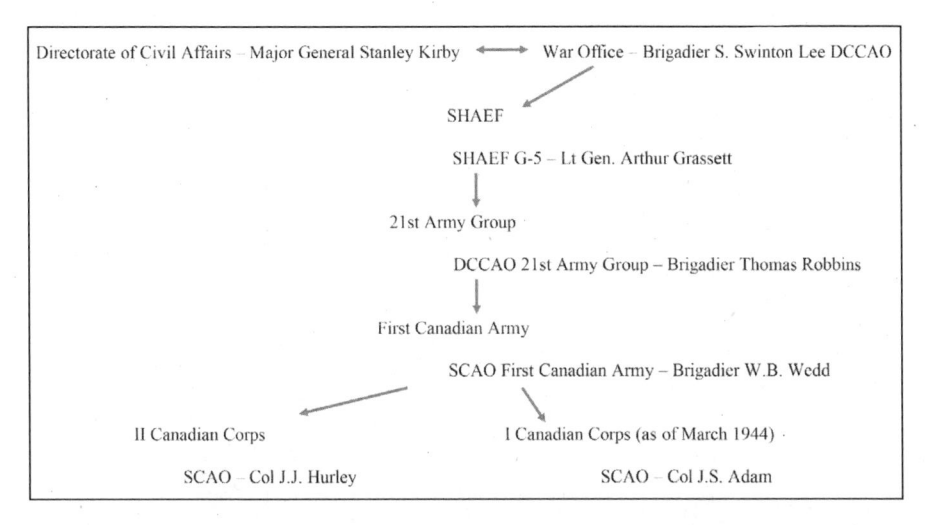

```
Directorate of Civil Affairs – Major General Stanley Kirby  ⟷  War Office – Brigadier S. Swinton Lee DCCAO
                                        SHAEF
                                        SHAEF G-5 – Lt Gen. Arthur Grassett
                                                │
                                        21st Army Group
                                        DCCAO 21st Army Group – Brigadier Thomas Robbins
                                                │
                                        First Canadian Army
                                        SCAO First Canadian Army – Brigadier W.B. Wedd

        II Canadian Corps                       I Canadian Corps (as of March 1944)
        SCAO – Col J.J. Hurley                  SCAO – Col J.S. Adam
```

Figure 5 Civil Affairs command structure

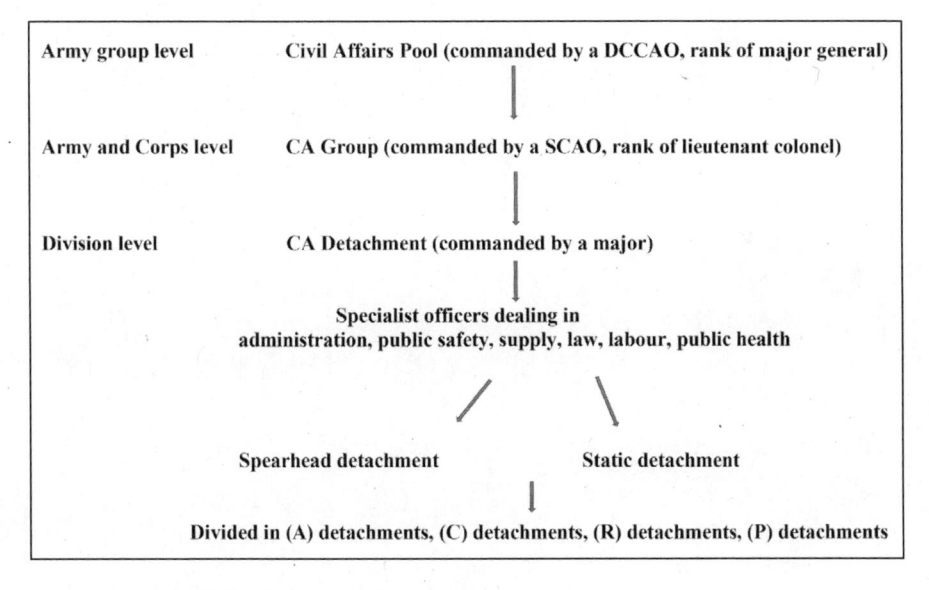

Army group level	Civil Affairs Pool (commanded by a DCCAO, rank of major general)
	│
Army and Corps level	CA Group (commanded by a SCAO, rank of lieutenant colonel)
	│
Division level	CA Detachment (commanded by a major)
	│
	Specialist officers dealing in administration, public safety, supply, law, labour, public health
	╱ ╲
	Spearhead detachment Static detachment
	│
	Divided in (A) detachments, (C) detachments, (R) detachments, (P) detachments

Figure 6 Civil Affairs organizational chart

SUBJECT: First Report - MEPPEL (MR 9556 - Sheet 3303).

225/5.

To:- C   HQ, 2 Cdn Corps. (2).
    AQ, 3 Cdn Inf Div.

GENERAL.
1.   MEPPEL was visited at 0900 hrs on 15 Apr 45. The Burgemeester was asked to give immediate instructions to the Police to keep the streets clear for military traffic, and issue orders with regard to civilian movement and restriction of all forms of civilian traffic. This was done at once, and the Burgemeester was then handed a complete set of proclamations and notices, which was posted by 1030 hrs. Morale was high. About 100 collaborators had been arrested, and it was thought that there were still a few more to be brought in. There are remaining approximately 100 Germans in the town, but these people were living there before 1940, and are not considered dangerous by the local officials. They should, however, be screened by FS. It is said that certain atrocities were committed at MEPPEL, and steps are being taken to collect evidence.

ACCIDENTAL DAMAGE.
2.   The Burgemeester reported that at 1310 hrs on 28 Jan 45, a British bomber crashed and destroyed a church and 120 houses. Sixteen people were killed. The crew were saved and looked after. In spite of the heavy damage, which, it is understood, was caused by bombs being released when the plane was in difficulties, everyone realised that it was an accident, and no complaints were heard.

SITUATION IN DETAIL.
3.   In view of the urgency to restrict civilian movement in four towns along the Divisional axis during the course of the day, it was not possible to spend much time making enquiries regarding the situation at MEPPEL. The following information, however, was given by the Burgemeester and other officials, who happened to be present:-

Burgemeester.	Mr. van NOOTEN. A Protestant clergyman. Speaks English and appears to be efficient. Former Burgemeester is said to be a man of weak character. Mr. van NOOTEN was, therefore, appointed in his place by the chief of the Underground.
Population.	14,000.
Refugees.	1,000. Chiefly from ARNHEM, NIJMEGEN, VENLO, and LIMBURG.
D/Ps.	31. 30 Poles and 1 Italian.
Water.	Good drinking water. Ample from deep wells at HAVELTE, 8 kms North of MEPPEL. Water is pumped into water towers in the town.

Sheet ..../2.

Figure 7 *Above, opposite, and following page* Sample spearhead detachment report – 225 CA Detachment Report from Meppel, 15 April 1945. Source: "225 Civil Affairs Detachment Copies of Reports from Files 2 July 44/10 May 45," RG 24 Vol 10567, LAC.

Sheet......./2.

Health.	General health satisfactory, though there have been some cases of diphtheria. No epidemics. There exists a Red Cross Hospital, under Dr. DHONT. Volunteer nurses.
Fuel.	1,200 litres of German petrol, which is being controlled by the Burgemeester, and used for essential services. No coal. Peat and wood from the demolished Church and houses is being used by the population.
Damage.	Apart from the damage already mentioned and about 20 farms, which have been burnt by the Germans during the past few days, there is practically no damage at MEPPEL. (Except telephone exchange, see below).
Electricity.	Nil. Normally from ZWOLLE, though it can also be had from LEEUWARDEN.
Gas.	No supply.
Public Safety.	Chief of Police, von WIJNNEN, who has an extremely bad reputation, fled with the Germans on 13 Apr 45. He took with him two constables. Present chief - BREEDVELD. Present strength of force 22, all of them said to be reliable. Responsible to Burgemeester only. Area of responsibility - gemeente of MEPPEL. There is a Police Station and 8 cells, each capable of holding 2 persons. There are no courts in the town. Courts at ZWOLLE.
Fire Brigade.	Voluntary Fire Brigade under VAN WERVEN. There is one motor pump, and one manual. All equipment available, and Fire Brigade able to operate.
Post Office.	Building intact and officials available. Booby traps are suspected and since the departure of the Germans, no-one has entered the building. Their fear of booby traps is possible due to the fact that the Germans blew up the telephone station.
Telephones.	Exchange recently blown up. Instruments available.
Schools.	All schools have been used as barracks by the Germans, and there has been no proper education of children since Sep 44. Buildings are in very bad condition, and schools will have to be re-equipped. Amongst the schools are 7 elementary, 3 high schools, 1 secondary, 1 teachers' college, 1 technical school, and one school for cookery. There has recently been private tuition for children. The Germans tried to introduce Nazism into the schools, but parents and teachers were warned. Teachers are available.
Accomodation.	ESSO and the GERMAN Bicycle Factory. A 3-floor building said to be capable of holding 1,000 people. Condition good, though a good deal of glass has been broken. There was a very large quantity of bicycles and material for the construction of bicycles in the factory, but all has been removed by the Germans. Factory will not be able to function for a very long time.

Sheet......./3.

Sheet......./3.

German War Material and Food Stocks. A few cars in bad condition. The Burgemeester has been ordered to freeze these until they have been examined. 3 lorries. These are being used for the distribution of food, and permission has been given for this to continue until they are officially taken over or permission given for them to be retained by the gemeente.

NOTE/ It is regretted that there was insufficient time to see the Food Controller. If possible, a further visit will be made to MEPPEL to collect this information.

Major,
Comd 225 Detachment, Civil Affairs.

B/L/A/
15 Apr 45.
CED/CSS/

Figure 8 Canadian zone of Military Government in northern Germany. Source: "Canadian Participation in Civil Affairs/Military Government Part V: Germany, General Historical Survey," June 1947, CMHQ Reports: Report 176, DHH.

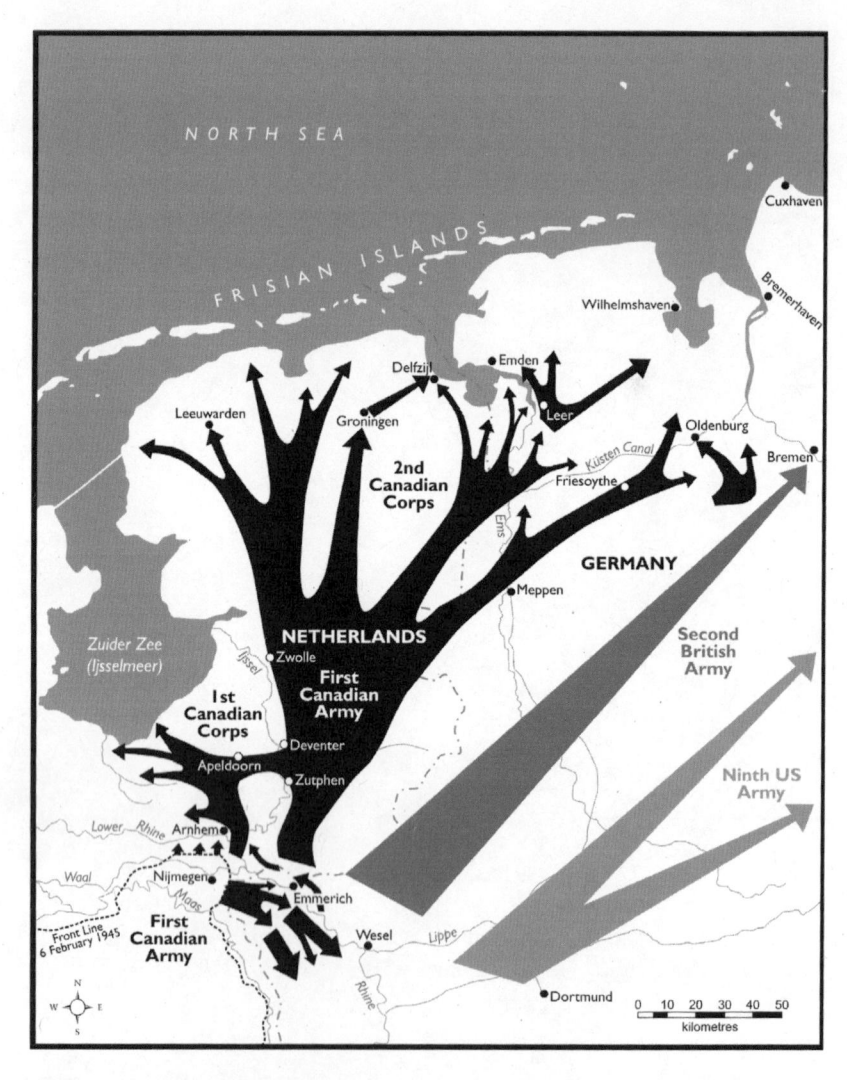

Figure 9 First Canadian Army advance into the Netherlands and Germany. Courtesy of Mike Bechthold.

CIVILIANS AT THE SHARP END

Introduction

"When elephants fight, it is the grass that suffers."
– Kikuyu Proverb

Dishevelled and lost they ambled down the road. The once proud soldiers of the French army were now beaten men in retreat, stunned by the ferocity of the German attack. They were not alone either. On both sides of them, as far as the eye could see, shuffled despondent civilians. Some were alone, others were travelling in small groups, and yet others were with entire families. They pushed carts, followed horse-drawn wagons, or carried everything they had upon their backs. The odd traveller stole a backwards glance, slight panic flittering across their face as they imagined a military horde descending upon them. Attempting to move in the opposite direction was the odd company of soldiers, hesitant looking but certainly not beaten. Several lorries honked their way through the teeming mass attempting to make room, yet nothing could fight against this wave of broken humanity. One soldier opened his door in an attempt to get a better look down the highway. "I get down from the lorry. A woman calls me over. I answer her. There are soon thirty refugees calling me, asking for advice, because I am a man, in uniform, and for hours they have found no one to ask, no official policeman, no agents, not even a local councillor ... Firefighters left with their equipment, agents with their authority and their coshes, but nowhere on the roads has there been anyone to put out fires or organize circulation at crossroads."[1] The sea of scared civilians and defeated French soldiers had flooded the highway, fleeing Hitler and his unstoppable army. There was nothing anyone could do.

In 1940, as the Nazi war machine stormed through Belgium and into France, millions of civilians clogged the road networks in an attempt to escape the German invasion. Lieutenant General Sir Henry Pownall, the chief of staff of the British Expeditionary Force, wrote of this situation in his diary, "Be it remembered also that we have behind us enormous quantities of pitiful refugees. They have encumbered our movements for many days. Now they are beginning to starve and will riot. What a situation!"[2] These waves of refugees disrupted the French and British retreat and created a complex set of problems, including homelessness, food shortages, medical emergencies, collapsed civil administrations, and disrupted economies. Allied planners feared a repetition of this chaos when they returned to the continent in 1944, and knew their soldiers would encounter multitudes of displaced civilians huddled in basements, hidden in forests, living in caves, and fleeing down roads, all trying to escape the destruction that war was to once again unleash upon their homeland.

In anticipation of their return to the continent, the British, American, and Canadian armies poised to invade Europe created a military branch to deal with the large populations of often hungry, sick, dirty, and homeless civilians. This obscure branch of the western Allied armed forces known as Civil Affairs (CA) became directly responsible for ensuring that civilians would not interfere with military operations in northwest Europe and the Allies' ultimate goal of defeating Germany and bringing peace to the continent. Furthermore, Civil Affairs would then be responsible for the military government of a conquered and occupied Germany. This book examines a series of case studies to show specifically how First Canadian Army Civil Affairs/Military Government (FCA CA/MG) dealt with civilian/noncombatant populations in key areas along First Canadian Army's liberation route. It demonstrates that while the work of Canadian CA/MG certainly sought to mitigate damage to civilian populations brought about by Canadian combat operations, its primary goal was operational in nature: to limit civilian interference in military operations and to quickly establish functioning political administrations to help support the on-going war effort. The selection of case studies in northern France, Belgium, the Netherlands, and Germany (where CA becomes MG) will not only illuminate this organization's unique position within the Canadian army but will serve to show the organization's flexible approach to increasingly challenging battlefield conditions. This is a combatant/noncombatant (CNC) relationship as yet unexplored in Canadian military history literature.

The function of Civil Affairs as described in a 1944 directive from the War Office was,

> First, to assist the military plans in the forward battle areas by liaison with the civil authorities and by controlling the activities of the local inhabitants in such a way as to prevent disorganization, disease and unrest hampering the activities of the fighting troops. Secondly, at a later state, to exercise administrative control and supervision, in such areas as may be directed by the competent authority, in order that the civil machinery may be set going as early as possible and in such a way as to benefit the Allied War Effort and to ensure the preservation of law and order.[3]

The War Office directive highlighted the overlapping jurisdictions of Civil Affairs and its better-known cousin, Military Government (MG). Military Government was primarily concerned with the occupation and governing of enemy territory. Defined by 21st Army Group as "the national territory of the Axis powers themselves."[4] Military Government controlled North Africa in 1942, Italy in 1943, and Germany in 1945. MG detachments had the same administrative tasks as most government branches normally associated with civilian rule: restoring and operating water and electrical services, transportation systems, and emergency response departments; distributing food; and even operating civil and criminal courts. Military governance often stayed in place until hostilities ceased, at which point a civilian control commission took over and prepared the country to reconstruct and reincorporate itself into the postwar world.[5]

Civil Affairs was responsible for two broad classes of territory as defined by the War Office: firstly, "territory of an allied state whose legitimate government recognized by His Majesty's Government is situated outside enemy control" and secondly, "territory lately in the military occupation of the enemy, the majority of whose population will welcome and assist the Allied operations, but which is not at present represented by an Allied government."[6] In this case Belgium and the Netherlands fall into the former category, France into the latter. "Stability, tempered by flexibility" became the guiding principle for Civil Affairs whose objective was to control the friendly noncombatant populations who found themselves liberated in these territories though temporarily occupied by the western Allies.[7] The organization was represented by field detachments connected to formations at various levels throughout the regular army chain of command. At headquarters, often at corps level and above, a small staff headed by a senior civil affairs officer (SCAO) commanded these Civil Affairs detachments. The SCAO coordinated the detachments in conjunction with military operational objectives. These CA detachments provided basic support services to civilians: food, medicine, and shelter. In addition, the CA detachments liaised with civilian officials and agencies so that the transition from enemy occupation to liberation could be carried out with minimum drain on military resources. CA liaisons were also present at the senior levels of the newly installed civilian governments. These CA officers (CAO) ensured that the administrative transition period, during which the military nominally administered daily state affairs, was limited to allow for a quick return to relative prewar normalcy and an efficient, functioning, friendly government on which the Allies could rely.

Sometimes CA would be challenged by competition for military resources. The military commanders' objective was to defeat the enemy by employing all resources at their disposal. CA had to use some of those military resources towards their own objectives, which were not necessarily congruent with those of the military commanders. This created an obvious tension. A Civil Affairs officer had to govern so as to help the combat forces, but his work was also judged by nonmilitary standards: the ability to comply with the rules of international law and, because military policy is but the instrument of national policy, by the ability to promote the nation's political interests. Whereas commanders had military and their political masters' priorities at heart, the CA officer dialogued with civilians and addressed their needs in support of those military priorities.

In July 1945, Major A.K. Reid, historical officer for First Canadian Army Civil Affairs branch, explained that "Civil Affairs or Military Government [was] that part of the Army by which a Commander-in-Chief discharges his responsibility of ensuring that the civilian population in a theatre of war does not interfere with military operations."[8] Allied armed forces in Western Europe operated, as a rule, under the assumption that although they recognized the primacy of military operations, they nonetheless understood the importance of an efficient transition to civilian government, "the C.-in-C. [commander in chief] will wish as early as possible to hand over civil administration to an indigenous government so far as compatible with military security ... [S]uch administration must, however, be subordinated to the military needs which arise during the course of the campaign."[9] Along with the prospect of liberating friendly countries, the potential threat to military operations posed by large refugee populations led planners to recognize the importance of providing basic support to the civilian populations coming under their care. The intent here was not altruistic humanitarianism. Refugees and unsettled rear areas could delay movements, restrict fields of fire and manoeuvre, and interrupt logistics. This civilian aid would therefore ensure that a friendly and helpful civilian population existed throughout the rear areas as the British, American and Canadian armies pushed towards their final objectives.

Civil Affairs has received little attention in Canadian military historiography. Within the Canadian postwar military academic community, plans were being made for an official volume on Canadian Civil Affairs, and Major A.K. Reid wrote several chapters for the Army Historical Section (later to become the Directorate of History and Heritage) in 1945. Due to significant budget cutbacks and a general lack of interest, however, this volume was abandoned. The early drafts provide a treasure trove of information in regards to the Canadian Civil Affairs story, though they are limited in their analytical depth. Official Canadian Second World War historian C.P. Stacey gives scant attention to the branch in his official history on the Canadian army in Northwest Europe.

The official histories by both the United States and Great Britain provide useful and important information in terms of Civil Affairs policy emanating from Washington, London, and the strategic planning committees. Harry L. Coles and Albert K. Weinberg's *Civil Affairs: Soldiers Become Governors* looks at the work of American CA operations from Italy to the liberation of northwest Europe (ending before the occupation of Germany and Japan), although it is limited in analysis as it approaches the narrative through the presentation of a series of primary documents pertaining to each chapter's subject matter.[10] Earl F. Ziemke, in the 2003 *The US Army Occupation of German, 1944–1946*, provides a more narrative approach to his analysis of the US army of occupation in Germany detailing the immense task facing the occupation of that country at the end of the war.[11] The most useful of the official histories for this study however is the 1961 British Official history by F.S.V. Donnison titled *Civil Affairs and Military Government in North-West Europe, 1944–1946* yet it contains few mentions of Canadian Civil Affairs.[12] Donnison's work, however, is an important foundation for any study of the Canadian organization as it provides significant analysis on the planning and execution of Civil Affairs from the perspective of the British War Office and eventually at senior command formations such as Supreme Headquarters Allied Expeditionary Force (SHAEF) and 21st Army Group. Donnison argues that while Civil Affairs endured a rough beginning with Allied Military Government in Italy, it became an essential, though continually misunderstood, component of Allied military success in northwest Europe.

Several more specific works have opened the door to a better understanding of the Canadian Civil Affairs experience. Cindy Brown and Amy Muschamp both provide unique glimpses into the workings of Allied Military Government (AMG) in Italy from 1943 to 1944. Brown focuses on the work of the AMG in Sicily and the small number of CAOs who were operating there arguing convincingly that AMG's work "made a significant contribution to the success of Operation Husky" and that AMG played a key role in the establishment of a working Sicilian government and other infrastructure essential to deliver the basic necessities of day-to-day life.[13]

Amy Muschamp's work sheds light on the complicated relationship between Italians living in the rural Molise region of mainland Italy and Canadian Civil Affairs officers working in the region. Muschamp argues that AMG policy in this rural and rather obscure region did more damage to the Italian civilians than the German occupation did, and thus provides a more nuanced examination of the complex relationship between AMG and Italian civilians.[14]

Terry Copp and Michelle Fowler have researched the reconstructive efforts of Civil Affairs in the destroyed city of Caen and the channel ports along the French coast.[15] They argued that the CA operations in northern France in 1944 were primarily focused on mitigating the urban damage caused by Allied bombing and that the Canadian CA experience specifically in Caen established a template for cooperation with French authorities that proved invaluable for future encounters with civilian populations in urban environments.[16]

Kirk Goodlet looks at the reconstruction of Zeeland province in the Netherlands during the last year of the war and argues that the decision to flood the areas of Zeeland province by the Allies was met with frustration and anger by local Dutch residents; however, the work by Canadian Civil Affairs to support and aid in the reconstruction of the region's dyke system played an integral part in mitigating this anger.[17] Goodlet further points out that the Dutch memory of liberation and reconstruction ignores the existence of Civil Affairs altogether.[18] As yet, no work has explored the Canadian Civil Affairs experience comprehensively, thus the story of Canadian Civil Affairs remained fragmented amongst these valuable yet focused studies.

Civilians at the Sharp End thus provides this comprehensive look at the Civil Affairs experience across northwest Europe. It is not intended as an all-encompassing history. Instead, it explores the most challenging obstacles faced by First Canadian Army Civil Affairs/Military Government from June 1944 until June 1945 and studies key points of contact between Canadian soldiers/officials and civilians in Belgium, France, the Netherlands, and Germany. Its primary argument is that Civil Affairs was essential in supporting military operations by dealing firsthand with the civilian populations encountered by First Canadian Army. Though the chapters are organized in a geo-chronological manner it is recognized that some chronological overlap occurs. For instance, CA operations in the Netherlands begin while CA operations in Belgium were finishing up and end fifteen days after Military Government in Germany was finished. Nonetheless, this structure better frames how Civil Affairs played a critical role in linking the Allied military machine and civilian populations during this intense period while addressing a number of complex issues surrounding relief and rehabilitation in these newly entered regions.

First Canadian Army Civil Affairs (FCA CA) was a highly adaptive organization. It faced and overcame a variety of challenging obstacles in the newly liberated areas of France, Belgium, and the Netherlands as well as the occupied region of northwest Germany. In each place it helped to restore effective civil life ultimately resulting in invaluable support to military operations in each country. After the hardships of war, the organization needed to provide civilian populations with food and medicine, to control and provide for thousands of refugees and displaced persons,[19] and to cooperate with, support, and at times govern newly established civilian administrations; all of this intended to ultimately support continuing military operations. While the general objectives of the organization remained relatively consistent, specific objectives changed and evolved with each new country encountered. Within each case study – France, Belgium, the Netherlands, and Germany – are embedded comparisons of CA/MG's objectives, tasks, and methodologies. The exploration of this tenuous balance between military operational demands with supporting civilian populations provide markers for the reader, allowing a greater comprehension of CA successes and an understanding of areas where CA fell short.

Because the history of Canadian Civil Affairs is closely linked to the history of British Civil Affairs, chapter 1 examines CA development within a British Commonwealth context. It begins with a brief summary of CA development in western military thought and ties it into the British Army's early use of CA in the Boer War and the First World War. The chapter explores the development of AMGOT in Italy during the Second World War, the AMGOT model's failures and successes, and the organization's influence on CA in northwest Europe. The chapter concludes with a detailed study of CA's organizational structure within the Allied military hierarchy.

Chapter 2 begins by analysing Canadian CA operations in northern France and focuses on how CA officers were able to cope with large-scale refugee movements during the battles for Caen, Falaise, and the capture of the channel ports. Organizational and doctrinal flaws were evident in these first major CA operations in the region and in many ways this period provided a crash course in Civil Affairs policies and practices. As a result of the obstacles, CA made changes, adjusted its doctrine, and learned valuable lessons.

Civil Affairs officers developed skills in France that would prove invaluable as the front moved north. Belgium, the focus of chapter 3, required a far more intensive and extensive role by CA to ensure that FCA military operations could continue and that Belgium could join in the fight against Nazi Germany as quickly as possible. Thus, the country's restoration to normalcy became an important element of the Allied military campaign through northwest Europe. While day-to-day CA tasks focused on controlling refugee movement and dealing with a rampant black market as well as uncooperative resistance groups, it also had to counter the threat of German V-weapons through an effective civil defence organization in the important port city of Antwerp all the while struggling with an ineffective Belgian civilian administration.

Chapter 4 focuses on CA officers' work combating the starvation crisis in the Netherlands during the "Hunger Winter" of 1944–45. The apogee of CA's relief effort occurred in the Netherlands. Officers tackled many of the same problems they had encountered in France and Belgium but on a much larger scale. The chapter examines some of the underlying tension between CA officers and the Dutch authorities and highlights the administrative weaknesses of the Netherlands Military Administration (NMA). Although CA's overriding objective was to limit the drain on military resources, CA resources were required for much longer and in a far greater capacity in the Netherlands than in any other place.

The final chapter finishes up in northwest Germany where Canadian Civil Affairs became Canadian Military Government. Though a much shorter period of operational responsibility than anywhere else in FCA's march across Europe, this region of occupied Germany posed similar challenges for the organization. Feeding tens of thousands of civilians and recently freed prisoners of war, caring for and controlling the movement of displaced persons, and maintaining law and order become essential in this region. These objectives were crucial building blocks in the reestablishment of a nascent German administration under the authority of the Allied occupation. When the Canadians handed over the region to the British, these building blocks were firmly in place.

The story of Canadian Civil Affairs/Military Government is a messy interaction between soldiers and civilians. Often initial projections had Civil Affairs playing a limited role as each country was expected to quickly establish its own independent war footing. In France this occurred relatively according to plan; in Belgium and the Netherlands it did not. CAOs had to quickly adapt to fulfil their responsibilities in these challenging environments. By the time First Canadian Army entered Germany its CAOs (now Military Government Officers or MGOs) were fully prepared for the requirements of widespread administrative responsibility. In all these cases, FCA CA/MG ensured that the demands of these countries and their populations did not significantly hamper or interfere with Allied military operations: a key contribution to victory in northwest Europe.

CHAPTER ONE

The AMGOT Model

"Mourning is in every household, desolation written in broad characters across the whole face of their country, cities in ashes and fields laid waste, their commerce gone, their system of labor annihilated and destroyed. Ruin and poverty and distress everywhere, and now pestilence adding to the very cap sheaf of their stack of misery."
– General William Tecumseh Sherman

The doctrine governing Canadian Civil Affairs was steeped in the British doctrine for dealing with civilian populations. Historically speaking this took the form of a military government administering occupied or captured territories and the civilian populations within. It is important to understand the historical development of this model within the British military in order to fully understand the organizational and operational context of Anglo-Canadian Civil Affairs during the Second World War. Early experiences from the South African War of 1899–1902 and the First World War established an administrative precedent for military government of occupied territory, but the size and scope of operations during the Second World War would ultimately force the British and her allies to evolve and adapt existing doctrine into a model that could cope with the demands of dense urban areas, larger civilian populations, and a constantly shifting front line. From East Africa to the Mediterranean, this evolution would finally manifest itself on the Italian mainland as Allied Military Government of Occupied Territories (AMGOT), becoming a controversial but important predecessor organization to Civil Affairs.

SOUTH AFRICA

Modern British military experience in dealing with noncombatants can be traced back to the Second Anglo-Boer War of 1899–1902. Franklin Donnison, official historian of British Civil Affairs in the Second World War, corroborates this when he writes, "The South African War is near enough in time to allow us our first detailed view of military government by British forces."[1]

Both the Orange Free State and the Transvaal were independent republics before the start of the war in 1899. British forces occupied these territories after a series of small military skirmishes and established military administrations. The British appointed Major General George T. Pretyman as military governor of the Orange Free State and appointed Major General John Maxwell as military governor of the Transvaal. As Donnison writes, "In the matter of military government, South Africa offers an example of the straight forward occupation and administration of enemy territory."[2] These governors and their staff were all military officers with no experience in military government; their department heads and local magistrates were often civilians. Sir Alfred Milner, the high commissioner in Cape Town, lent civilian officials to these military administrators to act as advisors until the military governance period had passed. In 1902, the British annexed the Boer territories to South Africa, and Milner became responsible for them.

During the military governance period, civilian officials and military officers clashed over jurisdiction and debated who should govern what aspects of the occupied territories; they questioned whether or not the essential responsibility of these territories should stem from a civilian or military authority.[3] This issue was never formally solved and would pose continued challenges to the issue of military government during the next conflict.

THE FIRST WORLD WAR

On the eve of the First World War most of the major powers of Europe recognized, at least on paper, the neutrality of peaceful civilian populations.[4] Civilians, generally speaking, were not to be targets of the belligerents. But the actions of the belligerents did not often match the professed belief in civilian neutrality. The British, for instance, had already broken this neutrality in the form of placing Boer civilians in concentration camps in South Africa. The 1907 Hague Conventions addressed the position of civilians during wartime in so far as they established broad guidelines by which they should be protected or at least civilian casualties limited by the belligerents in combat zones.[5] Even the 1914 British *Manual of Military Law* reflected the belief that as much as possible civilians should remain outside the scope of combat: "It is a universally recognized rule of International Law that hostilities are restricted to the armed forces of the belligerents and that ordinary citizens ... must be treated leniently."[6] Yet civilians were certainly targeted, either intentionally or not, even during the course of the First World War.

Mesopotamia

Mesopotamia offers an example of the growing complexity of military government. In October 1914 a British expedition sailed from Bombay to Mesopotamia to attack Turkish possessions in the Middle East. The India Office appointed Sir Percy Cox, head of the Foreign Department of the Government of India, to accompany this military expedition, an appointment quite common to other military operations conducted by the Indian government. Upon completing the expedition, he established an administration loyal to and governed by the British viceroy and the India Office. The expedition also protected the Anglo-Persian Oil Company while it installed wells and it confirmed that the various sheiks and Arab tribes in the Persian Gulf area were loyal to Britain.[7] The expedition captured Basra and soon after took various towns and villages along the Tigris River in its march towards Baghdad. Sir Percy Cox thus began the military governance of what is today central Iraq.

In February 1916, the War Office assumed command of all operations conducted by British Forces abroad. Cox was transferred from the Foreign Department of the Government of India to the India Office of Asquith's government in London. His title was also changed from chief political officer to civil commissioner. As Donnison writes, "The administration of Mesopotamia was thereafter conducted by civilians under the authority of the India Office under general military supervision."[8] Despite this change, the distinction between civilian and military administration was still quite unclear. Lt General Stanley Maude, commander of the military expedition, was technically responsible for the entire region, while Sir Percy Cox maintained a vague administrative control over the same region. He administered the territory as a civilian governor in all but name but at the same time was bound by Maude's operational goals.

German East Africa

During the campaign in German East Africa in 1916, the British military experienced another example of complicated military government. This time the acting commander in chief, General Jan Smuts of South Africa, appointed political officers to administer the British occupied territory of German East Africa. Once the British ceased active military operations in January 1917, Smuts appointed Horace Archer Byatt as chief administrator of all British occupied territories. Similar to Sir Percy Cox, Byatt was under the authority of the commander in chief but was directly responsible to the secretary of state for the colonies on all matters relating to civil administration. Once again, the civilian governor had to administer occupied territory while reporting to the acting military commander and to a separate governmental administrative branch in London.

Palestine and the OETA

This vague delineation of jurisdiction was not repeated in the volatile sands of Palestine where the administration of occupied territories had "none of the dual responsibility to both civil and military authorities."[9] In fact, it was here that the embryo for Civil Affairs was created.[10] The War Office appointed General Sir Gilbert Clayton to act as chief political advisor to General Allenby, military commander of the British force in the Middle East. Although Clayton was well versed in the issues affecting the Middle East, he was there in an advisory capacity with Allenby making all final decisions on territorial governance. It was made clear from the outset that Allenby was in charge of not only the military affairs in the region but also for the administration of the occupied territory, even though Clayton was appointed to assist Allenby in this. By October 1917 Clayton's efforts resulted in him being granted sole responsibility for Palestine's military administration. In this role Clayton created the first formal British military organization to deal directly with civilian administrative matters: the Occupied Enemy Territory Administration (OETA) was Clayton's brainchild and the ancestor to Civil Affairs. This organization's ranks included a number of officers who were previously civilians in the British Colonial Service. These men were tasked with administering the civilian population and coordinating relations between the occupying British and the local civilians. The success of this organization led to a further promotion for Clayton who was succeeded by General Sir A.W. Money in April 1918. Money continued running the OETA until the end of the war.

Germany and the Rhineland

The British occupation of the Rhineland after the First World War highlights the administrative evolution of military governance that was occurring within the British military during this period. While OETA was the ancestor, the occupation of the Rhineland is the earliest administrative model with some resemblance to the organizational structure that would become Civil Affairs. In 1918 the War Office appointed Lt General Sir Charles Fergusson as military governor for the British zone of occupation from Germany's western borders to the banks of the Rhine River. Fergusson's role as head of the military government was very similar to positions held by future Civil Affairs/Military Government commanding officers. As Frank Donnison writes, "He [Fergusson] was, in fact, senior staff officer for military government at Army Headquarters and would in the Second World War have been designated Chief Civil Affairs Officer or Director of Military Government."[11]

At Fergusson's headquarters, a small staff managed such matters as civil government, policy, personnel, circulation and war material, economics, labour, and imports and exports. None of the men appointed to head these specific sections were selected because of their specialized knowledge in these areas; "[Fergusson's] staff [appeared] to have been soldiers first and administrators afterwards."[12] During their occupation of Germany, the British implemented military government, and military administrators imposed pseudomartial law upon civilian populations while coping with administrative tasks that would have been better suited to civilian specialists, a trend that would be reversed in the next war.

The Interwar Period

After the conflict, the major powers did not attempt to further clarify military conduct towards civilian populations. Certainly the 1929 Geneva Convention was an attempt at codifying military conduct, but this convention ostensibly clarified and expanded previous conventions, focusing heavily on the rules and guidelines in regards to the conduct towards and treatment of prisoners of war. Nonetheless, the 1929 Geneva Convention and the 1907 Hague Convention created the most extensive codification of the conduct of warfare to that point in time. The rules did not address the responsibilities of armies towards friendly civilians nor did they provide any sort of legal template for the obligations of an Allied army towards a liberated population.

The international lack of interest in clarifying the relationship between soldiers and civilians was also reflected within the British military. The 1929 British *Manual of Military Law*, the document that would most inform soldier–civilian relations during the Second World War, dealt primarily with the constitutional and legal mechanics of occupation; for instance, distinguishing between unlawful assembly, riot, and insurrection.[13] Because Canada's military doctrine was so intrinsically tied to the British model, the 1929 *Manual* became the standard legal document for Canadian forces during the Second World War.[14] This manual was inadequate in addressing the issue of large civilian populations in a warzone. One can hardly blame the British for this absence of doctrine; no codification of the relationship between the military and civilian populations had been set through any international conventions. Because of the manual's vagueness, British military officials used local and short-term policy solutions, which became the accepted British model in Italy: ad-hoc responses to ad-hoc situations.

THE SECOND WORLD WAR

The first test for military governance of occupied territory in a Second World War context came in East Africa amidst the territories formerly ruled by Mussolini as part of his defunct Italian empire. By 1941 this empire was crumbling and the British had captured the Italian territories of Eritrea, Italian Somaliland, and Cyrenaica, and once again established military administrations.

Subsequently, the British liberated Abyssinia, an independent nation until it was conquered by Italy in 1936. The British elected to eliminate the term "enemy" in their acronym OETA, the Abyssinians not being considered an enemy people. The name was thus shortened to OTA (Occupied Territory Administration). Following the recapture of British Somaliland, the British renamed the organization as the British Military Administration (BMA), the acronym OTA bearing too much similarity to OETA.

During these early campaigns in East Africa, British administrators dealt with indigenous populations, reestablished a functioning democratic civil administration, and coordinated basic relief and aid. These operations provided a template that would be built upon in later Civil Affairs operations in Europe.[15]

With the knowledge that an invasion and liberation of Europe was necessary to win the war, the British War Office continued debating what to do with civilians and how best to govern them. The nations of Europe, occupied by the brutal Nazi regime, were predicted to be unable to govern themselves or sustain their own civilian populations once liberated. They had spent years being systematically exploited by the Nazis, administratively reorganized, and drained of resources. The War Office debates thus focused largely on questions of relief, field security, public order, and a legal framework for military commanders. The War Office had little to say about responsibilities towards civilian populations, and during these early discussions, direction was left to those at the military and political level on the ground.[16]

This British model was simply not yet sufficient to cope with the unique challenges and complexities of liberating large civilian populations in 1943, 1944, and 1945. Allied planners had to develop a coherent doctrine for the relationship between the military and civilians in both liberated and occupied territories, something that became a significant challenge. The experience of Allied Military Government in Italy highlighted this incredible challenge.[17]

ITALY AND AMGOT

Italy's political situation was precarious upon the eve of the Allied invasion. Since his appointment as prime minister in 1922, Benito Mussolini and his National Fascist Party had been moving Italy towards a one-party dictatorship. By the late 1920s this had been achieved and "Il Duce" and his fascists ruled at every administrative level throughout the country. In 1936 Mussolini and Hitler agreed to the Rome–Berlin Axis, effectively aligning the two powers. Mussolini believed this alliance offered the best chance of reestablishing Italian control over the Mediterranean and expanding his Italian empire. This alliance was formally cemented in May 1939 when both countries signed the infamous "Pact of Steel." Like Germany, Italy appeared poised to usher in a new era where Europe was dominated by the cooperation of these two totalitarian states. The war changed all that, of course. By 1943 Mussolini's hold on the country was falling apart. A variety of resistance groups had formed to challenge the fascist hold on the nation, morale was low amongst Italian soldiers and sailors after several years of defeats at the hands of the Allied powers, and Mussolini was even facing opposition within his own fascist party. On 25 July 1943, just over two weeks after the successful Allied invasion of Sicily, Mussolini was removed from power by senior members within his own fascist party, arrested, and imprisoned. With the backing of the Italian king, Victor Emanuelle III, Marshal Pietro Badoglio replaced Mussolini and immediately began negotiations for Italy's surrender to the Allies. When this finally occurred on 3 September 1943 Hitler rushed German troops into the country and effectively established a German occupation of the northern half of mainland Italy. Just over a week later Waffen-SS commandos freed Mussolini from prison and he was placed back in power at the head of a new Nazi puppet state, the Italian Social Republic. By 1945 as the Allies moved progressively northwards liberating more and more of the Italian mainland the puppet state was in near collapse. Mussolini attempted to flee Italy for Switzerland but was caught on 25 April by communist partisans. He would be executed a few days later, only two days before Hitler committed suicide.[18]

It was back in January of 1943 that President Franklin D. Roosevelt met Prime Minister Winston Churchill in Casablanca to discuss war plans in the Mediterranean. At that time the Germans and Italians were holding ground in Tunisia while being advanced upon from both the west and east by British First and Eighth Army respectively. By March the combined weight of both British armies began to break the German and Italian defences. In mid-April the British Eighth Army overcame the Axis defensive positions along the Mareth Line. At this point Axis troops began to withdraw from North Africa into Sicily. On 13 May the remaining Axis troops in Tunisia surrendered to the Allies and the battle for North Africa came to an end. All eyes were now on Italy.

Preparing AMGOT

Even though the war in North Africa was far from over when Roosevelt and Churchill had met at the Casablanca Conference they nonetheless began to make plans for a return to Europe via Sicily and the Italian mainland. As part of this invasion it was agreed that a joint Anglo-American Civil Affairs effort would support the invasion, an effort staffed primarily by American and British officers (though a small number of officers from various Commonwealth countries would also participate including thirty-nine Canadian officers).[19] It marked the first joint Allied CA effort of the entire war. Most of the American CA officers had been trained at the American Civil Affairs school in Charlottesville, North Carolina while a few of them had gained practical experience in running American Civil Affairs in North Africa.[20] The British contribution was an extension of the British Military Administration, most officers having gained experience in Africa and trained at the British Civil Affairs school at Southlands House, Wimbledon (which before the war had been a Methodist college for training women teachers).[21] A short two-week training course was subsequently given to both British and American AMGOT officers in North Africa in late June and early July 1943 as final preparation for the invasion of Sicily. At the same time this new Anglo-American CA organization was given the title of Allied Military Government of Occupied Territory to reflect the growing, multinational character of the organization.

The ultimate objective of AMGOT in Italy was to "administer the Allied Military Government under the Military Governor of the territory in accordance with rules and usage of international law."[22] In this case the military governor referred to General Harold Alexander, commander of 15th Army Group. The primary AMGOT directives supporting this objective were thus:

A. To relieve combat troops of the necessity of providing civil administration.
B. To restore law and order among the civilian population while procuring for them the necessary food supplies and where necessary providing relief and maintenance for destitutes within available army resources [destitutes refers to both "homeless civilians" and "refugees," often the two categories are used interchangeably to describe civilians encountered by AMGOT].
C. To assist in making available to the occupying forces the economic resources of the occupied territory.
D. To promote the political and military objectives of the Allied forces in connection with future operations through efficient government of the territory and the application of the policies toward the civil population laid down by the Commander-in-Chief.[23]

AMGOT included a number of key military officials who would later play a significant role in Allied Civil Affairs in northwest Europe. The chief civil affairs officer for Italy, essentially the man in charge of AMGOT, was British Major General Francis Rodd, Lord Rennell. In this capacity he oversaw CA operations while advising General Harold Alexander and his successor General Mark Clark, commanders in chief of 15th Army Group and ultimately the combined Allied military forces in Italy. In the spirit of cooperation that characterized AMGOT, his deputy was American Brigadier General Frank J. McSherry. Advising Supreme Allied Commander (SAC) General Dwight D. Eisenhower at Allied Forces Headquarters (AFHQ) was American Colonel (later Brigadier General) Julius C. Holmes on behalf of the Military Government Section. This section later became the G-5 division of Supreme Headquarters Allied Expeditionary Force (SHAEF). G-5 would be responsible for all of Civil Affairs within the western Allied forces. It was first headed by British Major General Lumley, but in April 1944 he was replaced by Lt General Alexander Edward Grasett from Toronto. The *Hamilton Spectator* was quick to celebrate a Canadian becoming responsible for Allied Civil Affairs in its 11 May 1944 piece titled "Toronto Man in Leading Role" exclaiming,

> A hand-picked force of several thousand British, Dominion and American experts in civil administration was ready to-night to accompany the Allied invasion spearheads to the European continent to aid in the immediate restoration of normal civilian life in the liberated territories. For many months these experts have been trained at a secret school under the newly-established civil affairs branch of supreme headquarters. It can now be revealed that the section of supreme headquarters was organized under Lieut.-Gen. F. Grassett [sic] of Toronto, as assistant chief of staff directly responsible to Gen. Dwight S. [sic] Eisenhower.[24]

The Allies encountered many challenges when developing AMGOT policy prior to the invasion. One of the first was finding an effective way to educate most soldiers on what exactly AMGOT was supposed to be doing and how AMGOT was supposed to be working within the structure of the larger invasion force. In preparing for the invasion, AMGOT issued several pamphlets and handbooks designed to inform the regular soldier on the functions of AMGOT and its relationship to the rest of the military.[25] A *Pamphlet for Troops* was issued to all officers from the company level upwards detailing AMGOT's role and purpose, how its organization was structured, and how it was to work with other units. It identified the broad objectives for AMGOT while also outlining expectations for cooperation between AMGOT and combat units. A series of pamphlets were also issued to AMGOT officers to provide them with broad operational guidance: the *AMGOT Bible* and *Dos and Don'ts in Italy*. These included missives on how to interact with local females and which municipal officials to trust, along with brief historical sketches of specific regions.[26]

This literature was part of a broader initiative in predeployment preparation. Part of this preparation included a six-week training course attended by several hundred British and American CA officers at the town of Chréa in Algiers. The course covered a variety of topics and was mainly lecture based, including Lord Rennell as one of the lecturers. Overall, the training was thought to be of limited value to the men. It seemed that historical lessons from past military government operations were of little to no help when the men were faced with real-time challenges in Italy.[27]

There was also significant disagreement over administrative policy between the British and the Americans. The Americans favoured a direct approach in the form of traditional military government. Used by the Americans in the Civil War, 1861–65, and later in the Philippines, 1898–1902, this approach involved directly controlling the territory with military-appointed governors and very little cooperation with local civilian administrators. The Americans' experience in North Africa from 1942–43 further cemented their belief in this approach. Military officials witnessed numerous civilian agencies chaotically struggling for control over the region's administration.[28] The director of one of the many reconstruction agencies involved in North Africa noted to President Roosevelt, "this ... disunity and competition among American agencies [played] into the hands of the enemy and [confused their] allies."[29] The Americans were convinced that civilian agencies and a civilian administration were far too inefficient for territorial administration and therefore preferred a more direct, militarized, and centralized approach.[30]

The British favoured a more indirect approach. Drawing from their experience in administering numerous foreign territories throughout their empire and beyond, they wanted to blend military administration with cooperative civilian officials. They also recognized that a direct approach would require more trained soldiers to work in administration putting further strain on manpower, manpower the British were focused on conserving for the big push into northwest Europe. Eventually the decision fell to General Alexander, commander of 15th Army Group, who decided to employ the indirect approach, albeit on a region-by-region basis.[31]

Alexander's decision came only weeks before the Allies launched their invasion of Sicily. The plan called for US 7th Army under General George S. Patton to land on the southern beaches of the island between Cape Scaramia and Licata, seizing a crucial port and a number of important airfields. US 7th Army would also be protecting the left flank of British Eighth Army, commanded by General Bernard Montgomery, who would be landing at the same time between Syracuse and Pozzalo. Eighth Army, of which 1st Canadian Division and 1st Canadian Tank Brigade were a part, would seize the important airfield of Pachino and begin moving northwards towards the Catania plain, one of the few regions of open flat terrain on the island suitable for the use of armoured vehicles. Once these initial objectives had been seized, essentially seeing the Allies entrenched in the southeastern corner of Sicily, the two armies would then fan out and complete the conquest of the island.[32]

Late on the night of 9 July 1943 the Allies launched Operation Husky, the largest amphibious assault the world had ever seen. A small number of AMGOT officers landed on the morning of 10 July with the first waves of assaulting troops, included one Canadian, Captain (later Major) Alexander S. O'Hara. By 19 July 150 AMGOT personnel were in Sicily, of which six were Canadian.[33] From July into early August the Allies fought a series of hard-pitched battles across the island while significant numbers of Axis troops escaped across the straits of Messina onto the Italian mainland. The remaining Axis troops stationed on Sicily finally surrendered to the Allies on the 17th of August. The Allies then crossed from the island to the Italian mainland in early September 1943 and on 8 September the Italian government formally surrendered. After the armistice with Italy AMGOT's name was shortened to Allied Military Government (AMG) to reflect an emerging political alliance with the new Italian government (Italy would officially join the war on the side of the Allies on 13 October) and to allay some fears amongst Italian leaders of direct Allied control of the country (for consistency I will refer to the organization as AMG from here on out).[34] As the Allies continued the push northwards, more and more territory was incorporated into the military government administration and the organization continued to grow in size. At its peak AMG in Italy would boast 829 American officers with 1,060 enlisted men and 895 British officers and 1,031 other ranks (including thirty-six Canadian officers and a small number of other Commonwealth soldiers).[35]

Administrative Problems

Administrative issues plagued AMG almost from the very start and General Alexander's decision to approach AMG policy on a region-to-region basis was certainly to blame. The most obvious consequence of this policy was a lack of centralized decision making. AMG officers tended to implement AMG policies locally without thought for how it might work in a larger system or in other regions. As well, short-term solutions were often applied to specific regional issues, usually at the cost of more effective long-term nationwide policies. The Allies never viewed Italy holistically but as a series of operational phases with subsequent British or American military governments. Italy's rapidly changing status from an enemy belligerent to a neutral nation to an ally, coupled with the general view at Allied Forces Headquarters that regionalism better suited Italy, further reinforced this regionally based policy.[36] Unfortunately, AMG's parochial approach hurt its overall effectiveness.

Further hampering effectiveness was the absence of any efficient means of communication and a shortage of transport, which created serious obstacles to any attempt to centralize policy between the various AMG control zones.[37] Due to the lack of telegraph or telephone lines, officers frequently travelled long distances to communicate with their counterparts in other regions, and they were often frustrated by the lack of available transport needed for these laborious attempts at communication. During the first months of invasion, "officers with the assault formations were only provided with a nominal scale of transport ... [AMG] officers therefore had to depend in the initial stages on locally requisitioned vehicles, and the use of combat units' M.T. [Motor Transport]."[38] As British official historian and AMG veteran Charles Harris argued, the lack of communication and transportation resulted in an "involuntary decentralization which did not always entail the advantages claimed for this type of organization ... In fact for a long time each province remained ... a law unto itself."[39]

General Alexander's preference for a regional approach to AMG doctrine also meant a lack of consistency in terms of AMG cooperation with qualified civilian officials. Various commanders of AMG districts preferred to work with military officials and without any overriding direction from Alexander to cooperate with civilians continued to do so. Upon entering Italian territory, most military commanders removed any civilians who were deemed to have ties to the previous fascist government. This policy was often applied quite recklessly and created a serious disruption in civilian administration. Crucially, Italy's status as an enemy belligerent until September 1943 meant officials based this removal policy on the concept of military government of an enemy state, not civil management of a liberated ally. As well, the military recruited any and all well-organized community groups to fill the administrative gap left by the removal of fascist officials. Interestingly, the Catholic Church, labour groups (including organizations with strong communist leadership), and members of organized criminal gangs masquerading as legitimate administrative options filled many of the local positions.[40] The military relied on these groups for local knowledge. Often local leaders exploited this relationship and guided provincial policies to achieve their political, social, or economic objectives. Policies were rarely in line with national or even provincial directives. Attempts to indirectly administer the various regions increased policy discrepancies that became serious issues later in the campaign. This meant far more direct involvement for AMG officers than initially anticipated and whether undermined by Allied policies or circumstances of their own making, the ability of the Italians to govern themselves could not be achieved except without substantial Allied support.[41]

During the liberation of the Italian mainland, AMG had considerable difficulty cooperating with combat units, thus hurting their ability to gain any long-term large-scale successes. This largely stems from the general failure of combat commanders to understand AMG's scope and their own responsibilities for assisting the organization.[42] Military commanders failed to recognize organizational issues primarily because AMG operations tended to be conducted separately from military operations; in essence, AMG was a pseudoseparate branch with a separate chain of command. The major administrative problem lay in the lack of communication between CAOs at the corps and divisional level. The SCAO (senior Civil Affairs officer) of one corps or division in Italy rarely had contact with his equal in another formation. The Allies had unintentionally built AMG into a secondary and almost independent command structure, one parallel to the army yet relatively isolated from its hierarchy and decision making. This was further amplified after combat ended and the two organizations, AMG and the army, had almost nothing to do with each other. Therefore, many combat officers saw AMG as acting independent of military command and ignored it. Officials designed AMG to limit the burden of civil administration on operational commanders and instead it severed the links between military formations and AMG officials, and formations lost interest in civilian matters and with it any sense of obligation to help.[43]

While cooperation with combat units and commanders was difficult, the actual execution by AMG personnel of their operational duties could be effectively carried out. Both during and after combat, AMG controlled civilian movement, administered medical aid, supplied food, engineered sanitation lines, established local administration and police forces, and rehabilitated infrastructure. At the front lines of AMG operations were mobile detachments led by a Civil Affairs officer attached to corps and division headquarters and backed by a small team, including one or two specialist officers and several ORs (other ranks). These men would be the first to assess the situation at the front and deal with any immediately pressing problems. As Rennell describes, "The officers in the mobile parties are specialized, mainly experienced young officers good at improvisation, and they need to be good at that."[44] Generally they would find a town that lay in ruins, debris filled streets, dead bodies of soldiers and civilians lying exposed to the Italian sun. The local government would have fled or been removed. The inhabitants would be scattered into the countryside or huddled in basements, makeshift air raid shelters or caves.[45] Electricity, clean running water, and food supplies would be scarce or nonexistent. The first officer into this mess would report on these conditions to a provincial SCAO stationed at army headquarters. This SCAO, in turn, reported to AMG officials at army group headquarters. Once the initial reports were received from the front line a larger more permanent CA team would be sent from army HQ to deal with longer-term issues and provide a more permanent CA presence. These more permanent teams generally focused on cities and towns within their respective regions, as more CA problems arose in urban areas than rural. By the winter of 1943 US Fifth Army had seventy-one AMG officers and British Eighth Army had seventy-four operating within this system.[46]

That winter, AMG's organizational struggles became more difficult when, in November 1943, the Allies established the Allied Control Commission (ACC) for Italy. The creation of the ACC came as a result of a conference between representatives of Great Britain, the United States, and the Soviet Union in Moscow the month before. It was in Moscow that all three powers formally agreed that fascism in Italy had to be destroyed and a democratic government established.[47] By this point the Allies were facing the German Winter Line, a series of defensive positions running across the peninsula anchored in the west on the mountains above the town of Cassino and in the east on the town of Ortona. A large swathe of Italian territory to the south of the battle zone, the so-called "King's Italy," was out of range of AMG and now being run by an interim Italian government under Marshal Pietro Badoglio. The ACC had five key objectives: to organize military government operations; to give practical help to civilians to prevent disease and unrest; to prepare the governmental administration and economy in such a way that it could be returned to civilian control as quickly as possible; to supervise and execute the terms of Italy's surrender; and to be the liaison between the Allies and the new Italian government.[48] The ACC was designed to support the Badoglio government's transition back to full Italian sovereignty in line with the Moscow Conference's broad objectives while also ensuring that the new Italian government and its people operated in a capacity that supported the Allied war effort (the Badoglio government declared war on Germany in October of 1943).[49]

The ACC was a complex organization. It was essentially a separate organization, independent from 15th Army Group's chain of command, staffed by both civilians (generally diplomats) and soldiers. Its first commanding officer was Major General Kenyon A. Joyce and then American Rear Admiral Ellery W. Stone. The headquarters for this organization was located in Taranto and was answerable directly to General Eisenhower. This situation meant that when a dispute arose between any formation within 15th Army Group and the ACC, General Eisenhower himself would have to be involved as the supreme commander was the only point in the broader military chain of command where the two organizations finally met. This organizational flaw would seriously tarnish ACC's reputation amongst 15th Army Group's commanding officers.

The plan was for AMG to be merged into the ACC's chain of command while also operating within 15th Army Group's chain of command, straddling the two organizations so to speak. The ACC had similar objectives to AMG though designed to operate in the rear areas that were no longer within the army or AMG's jurisdiction: essentially territory that was no longer close to the battlefront or had very little strategic importance to military operations. ACC objectives were widespread but they also included AMG's objectives. This meant ensuring that rear areas facilitated the movement of supplies and troops to the battlefront, supporting combat troops when needed, providing any immediate practicable help to the civilian population, preparing the governmental administration and the economy to be turned over to the civilian control as quickly as possible, and supervising the execution of the armistice surrender terms.[50] These operational objectives were designed to facilitate the country's long-term rehabilitation. The ACC was divided into five independent subcommissions (Navy, Army, Air Force, Communications, War Materials Disposal) along with a number of sections: Regional Control and Military Government (with subsections covering refugees, displaced persons, and general government), Economic (with subsections covering finance, works and utilities, food and agriculture, labour, industry and commerce), Administrative (public education, legal, interior/local government, monuments and fine arts and property control), and a short-lived Political section (which transformed from a commission to an advisory council to the Badoglio government).

Through these subcommissions and sections, ACC headquarters continually stayed in contact with the new Italian government and, in fact, shared a de facto position within that government.[51]

There was very little clarification regarding operational boundaries and within a month of the ACC being established Civil Affairs in Italy descended into a messy patchwork of jurisdictions. At the front were areas generally under AMG control, working in accordance with US Fifth or British Eighth Army HQ. Rear areas, otherwise known as "King's Italy," were controlled by the ACC. This area often included AMG units operating either permanently or temporarily in the region and now responsible to ACC and not army headquarters. Any territory in between front and rear areas had both organizations operating at crossroads to each other with no real distinction of who was in charge. The frustration of AMG personnel with the ACC was most acute in the rear areas. Once operating in these areas AMG personnel were suddenly disconnected from the military chain of command as they were now responsible to the ACC who reported to a whole different headquarters in Taranto. This was a wholly inefficient system. The boundaries distinguishing the two areas, forward and rear, were often poorly defined and it took weeks determining where one stopped and the other began. Further complicating this issue was the location of ACC officials; accustomed to traditional administrative methods, they rarely left their headquarters and remained well back from active operations and completely detached from local or even regional issues.

ACC–AMG tension was exacerbated because of ACC's approach to civilian relations. The ACC, for instance, saw labour activity and strike action as a return to normal political life.[52] AMG officials would never tolerate labour strike action that might prevent military operations or manoeuvres from being carried out. AMG officials accused the ACC of operating too slow, of having little to no experience, of not appreciating the realities of the forward areas, and, finally, of sullying the AMG name. Lord Rennell wrote to Sir James Grigg, the secretary of state for war at the War Office, and spoke of ACC operations as a "dogs breakfast and & catshit!" Rennell had developed an opinion of the ACC that the "number of officers, and in many case their training and background, leave me in doubt whether any Italian Government would ever survive being overlaid by such a nursery governess."[53] Another AMG officer wrote of the frustration with ACC officials, "When you give an order to an Army officer you can expect it to be carried out, but when you give an order to an ACC officer it becomes a basis for negotiation."[54] Often General Eisenhower was forced to arbitrate disputes between the ACC and AMG as his position was the only connection between the ACC and the regular military chain of command. The struggles of the ACC to work within the 15th Army Group framework contradicted the original cooperative philosophy of AMG. Unfortunately, AMG became lumped in with broader frustrations over the ACC. Consequently, many senior military officials viewed AMG efforts as inefficient and insufficient.

The AMG–ACC model also suffered from issues with the Italian political administration. The Badoglio government, in power from July 1943 to June 1944, was run by only a small handful of ministers who inspired very little confidence amongst the Allies. Part of this was their disconnectedness from regional political matters due to a lack of communication and transportation as a result of the ongoing fighting. The government was temporarily seated in the town of Brindisi, deep in the Italian heel, and thus fairly isolated. Another reason was simply a lack of competence, as Allied officers questioned the ability of the members of the tiny Badoglio government to effectively govern.[55]

The Allies pursued a policy of "defascistisation" in every region they entered, routinely removing any local officials deemed either to be fascist or having fascist sympathies. One of the unintended consequences of the removal of so many local officials, however, was to contribute to a growing political instability.[56] So many officials were removed that in many regions a significant political and leadership vacuum developed. Into this vacuum stepped groups and individuals with varying abilities and qualifications. AMG officers often relied upon the church to decide who would be suitable for these new administrative positions. Though even the church could not prevent various unsuitable groups from taking power in regions. Most infamously, some AMG officers utilized local Mafioso in Sicily to help fill the power vacuum, though the traditional narrative of the AMG reintroducing the Mafia to Sicily has been debunked.[57] In many instances new ideological groups took over where the old Fascist ones existed, like many of the labour organizations that quickly found themselves run by Communist groups. Many of these groups sought to challenge the political legitimacy of Badoglio's government and even the monarchy, seeing them as fascist sympathisers.

The situation began to improve by June 1944. The King abdicated on 5 June, Badoglio stepped down on 18 June and a new coalition government led by Ivanoe Bonomi took office. By this time Rome had been captured and the government could now take its official seat in the traditional capital. Yet the Bonomi government continued to struggle with many of the same issues as the Badoglio administration. It relied heavily on Allied support to ensure it could effectively govern those areas deemed under its authority, and thus both the ACC and AMG continued to play an involved role in Italian political administration. Be it the failure of the Badoglio government, the limitations of the Bonomi government, or a result of Allied policy, an effective Italian administration could not survive without substantial Allied support.[58]

Partisans

Resistance groups only began to pose a problem for AMG as the Allies got closer to Rome. Various partisan groups had been active since Operation Husky, supported by Allied military agencies. As the Allies approached Rome more and more of these partisans came under the authority of the Allies. The problem was the resistance movement in Italy was not centralized at all. Elements comprising the "resistance" actually represented a wide range of anti-Fascist political parties and patriot groups. Mixed in there with Italian partisans were last minute "patriots," Italians who had formed bands only in the final days of liberation and now sought full recognition as resistance members. As well, many groups consisted of Italian military deserters, escaped Allied prisoners of war, even Yugoslavs and Russians. Broadly speaking the Allies divided the resistance movement into two groups. Those loyal to the Committee of National Liberation (CNL), a committee made up of a wide variety of interest groups from both the political right and left and led by Ivanoe Bonomi. The second group comprised those parts of the Italian army's underground resistance network and loyal to the King and the current Badoglio government. As the Allies pushed northwards

Rome fell into the murky jurisdictional waters of the ACC, and thus the ACC dealt with the resistance leadership while AMG dealt with partisans on the front lines. The ACC in fact created a special section to deal with the resistance movement, and shortly after the liberation of Rome the ACC sat down with the leaders of both groups to bring some sort of centralized control to the whole affair. Meanwhile more and more partisan groups were uncovered as the Allies continued northwards. The main difficulty lay in convincing many of these armed partisans to disarm and return to civilian life. Both the ACC and AMG sought to provide incentives for these men to do so. Many were offered employment, some, after being properly vetted, were given positions in local government, and others were allowed to volunteer to serve in the Italian army. While numerous armed bands of a variety of political and ideological leanings would make any government nervous, ACC and AMG personnel were able to navigate this complicated arena in a way that limited strain on military resources and skilfully maintained order.

Population Control

Population control was one of the greatest challenges for AMG. Thousands of civilian refugees were encountered as the Allies moved up through Sicily and mainland Italy. Many of them were attempting to flee the battle zone or return to their homes after combat had passed by their villages and towns. These large, seminomadic groups threatened military roads and supply lines by clogging up traffic. Health and safety concerns were also a serious issue as any outbreak of disease amongst the civilians could pose a threat to military personnel. Angry, restless, hungry, and desperate civilian refugees could pose a threat to law and order in the Allied rear areas if they were not cared for. Finally, civilians were also seen as a potential security risk and rumours swirled within the Allied ranks of Italians betraying their liberators to the Germans.[59] AMG was responsible for mitigating any issues that might arise from this growing issue of population control. In Sicily, the number of refugees helped by AMG numbered in the several thousand. As the Allies moved northwards on the Italian mainland the numbers increased dramatically. By November of 1943 the civilian refugees encountered were reported to have increased a hundredfold. Adding to this confusion was now thousands of Italian soldiers attempting to return home, either after deserting or being demobilized. By early 1944 AMG was coping with tens of thousands of refugees. A refugee camp at Campobasso reported processing on average 600 refugees a day during the month of February. By the end of that month AMG officials estimated that they had helped evacuate and move approximately 47,000 refugees. In March Mount Vesuvius erupted forcing CA officers to cope with an added 20,000 refugees fleeing the ash and poisonous smoke from the legendary volcano. Numbers continued to rise as the Allies pushed northwards. By the late spring and early summer of 1944 the monthly flow of refugees was somewhere between 10,000 and 15,000 civilians. It was estimated that Rome's population upon the city's liberation in June 1944 was 2 million people, an increase from 750,000 only a year before. In order to effectively cope with these unprecedented numbers AMG established forward reception centres. Refugees would be temporarily sheltered, receive medical aid and food, and then be transported or directed to permanent and semipermanent camps farther in the rear organized and operated by ACC representatives. Billeting for these civilians fell under the responsibility of local Italian authorities once civilians were established in the ACC controlled areas in the rear.[60]

Food

While AMG was successful in preventing any large-scale problems arising from population control, the issue of food supply was far more vexing. For much of the campaign, the average ration for an Italian citizen remained below the 2,000 calories regarded as sufficient by Allied authorities. Reasons for this inability to adequately feed the Italian people started in the early planning stages. Intelligence about conditions in Sicily and on the Italian mainland were limited and presented a far more positive assessment of available food stocks. Planning for food relief (which required orders placed generally three to six months in advance) was based on poor intelligence and proved insufficient for the demands at the sharp end. As well, Allied propaganda coming into Italy through BBC radio broadcasts boasted that food supply under the Allies would be better than under the Germans. Lord Rennell commented on this: "The things they had been promised by the BBC and American radio speakers had in fact not arrived. Propaganda had done more harm than anything else that had happened."[61] After liberation, hungry Italian civilians were constantly questioning Allied soldiers about when the supposed food supplies would arrive.[62]

Though poor planning certainly contributed to the growing food crisis in Italy there were other issues compounding the problem. The first was German theft and sabotage. The Germans looted and plundered most remaining food stocks during their retreat northwards, leaving the Italians reliant on whatever the Allies could supply. The Germans also destroyed and disrupted much of the infrastructure required to harvest and produce food. The destruction of power lines and the stealing of electric cables meant that many of the larger mills could not function until electricity was restored. Some three million German mines were buried throughout the countryside in Allied-occupied areas making the day-to-day life for farmers dangerous.[63] By spring of 1944, approximately 100,000 mines were being cleared a month, with millions more to go.

Further hampering the ability to get food to the Italians was a lack of transport. What the Germans had not taken or destroyed, the Allies requisitioned for military purposes. Soldiers transporting supplies and munitions even seized mule trains. AMG struggled to convince forward elements to give up some transport in order to provide food for the civilians. Though military necessity would always trump CA operations, a greater balance in Italy needed to be struck. The failure to find this balance meant simply that food did not arrive in sufficient quantities or in a timely manner. In September 1944 the ACC reported that infant mortality was quadruple prewar levels, the general mortality rate had doubled within a year, tuberculosis had tripled, and most Italian adults had lost 2.26 to 4.5 kilograms (5 to 10 pounds) in weight.[64]

The demand for food meant that an existing black market expanded dramatically and AMG personnel would find no answer to solving the black market problem in Italy. Prices soared to ten times that of official prices. Italians became increasingly frustrated with the perceived failure of AMG and the Allies to do enough to curb the market. Nearly one hundred AMG officers with the Public Safety section, some with civilian police experience, led the Italian police in a campaign against black market activity. At its peak in the first months of 1944, 3,000 prosecutions against black marketeers were processed a month. Wage control measures were also implemented, though sporadically and without any official policy. The British and Canadians withheld portions of servicemen's pay in order to prevent a rise in purchasing power by the average soldier. The Americans did not employ this policy. Some wage control measures were used with hired Italian labour but this was inconsistently applied. The flood of Allied goods arriving in theatre also fuelled the black market. Either through theft or the sale of goods by military personnel, the black market soon offered a wide range of Allied food and supplies. The black market continued to thrive for the duration of the war and would prove to be a reoccurring thorn in the side for Civil Affairs in Europe.

Naples

No city, town, village, or region posed as great a challenge to AMG as that of Naples, and in many ways the AMG experience in that city became a metaphor for its time in Italy. As one AMG officer put it, "Naples ... represents military government at, let it be hoped, its worst. During that period of time Naples was probably the worst-governed city in the Western world."[65] In September of 1943 distressing reports were streaming into AMG of significant food shortages, starvation, lack of clean water, spreading diseases (in particular typhus), and a complete absence of medical personnel. The Germans had stripped the city of all its food, medical supplies, and transportation before retreating. They had destroyed the city's largest aqueduct, preventing most of the city's fresh water from coming in. The Germans had also stripped the city of its electric cables and blown up the power station, completely shutting down the electric grid.[66] Close to one million people still remained in

Naples with tens of thousands of them living in makeshift air raid shelters. These cramped, unhygienic spaces facilitated the rapid spread of disease amongst the Neapolitan population.

In response to these reports Lord Rennell requested supplies and reinforcements directly from the Military Government section at AFHQ. He asked for additional medical supplies in terms of typhus, typhoid, and cholera vaccinations, but these were rejected as AFHQ deemed the amount of vaccines in-theatre sufficient. In fact, AFHQ reported to the combined chiefs of staff that there were no epidemics in the city, a serious intelligence error stemming from inaccurate reports submitted by AMG officers in the Public Health section. Rennell also requested stores of food. This request was granted. AMG received 1,200 tons[67] of flour, 650 tons of dehydrated soup, 175 tons of milk, and 75 tons of army biscuits as an emergency supply.[68] As well, several AMG and US 5th Army medical teams were moved into the region to support the Public Health section of AMG.

The Allies captured Naples on 1 October with AMG personnel in fact entering the city hours before the first combat troops.[69] The city was even worse than reports had described. The city was demolished. Hundreds of bodies lay unburied in the streets. Most Neapolitans were malnourished, unwashed, and suffering from some sort of illness. Almost the entire city's infrastructure was broken down. The immediate concern was reestablishing running water. Within four days Fifth Army engineers had some water coming in from the main aqueduct while AMG had taken charge of a secondary aqueduct. AMG also oversaw the construction of a saltwater distillation plant in the bay of Naples. Regardless of these early measures, all water had to be rationed and guards were posted at any water collection point as long lines of dehydrated Neapolitans stood with buckets and pails to accept their limited yet life-saving amount. Within two weeks full water supply was up and running.

While water was fairly effectively dealt with, food supply proved far more complicated. In fact, food supply for the civilian population would take months to reach adequate minimal levels. Initial supply came from a combination of emergency rations on hand by the forward units, the supplies requested by Rennell, and the discovery of stocks of food hidden by the Germans in the surrounding countryside. This, however, was not nearly enough. Even when the port was opened on 7 October and 200 tons of milk and flour were being unloaded per day this was still insufficient to meet the basic needs of the civilian population. There were numerous reasons why civilian food supplies only trickled into Naples. Firstly, the military had priority on supplies. So food, trucks, boats, docking berths, roads, and personnel were allocated for military needs first, civilian needs second. Administrative failure also played a role. Lord Rennell had requested further food stocks from the Military Government section at AFHQ to arrive in November. The paperwork was lost. As well, by November the ACC had officially been placed in charge of feeding the Italian population. Yet, the ACC had very few personnel operating in Naples and no organization to actually deal with food supply. As a result, ACC and AMG struggled with each other and the army in an effort to provide food for the Neapolitans. Even when supplies trickled into Naples there was such a shortage of civilian transport that it was hardly possible to move any large quantities into the city as the Germans had destroyed or taken all mechanical transport.

The food situation was such a mess that by December of 1944 drastic action had to be taken and the responsibility for feeding the Neapolitans was taken away from the ACC and placed into the hands of an advanced AFHQ administrative section (code-named FLAMBO). Though a temporary measure, the immediate result was that military resources were redirected to AMG in order to help feed the population. General Eisenhower recognized this growing problem and the importance of it being solved when he wrote, "The primary interest of this headquarters in meeting the minimum food requirements in Italy is to avoid interference with military operations. It may be an over-riding military consideration that the civil population be fed."[70] By the beginning of January 1944 the food situation had been stabilized and military operations continued unimpeded.

Food supply was not the only major problem, the spread of typhus proved to be another serious challenge for AMG. The poor intelligence and failure of Public Health AMG officers resulted in a typhus outbreak amongst the civilian population, posing a threat to the health of Allied soldiers. One senior AMG officer said, "The typhus scare might never have developed had senior CA officers paid more visits early on to the poorer quarters, and especially the air-raid shelters."[71] Typhus outbreaks had occurred as early as July 1943 but as the winter drew near and malnourishment increased, more and more cases began to be reported. By late November AMG, ACC, and army medical personnel were dealing with hundreds of typhus cases. The threat of a widespread epidemic was real.[72] The problem was that no one organization was taking charge of the typhus crisis. Though AMG medical teams were generally on the front line of response, ACC was supposed to be the organization in charge. Yet, Naples in November consisted of numerous headquarters, AMG, ACC, US Navy, AFHQ, army, and several civilian agencies. There was considerable jurisdictional overlap and lack of any clear authority or efficient cooperation. At the core of the issue was once again the inability for AMG and ACC to effectively sort out administrative responsibilities.

It was FLAMBO that was ordered to step in and take ultimate authority by late December. It established a Typhus Control Board that finally provided a centralized authority in regards to typhus issues. Public dusting stations were established, population control measures were put into place, soap was distributed to the population. Though January saw the typhus outbreak peak at 300 cases per week, by February 60,000 Neapolitans were being dusted per day. Incredibly, the typhus outbreak amongst the civilian population never was transmitted to the military; very few cases of Typhus amongst soldiers were ever reported.

Naples speaks to the broader perception of AMG in Italy. The administrative issues plaguing ACC in turn plagued AMG. As one American AMG officer wrote, "it should be made clear that ACC in its darkest hours would probably appear bright if compared to what might have been had ACC not been there. But that is not good enough; it does not vindicate us."[73] Most military personnel failed to differentiate between ACC and AMG, and thus both were seen as failures. Even though ACC would not appear again until the occupation of Germany, the damage was done. Senior military commanders aggressively denounced anything hinting of AMG policy. Any mention of using the Italian model for northwest Europe was dropped by early 1944.

Despite vehement denunciation, institutional growth and development had occurred. AMGOT may have experienced numerous growing pains inevitable to any organization's early development but Civil Affairs doctrine evolved during the Italian campaign. This doctrinal development was rooted in the process of learning from mistakes and many of the most successful solutions to CA issues within Italy came after problems with current methods were realized. Despite these areas of localized success the lack of uniformity in policy, limited to no cooperation between AMG and the army, and the aura of inefficiency as a result of jurisdictional squabbles between it and the ACC, led to politicians and military commanders regarding AMGOT as a failure.[74]

The War Office, the Civil Affairs Staff Centre (CASC) in Wimbledon, and even small groups of Allied officials not directly involved in the Italian campaign had a far more favourable view of AMGOT. They believed that, while there were problems, it was not broken.[75] Clearly, the experience gained in Italy could provide a foundation for Civil Affairs policy in northwest Europe, whether military commanders agreed or not. Regardless of all its perceived failures, the Italian campaign certainly illustrated one important overall lesson: that Civil Affairs doctrine would fall victim to both predictable and unpredictable circumstances during operations in industrialized European nations with large populations and urban centres. An AMGOT report in December 1943 stated, "It has been realized ... that the success or failure of any operation may depend upon the way the civilian population (refugees) are handled particularly in thickly populated areas such as Northern France ... The problem of handling refugees and restoring order in liberated or occupied territories is now considered of sufficient importance."[76]

Some European leaders-in-exile, most notably Charles de Gaulle, were still concerned about AMG's intervening role in the new Italian administration and possible infringements on the sovereignty of their own nations. De Gaulle appointed Mr Francois Coulet as Rouen regional commissioner in June 1944 (Rouen being the capital of Normandy), two months before the region was even liberated. Coulet was also suspicious of Allied authority and feared that the Allies were going to follow the AMGOT model when liberating France. Mr Coulet and de Gaulle were both aware and sceptical of AMGOT's shortcomings: provincialist policy; failure to quickly establish an efficient, autonomous, and indigenous civilian administration; and lack of cooperation with both the ACC and combat military personnel.[77] Both men were concerned that an institutional failure would be disastrous for a newly liberated France. In fact, during the first few days of the invasion of France in 1944, Coulet refused to use the term *Civil Affairs* in his communiqué with Allied officials because he, like many within the Allied administration, associated Civil Affairs with AMGOT.[78]

A TUMULTUOUS BEGINNING

In Italy, AMGOT personnel and planners learned many valuable lessons and gained much-needed practical experience that would play a fundamental role in the approach to Civil Affairs in northwest Europe. Unfortunately, Civil Affairs officers had a difficult time overcoming AMGOT's negative public perception, and many senior military commanders continued to resist and even show outright hostility to the AMGOT/Civil Affairs model. Commanders like Eisenhower (SHAEF), Montgomery (21st Army Group), Gen. Harry Crerar (First Canadian Army), Gen. Guy Simonds (II Canadian Corps), and Gen. Charles Foulkes (I Canadian Corps) understood that dealing with civilian populations was a reality of the battlefield and Civil Affairs was the only branch of the military trained and prepared to take on this complicated and challenging task.

Though AMGOT received significant negative criticism it was a vital "stepping-stone" organization for Civil Affairs. By the time the Allies invaded northwest Europe in June 1944 Allied Civil Affairs administration had developed a bedrock of information and experience, and Allied leadership understood that success depended on military and CA formations continuing to liaise and cooperate. This is a direct result of the struggle by AMGOT in Italy. One almost comical event highlights the difference between the organizational acceptance of Civil Affairs in northwest Europe versus the marginalized nature of AMGOT in the Italian campaign. During Operation Husky, CA officers were forced to stow away on ships in order to participate in the beach landings as they had been forgotten when planners drew up each ship's manifest. During the

Normandy invasion, CA officers, supported by a large and functioning administrative network, landed within hours of the first wave hitting the beaches.[79] It was here that the Civil Affairs branch of First Canadian Army encountered new and daunting challenges in the concentrated urban areas of northwest France. These challenges provided an opportunity for Canadian CAOs to showcase their unique and often overlooked talents. More important, their contributions in France would prove how important Civil Affairs truly was to Allied military operations.

CHAPTER TWO

A Battlefield Classroom – Civil Affairs in Northern France

"Every gun that is made, every warship launched, every rocket fired, signifies in the final sense a theft from those who hunger and are not fed, those who are cold and are not clothed."
– Dwight Eisenhower

On 6 June 1944, as the Allies fought for a hold on France's northern shores, Civil Affairs officers began conducting a wholly different type of campaign. This battle was not fought with shells and bullets but with supplies and knowledge. SHAEF directed Civil Affairs to provide relief to the beleaguered and destitute civilians of war-ravaged Europe. In northern France, the men that would make up Civil Affairs First Canadian Army received their "trial by fire" and developed the skills necessary to handle the myriad problems that lay ahead. The experience of Canadian Civil Affairs detachments in northern France helped forge an operational template for dealing with civilian populations that would be utilized by First Canadian Army for the remainder of the war. They moved large numbers of refugees to safe zones, provided relief and medical aid, reestablished infrastructure, arrested and removed collaborationists, and facilitated the transition from a pro-Nazi regime to a democratic member of the Allied nations. Canadian Civil Affairs officers came to face-to-face with a civilian population traumatized by years of occupation and the sudden and violent arrival of the Allied war machine. Despite the challenges, by late October 1944 a demonstrated and validated operational model for dealing with urban civilian populations was in place that began to displace the sour memories of AMGOT's shortcomings in Italy.

FROM AMGOT TO CIVIL AFFAIRS

The negative perception of AMGOT amongst senior military commanders and Allied leaders resulted in a complete name change before the invasion of France. The adoption of the title *Civil Affairs* for the organization was born out of the necessity for a public image makeover prior to the invasion of northwest Europe. The use of the term *military government* or even simply *government* carried connotations of Allied military control, a disconcerting idea in European countries that were to be liberated. Though obviously far more tyrannical, the Nazi occupation had been a form of military government too. Furthermore, the organization's name had to be revamped simply in order to convince senior military commanders that this was not the AMGOT organization that had developed such a bad reputation in Italy.[1] Although already in use in various faculties throughout British and American command, the Allies officially incorporated the term *Civil Affairs* into the Field Service Regulations in early 1944.

Civil Affairs in northwest Europe dealt with civilian populations in highly industrialized areas and presented an improved model of civil–military cooperation. Cooperation that borrowed elements from the Italian AMGOT experience but also identified and mitigated any administrative dangers carried over from the Mediterranean. The organizational objectives in Europe were

> A. To ensure that conditions exist among the civil population which will not interfere with operations against the enemy (including enforcement of the terms of surrender) but which will promote such operations to the greatest extent possible.
> B. To carry out, through the Allied National authorities concerned, the political and economic policies of the Supreme Commander towards the people of liberated territories and for the establishment of law, order and normal conditions, in pursuance of the

principles of international law and directions from the Combined Chiefs of Staff.

C. To advise and assist the Allied national authorities concerned in matters relating to the control, care and repatriation of Allied and enemy displaced nationals.

D. To protect Allied property.[2]

To complete these objectives CAOs had three primary tasks: first, to "exercise administrative control and supervision ... in order that the civil machinery may be set going as early as possible and in such a way as to benefit the allied war effort."[3] Civil Affairs officers sought to aid and cooperate with local populations to reestablish indigenous administrations and avoid any lengthy, complicated period of military government. Secondly, CAOs were responsible for ensuring that refugees did not impede military operations or activities (as they had in 1940). This meant responsibility for controlling their movement, as thousands of civilians fled or were forced from their homes due to fighting.[4] This responsibility also included efforts to limit disease, disorganization, and general unrest amongst civilians. Finally, CAOs would be responsible for liaising between the civilian population and the military.[5] Like the operational objectives, these tasks were broad and encompassed innumerable obstacles and a vast multitude of tasks.

Training

Civil Affairs officers were primarily trained in England at the Civil Affairs Staff Centre in Wimbledon. Candidates for the centre were required to have working knowledge of a European language as well as experience in one or more specialized subjects such as finance, law, art, trade and industry, fire and civil defence, or engineering to name just a few. The curriculum covered both military and civil studies related to a specific country: France, Belgium, Holland, Luxembourg, Denmark, Norway, and Germany. A candidate for Civil Affairs would have to complete a six-week course (though the very first course held was thirteen weeks in length, upon completion the War Office deemed this far too long because of an overseas demand for CA officers). The course would include a series of lectures given by outside scholars, government officials, and researchers supplemented by study groups looking at a variety of topics and regions. The final month of the course would involve an exercise whereby students would be faced with a series of CA obstacles during a pretend military operation. After the course ended, CA graduates would often go on to receive additional training focused on their specialized areas (civil defence, finances, legal, etc.). Each course would have on average 150 to 300 students and by late September 1943 the course had already graduated 1,300 officers. At its peak the centre included students from all over the Allied world: the British Commonwealth, the United States, Britain, Belgium, Czechoslovakia, France, Luxembourg, the Netherlands, Norway, and Poland. After completing the course officers were grouped into specialities or "functions" according to their civilian experience and recent training. Most graduates were immediately sent to the front to gain practical experience with Occupied Territory Administration (OTA). The earliest graduates were sent to the colony of Tripolitania but after July of 1943 graduates were sent to Italy.

The invasion of Sicily in July of 1943 and subsequent liberation of mainland Italy meant that more trained CA personnel were needed as AMGOT's role expanded. This provided a convenient excuse for a decision by the War Committee of the Canadian Cabinet to start a Civil Affairs training course at Royal Military College in Kingston, Ontario. There was significant support for this endeavour within Canada; Prime Minister William Lyon Mackenzie King supported it, Minister of National Defence J.L. Ralston was one of the first to propose it, both Vincent Massey and Charles Ritchie (stationed at Canada House in London) in the Department of External Affairs voiced support for this program, and Brigadier General Kenneth Stuart, Chief of the Canadian General Staff and the man who had the final word on its execution, cabled his consent for the program. Unfortunately, the War Office in London was not so keen, saying that, "the objects of the school [in Canada] could better and more economically be achieved by accepting added vacancies at Wimbledon where specialist instructors and complete facilities were readily available."[6]

Contributing to this British position was the fact that the Americans were running a Civil Affairs course in Charlottesville, Virginia and offered limited vacancies available to Canadian soldiers. The School of Military Government (SOMG) in Charlottesville was established in May 1942 on the University of Virginia campus. Its curriculum was modeled along the lines of the British Civil Affairs training centres in England with two British CA veterans of North Africa brought in as part of the permanent faculty. Graduates from the SOMG were intended to become the administrative and advisory assistants to military governors with an emphasis on the eventual military government of Italy, Germany, and Japan.[7] To supplement the SOMG further, Civil Affairs Training Schools (CATS) were established throughout the United States at Yale, Harvard, Princeton, Stanford, and at the Universities of Michigan, Chicago, Pittsburgh, Boston, Wisconsin, Northwestern, and Western Reserve.[8] The CATS differed slightly from the SOMG in that they were far less concerned with high level regional and national planning and focused curriculum more on the day-to-day work of running an occupied city or town.[9] With access to schools in Britain and the United States the War Office frankly could not understand why a separate Canadian school was needed at all. Even Toronto-born Brigadier General William Basil (W.B.) Wedd, SCAO for First Canadian Army, voiced his displeasure for a Canadian program: "I have always felt that it [the training course in Canada] was basically unnecessary and that all Canadian graduates could be trained at Wimbledon."[10] Regardless, Massey cabled Ottawa ensuring that no one was "discouraged by the War Office views" and with General Stuart's support the course went ahead as planned.[11]

The creation of the Canadian CA school was a calculated move on the part of the Canadian government. The school ensured that enough Canadian officers would be trained for both CA and MG work with Canadian units overseas while also asserting a level of sovereignty over Canadian CA/MG personnel. Up until late 1943, when final steps were being taken by the Canadian government to approve the school's creation, the War Office had yet to ask for any significant formal commitment of Canadian CA officers to be trained in England. At this point the War Office had complete control of who could take the CA course at Wimbledon and in turn controlled where trained CA officers could be appointed. In fact, "candidates from Canada were nominated only when requests were received from the War Office."[12] Only twenty-seven Canadian officers had been trained at Wimbledon and were still waiting deployment overseas. It seemed to the Canadian government that the War Office was not overly interested in getting any large numbers of Canadians to train at Wimbledon.[13] Certainly the Canadian government was aware that if this policy continued it was very likely the vast majority of CA officers eventually serving in Canadian formations would be British. The Canadian CA school was a way by which the Canadian government could ensure that Canadian military personnel were being trained for CA work overseas while also decentralizing British control over CA personnel training and selection. Within a month of the Canadian War Cabinet approving the creation of the Canadian school the British finally sent a formal request for Canada's CA commitment to be 319 officers and 419 other ranks. The Canadian school could now help ensure that commitment.

Overseen by the Canadian National Defence Headquarters, the Royal Military College (RMC) in Kingston, Ontario, opened its first CA course in conjunction with the Department of External Affairs in December of 1943. The qualifications for CA school candidates seemed to be a combination of age, civilian experience, and language abilities. Generally, a candidate would be expected to have some sort of real world experience in a particular specialized subject (law, finance, art and architecture, politics, health, history) and speak one or more European languages other than English. Candidates were certainly considered "of a high standard ... between the ages of 35 and 50 ... and were officers rendered available for other than normal military duties."[14] An article in the *Hamilton Spectator* wrote, "It is understood that there is a considerable number of suitable men in the Canadian forces too old for combatant service in the ranks they now hold. The experience of the present war has shown that advancing Allied forces face many problems which are of a non-operational character but which they must be prepared to meet."[15] Mollie McGee of the *Globe and Mail* wrote, "half of the G5 officers [CAOs] have been drawn from civilian life ... Ages vary from 22 to 58, the average just above 35 years. They include a mayor, a corporate lawyer, a policeman, an internationally known authority on gas surveyage [sic], governors and college presidents."[16] The University of Alberta's dean of arts at the time, professor G.M. Smith, was appointed director of Civil Studies at RMC. In conjunction with Major T.F. Gelley, a member of the RMC directing staff, and Wimbledon school administrators, Smith began organizing the curriculum. Subsequently, the college offered three full courses and a partial postgraduate course in Civil Affairs. In total, 141 CA officers completed the RMC CA staff course with another 273 Canadians completing their training at Wimbledon.

The Civil Affairs training curriculum in Canada was meant to be the same as in England. To ensure this, two senior instructors were brought over from Wimbledon, Lt Colonels L.T. Neck and J. Campbell, to help foster consistency in what was being taught to Civil Affairs recruits in England, "thereby ensuring close co-ordination of the British and Canadian courses."[17] The curriculum in England suffered from being too broad and, besides providing general background knowledge on a specific country, its language, and perhaps one subject within the CA mandate, most graduates in England learnt their skills on the job. This broad curriculum of course carried over to the Canadian school. Students were first given instruction in military organization, specifically how to carry out the duties of a staff officer. They were then divided into specialist groups where they studied history, government, and local administration of a specific country. Finally, they were further divided into specialist functions: finance, law, supply, trade and industry, relief, fire and civil defence, public safety, labour, and engineering. Canadian administrators had insufficient time to improve on any faults that lay within the Canadian curriculum because the demand for CA officers became so great that most recruits were sent to the front before completing the course.

The opening of the Canadian CA school coincided with an ongoing discussion amongst senior Canadian politicians and military officials about the prospect of creating an all-Canadian Civil Affairs Group that would eventually operate as part of First Canadian Army. As early as 1942 the idea of an all-Canadian civil–military liaison group had been discussed. A proposal to General McNaughton (commander of First Canadian Army until December 1943) addressed the potential for French Canadian officers to be warmly received within liberated France and play a significant role in the liaison between the Allies and the liberated French population. That early in the war however, McNaughton and others in his command felt that steps should be not be taken without the order emanating "from the War Office so as to ensure there is no duplication between our own efforts and those of the British."[18] The idea of an all-Canadian CA group was revitalized in early 1944 after the British had formally requested the Canadian contribution to Civil Affairs. The size of the Canadian contribution was roughly equivalent to the size of an entire Civil Affairs Group and Major General Stanley Kirby at the Directorate of Civil Affairs (DCA) recommended that an all-Canadian Civil Affairs Group be created to eventually operate within First Canadian Army. Lt General Kenneth Stuart (interim commander of First Canadian Army until March 1944) supported this "Canadianization" policy. Even Brigadier Wedd voiced his support for this move. Part of the reason, Wedd identified, stemmed from the dissatisfaction of Canadian CA officers currently serving within British units. Many felt they were not being actively used and were concerned "that they are being lost sight of from a Cdn [Canadian] army standpoint and not being considered for promotion, etc."[19] Wedd further stated, "I believe that under present conditions there is a great risk of Cdn [Canadian] offrs [officers] employed on Civil Affairs work with Br[itish] Groups being over-looked."[20] He went on to advocate, "I think it would be an advantage to form a Canadian Detachment Group."[21]

Wedd's recommendation would not be acted upon. The War Office and the Combined Chiefs of Staff had already decided on a policy in regards to the nationality of each formation's CA personnel. Civil Affairs staff at formation headquarters (generally army and corps) would be the nationality of that formation (so First Canadian Army and II Canadian Corps HQ would have all Canadian CA staff officers) while detachments were to be internationalized as much as possible. Internationalization in this context referred to a mixture of American and "British" personnel, the term "British" included soldiers of the Commonwealth as well as miscellaneous nationalities from around the globe.[22] This policy towards detachments was, as Wedd later explained, to "prevent civilian populations 'playing off' one detachment area against another."[23] This internationalization policy was later rescinded in the fall of 1944 on account of Soviet concerns that it was enabling too much close cooperation between the western Allies, from October 1944 onwards all CA detachments in 21st Army Group would consist of Anglo-Commonwealth personnel only.[24]

The issue of an all-Canadian CA Group was never really discussed again once active operations commenced in France in June 1944 and the RMC course would be cancelled shortly after the invasion of northwest Europe. Simply put, it would be difficult to separate Canadian and British CA personnel while the Allies were desperately fighting for a foothold on the continent. As well, with most Canadian CA officers then either engaged in active operations or about to be sent overseas, any dissatisfaction over inactivity disappeared.[25] By late August 1944, the Allies were rapidly advancing in northwest Europe and had liberated large swathes of French territory. The Allies needed CA officers so desperately that the RMC course was disbanded to allow all of its students to transfer immediately to overseas units. Wedd lamented the state of his officers: "The way in which Civil Affairs officers will carry out their duties is still undefined in many respects. Some of the officers selected have not been able to even attend a Civil Affairs course of instruction."[26] They would have to learn on the job.

The Structure of Civil Affairs

The DCA headed by Major General Stanley Kirby was the primary body responsible for the philosophical direction of Civil Affairs in northwest Europe. Kirby was a professional officer who rose to the rank of captain during the First World War and served most of the interwar period in India, obtaining the rank of deputy chief of General Staff for the British Army. As commander of the DCA, he ran a staff of sixteen lieutenant colonels, two colonels, three brigadier generals, and one major general, all with varying specialties, including technology, economics, government, personnel, and training.

The DCA was responsible for keeping relevant civilian officials informed of CA work. To ensure frequent contact Kirby worked closely with Brigadier S. Swinton Lee at the War Office. Lee was appointed as acting deputy chief civil affairs officer (DCCAO) for the War Office in December 1942. Lee was essentially the man responsible for liaising between the civilian government and the DCA in all matters pertaining to Civil Affairs.

The DCA staff also worked in an advisory capacity to SHAEF. It was the G-5 branch of SHAEF, commanded by Toronto-born Lt General Arthur Grasett, which issued orders for Allied Civil Affairs operating in theatre. Civil Affairs officers were integrated into the headquarters of most Allied military formations. Starting with 21st Army Group, eventually commanded by General (later Field Marshal) Bernard Montgomery, CA officers were attached to headquarters extending katabatically through the various field armies, including First Canadian Army, to corps, and eventually to division level.[27]

The DCCAO for 21st Army Group was Brigadier Thomas Robbins, formerly the commandant of the Civil Affairs school at Wimbledon. Reporting to him was the SCAO for First Canadian Army, Brigadier Wedd. Wedd was an officer in the Canadian Corps during the First World War and was even wounded at the Battle of Mount Sorrel in June 1916. He was appointed SCAO First Canadian Army in February 1944. As one historical officer noted, "Brigadier Wedd, in addition to his military qualifications [D.S.O., M.C., E.D. veteran of the First World War] possessed a background of experience in civilian life ... He had for some years been the European representative of the Massey-Harris company and many years residence in Europe had made him familiar with the language and characteristics of the people in the countries through which the Canadian Army was to pass."[28] In contrast, many of the British appointed officers were career officers with little civilian experience. This gave Wedd a distinct advantage in terms of the flexible problem solving required of a Civil Affairs commander.

Civil Affairs was organized by pools, groups, and detachments. A pool was generally attached to an army group formation, such as 21st Army Group, and contained three to five groups. Each group, commanded by a senior Civil Affairs officer (SCAO) at the rank of lieutenant colonel, consisted of roughly 240 officers and 360 other ranks divided into a number of detachments. Generally, one to three groups would be attached to an army formation, such as First Canadian Army. A SCAO, and his small supporting staff, would be attached to headquarters at the levels of army, corps, lines of communication, and lines of communication subareas and would liaise between field detachments and unit headquarters. This was the crucial link in making sure that cooperation existed between combat and CA formations. The SCAO would be responsible for a number of detachments, to which specialist officers could be added as necessary. Depending on the situation at the front line the SCAO would send out specific detachments from the group. A detachment, commanded by a major, could contain between six and ten officers who specialized in various areas of CA, such as administration, public safety, supply, law, labour, and public health; the detachments were augmented by several other ranks as well as the necessary equipment and material. The detachments were flexible in that they could be temporarily attached to a corps, division, or even a battalion depending on the requirements of the operational situation. Regardless, once a detachment had established its operational presence in an area it was responsible to the local formation commander (usually a division commander but sometimes a brigade or even a battalion commander) while reporting back to the SCAO at headquarters.

Detachments were formally divided into two general types: spearhead and static. Spearhead detachments followed closely behind their assigned division, having a representative (often the detachment commander) present in the division headquarters while the men of the detachment worked within the division's area of operation. The attaching of spearhead detachments to divisions was something not anticipated prior to the actual invasion (detachments were originally supposed to cooperate with and answer to corps HQ) but quickly became standard practice within both Second British Army and First Canadian Army. These spearhead detachments facilitated a rapid assessment of the primary civilian problems affecting newly liberated areas and enabled the provision of immediate and short-term relief. Static detachments then established their bases of operations at major towns or city centres and made longer commitments to local rehabilitation.

Static and spearhead detachments were further subdivided into several classifications. Area (A) detachments were basic static detachments providing administrative support for their specific locations. Provincial (P) detachments would administer larger areas and often command several area detachments within their operation zones. Corps (C) detachments were the basic spearhead detachments (confusingly, they would work alongside divisional troops while reporting to corps HQ). (C) detachments would enter an area right behind the first wave of troops, make a preliminary report on local conditions, and submit the reports to corps headquarters. Besides producing a preliminary report, a (C) detachment's primary function was to reestablish a reliable police presence in the town. Relief (R) detachments would follow after (C) detachments and were static and designed to set up relief camps for displaced persons, refugees, and civilian casualties. These detachments would often have Red Cross or civilian medical teams attached to them and would usually contain an officer from the army medical corps. Any or all of these detachments could be working at the corps or divisional level depending on the specific operational circumstances.

Typically, spearhead detachments arrived in villages and towns alongside front-line troops. They executed a variety of projects, including providing immediate medical aid, restablishing running water, electricity, and local industry, resolving financial issues, liaising with local resistance groups, and controlling refugees. They often moved quite quickly and sometimes stayed in one place for only a couple of days before moving on. While the civilians celebrated liberation, CA soldiers determined the names of reliable local officials and which officials were considered collaborators. They also arranged some sort of administrative hierarchy and filed a comprehensive report on local needs to give the static detachments some idea of what to expect. These reports could range from serious issues to mundane day-to-day issues. For instance, Captain Pury, a CA officer reporting directly to 21st Army Group headquarters, wrote about the general friendliness of the inhabitants of a village he visited along the front line but cited a complaint from a farmer who had "lost two mules. [The farmer] said he had noticed soldiers carrying shell cases and he surmised they had taken the mules to help them in this job. He then chuckled and said in the last war he had done the same thing and could not blame them."[29]

In sharp contrast to spearhead detachments, static detachments often stayed in one town or village and worked out towards the surrounding area. A formal hand over was supposed to occur between the spearhead and static detachments in order that they could be apprised of the issues affecting that town or region. Complications arose when the spearhead detachments were ordered to move on and the static detachments had yet to arrive. In many instances it was not possible for the spearhead detachments to remain behind in order to hand over the town.[30]

The information from this "hand over" was certainly important. Often officers in static detachments collected numerous reports filed by spearhead detachments and fused them into more general reports for senior commanders. Corps and army headquarters then compiled these reports into general surveys issued fortnightly. One such report by First Canadian Army discusses a variety of topics, such as fire and civil defence, resistance groups, prisons, courts, and finances.[31]

Static detachments were in a better position to assume control of many long-term projects started by spearhead detachments. They continued to vet local officials, reestablish basic industry and self-sufficient supply systems, and recovered water, gas, and electrical utilities. Static detachments also often set up local police forces and disarmed resistance groups and, of course, continually transported and controlled refugees and displaced persons.[32]

These detachments relied heavily on the standard military supply network during the initial contact phase with civilians. Once static detachments securely integrated with local authorities and established some form of civilian administration, they would begin using separate CA logistical supply networks. The CA supply network consisted of two types of depots. The base port depot (BPD) was the primary point of supply delivery to the continent, and the Civil Affairs inland depot (CAID) provided immediate supplies when requested by CA formations. Although combat formations could draw on the CA supply network in cases of emergency, Civil Affairs designed these depots to keep civilian stores separate from the military supply network and to track what supplies went to what countries for billing purposes.

The CA supply network controlled supplies for a variety of specific civilian needs. For instance, the memoir of Lieutenant Colonel Jefferey Williams recounts the time when the Polish Armoured Division of II Canadian Corps requisitioned 250 brassieres for women recently liberated from a concentration camp.[33] CA logistics would often control unusual orders of this sort.

Civil Affairs in France

Planning for Civil Affairs in France began well before the spring of 1944 and was based largely on both the positive and negative lessons learned from AMGOT operations in Italy. These lessons of Italy were, in turn, shaped by practical discussions at Chief of Staff Supreme Allied Command (COSSAC, which eventually became SHAEF), the War Office, Administration of Territories (Europe) Committee (or AT(E)), the Washington and London Civil Affairs centres, and 21st Army Group (the higher formation responsible for the invasion). After a number of joint meetings, COSSAC released its first significant manual, *Military Manual of Civil Affairs in the Field*, in February 1944.[34] In March 1944, COSSAC released *Civil Administration Instructions for Normandy*, which was followed by *Technical Instructions for Normandy* in May.[35] The objectives for CA in France were defined as,

> A. Keep the civil population from impeding the troops. This implied:
> a) Establishing law and order
> b) Preserving the population from want, disease, and fear.
> B. Assisting in the restoration of the economic life of the community and thus transform the civilian population from a liability to an asset by:
> a) Procuring civilian labour for military purposes thereby providing employment as well as helping the services, army, navy and air force.
> b) Making available economic resources of the territory thereby saving shipping, tonnage and inland transport.[36]

Within these broad operational objectives, "the maximum encouragement was to be given to local officials and organs of government ... to aim at the earliest possible restoration of National authority."[37] Key tasks for CA officers to fulfill these broad objectives were as follows,

> A. Reestablishment of an efficient administration and orderly social life, i.e., police, justice, essential amenities and utilities.

B. Regulation of food supply, the institution of relief measures, *provisional and temporary* (author's italics).
C. Promotion of production for:
    a. Military necessities
    b. Essential civilian needs
D. Promotion of useful employment in addition to finding labour for the services.
E. Institution or improvement of air raid precautions and fire defence.
F. Institution of information bureaus to help displaced and missing persons and to maintain the morale of the population.[38]

Allied planners had hoped to have these instructions in play much earlier than that spring of 1944. The delay in issuing these technical instructions was the result of strategic disagreement between President Roosevelt and Prime Minister Churchill on CA policy towards the administration of liberated France. Roosevelt wanted direct military control of the liberated areas until elections could be held. Yet this more direct form was negatively associated with the AMGOT model.[39] Churchill lobbied for an indirect approach, one that saw CA officers as advisors to newly appointed French administrators. He argued this would reduce the strain on military resources.[40] Both leaders failed to come to any understanding, and Eisenhower was left to decide, ultimately opting for Churchill's indirect approach. Eisenhower's last-minute decision further served to mollify a vocal Charles de Gaulle, who was concerned about any infringements on the autonomy of a new Free French government.

One of the major concerns for Civil Affairs in France was the large numbers of refugees and displaced persons that were going to be encountered (a refugee was considered a temporarily homeless civilian from the region currently within the military jurisdiction of Civil Affairs, while a displaced person was a civilian originally from a region, province, or country outside of the current jurisdiction of Civil Affairs). The CA policy towards refugees and displaced persons in France came directly from SHAEF,

A. To prevent any hindrance to military operations which might be occasioned by their massing or uncontrolled movement.
B. To prevent the infiltration of enemy agents posing as refugees or displaced persons.
C. To prevent outbreaks of disease among refugees and displaced persons which might threaten the health of the military forces.
D. To relieve as far as practicable, conditions of destitution among refugees and displaced persons which might adversely affect military operations.
E. To assist the French authorities, when the military situation permits, to set up an organization to effect the rapid and orderly repatriation of displaced persons.[41]

It is clear here that at all times Allied military operations were a priority, yet as the Allies planned and developed Civil Affairs policies they had to clearly communicate to the Free French and de Gaulle their intentions to infringe as little as possible on French administrative sovereignty as long as that sovereignty supported the military objectives of the Allies.[42] This rhetoric can be seen clearly in the following comment towards refugees and displaced persons:

> The French authorities will have full responsibility for refugees and displaced persons. However, in the Forward Zone in emergencies affecting military operations or where no French authority is in a position to put into effect the measure deemed necessary by commanders, the latter may as a temporary and exceptional measure take such actions as is required by military necessity. Moreover, in the Military Zones, commanders may take, or cause the services in charge of installations of military importance to take such measures as are necessary for the conduct of operations and, in particular, those necessary to assure the security and efficient operation of such installations.[43]

While Allied planners sought to convey their intention not to impede upon French sovereignty they had to make it clear that there was a very real possibility for assuming control when and where military operations deemed it necessary.

THE NORMANDY BRIDGEHEAD

Once the Allies were ashore, one of the first CA objectives in northern France was to establish a functioning civil administration in place of the crumbling German military one. On the eve of the Allied invasion, the German military administration of occupied France was a mess. Occupied Zone North (Vichy France having been fully occupied and renamed Zone South in 1942) was controlled from Paris. The administration of France was overseen by the MBF (Militärbefehlshaber in Frankreich) commanded by General Carl-Heinrich von Stülpnagel (who in July 1944 would be complicit in the attempted assassination of Hitler). The MBF was subordinate to supreme command for German forces in the west, known as Ob West. Ob West answered to the Wehrmacht's high command, OKW (Oberkommando der Wehrmacht), who in turn answered directly to Hitler.

The German military administration operated as a multitiered administration with military officers placed in charge of key towns and cities. These local administrators were subordinate to German officers in charge of individual *departments* who were in turn answerable to officers in charge of larger regions made up of several *departments*. While MBF was responsible for both security and civil affairs most German soldiers had little experience with the latter. From the very early days of occupation, the MBF began recruiting French civilian bureaucrats and integrating them into the larger MBF administration, even giving them uniforms and rank. By 1944 these French soldier–bureaucrats were an integral part of the administrative staff of the MBF, overseeing the French economy and government.

By 1944 the German military administration of France was an absolute mess. While on paper it was supposed to run as the multitiered system overseen by the MBF, in actuality it resembled a patchwork of competing feudal kingdoms, indicative of the larger chaos that was the administration of the Nazi empire. Since 1941 Hitler had continually allowed a variety of groups to become operationally active throughout occupied France, independent of the MBF. Senior Nazi officials like Heinrich Himmler, Joachim von Ribbentrop, and Hermann Göring all had carved out a piece of occupied France for themselves and their retainers. Himmler's SS was particularly aggressive in challenging the MBF for jurisdictional control and by 1944 the MBF was constantly clashing with Hitler's feudal lords. Meanwhile parts of the northern coast, including the Nord and the Pas-de-Calais, were under strict military government overseen directly by the Wehrmacht's General Alexander Von Falkenhausen (who was also in charge of the military occupation of Belgium).

The Allies invaded a France that had suffered nearly four years of this chaotic Nazi administration. By 1944, many of the French officials cooperating with the German military administration in northern France held pro-Nazi sympathies, and CA personnel faced a very complicated vetting process. The operations in Italy had shown that dismissing every official who had worked in the preliberation administration created serious administrative gaps. Once on the ground, CA officials would have to decide for every level of government who were Vichyites and who were in favour of an independent France but had chosen to stay and attempt to work within the German occupation system.[44] This meant vetting countless prefects, subprefects, and mayors throughout the administrative chain of command.[45] In order to not be seen as infringing on French sovereignty this vetting would end up being a cooperative process with delegates of the nonrecognized Gouvernement Provisoire de la République Francaise (GPRF). The GPRF had a somewhat confusing role amongst the Allied powers. Originally formed in June 1943 as the Comité Français de Libération Nationale (CFLN) its leadership was initially shared between General Charles de Gaulle and General Henri Giraud though by November of the same year de Gaulle presided over the CFLN alone. It was, in the eyes of the French who recognized its authority, a provisional government directing the Free French war effort. The Allied powers were of a mixed mind towards the function of the CFLN. The Soviet Union was far more open to recognizing its role as a provisional government, though was hesitant to contradict the Americans. The Americans and British recognized the CFLN's authority only in so far as it directed the war effort and both powers were careful to avoid any language that could be construed as recognizing a new permanent French government.[46] Yet by 1944 the CFLN under de Gaulle was in no uncertain terms the administrative body leading the Free French and would be essential in helping to establish a new French government upon liberation.

De Gaulle, Roosevelt, and Churchill's deteriorating relationship further complicated the issue of policy towards a new French administration. Diplomatic relations became strained throughout 1944 as de Gaulle pressed for the CFLN's sole authority to choose the new French administration. The Allies felt it was imperative that the French people choose their own government democratically. As the SHAEF handbook for Civil Affairs in France noted, "The delicacies of the political situation lends additional emphasis to this point. The utmost care must be taken that no impression is given which may be construed as forwarding the political interests of any particular group, faction or party."[47] At the same time the Allied leadership recognized de Gaulle's popularity and the reality that his officials would be the ones on the ground working closely with many CA officers. The "French authorities have the responsibility of reorganizing and re-establishing French administrative and judicial services ... the French Committee of National Liberation is the de facto authority in the liberated area of France."[48]

This confusing situation was made worse because until 12 July 1944 the Allies did not officially recognize de Gaulle's provisional government (the CFLN changed its name to the GPRF in early June 1944). SHAEF was particularly unsure of how exactly the French public would receive the Gaullists and wanted to avoid simply replacing a German occupying regime with an Allied backed regime without public support. It would be circumstances on the ground, though, that dictated the process. Charles de Gaulle came ashore at Courseulles-sur-Mer on 14 June 1944 "totally unexpectedly" and almost immediately upon liberation of any Norman communities replaced most administrative positions with deputies and civil administrators of his choosing and "although opinions differed slightly on the warmth of his reception by the inhabitants, his visit did give the effect that they had their sovereignty back."[49] As another CA officer observed, "De Gaulle has staged a very clever coup."[50]

Canadian detachments working in Normandy were therefore faced with a policy paradox. As soon as British and Canadian troops entered Caen on 9 July, Gaullist officials set about appointing a new prefect, a new secretary general and a new mayor while also appointing a new head of police, all of whom were known Gaullists.[51] II Canadian Corps CA officers worked closely with many Gaullists in an administrative capacity even while Allied authority balked at CA's unofficial endorsement of what was becoming de Gaulle's provisional government. Frankly, there was really no alternative but to cooperate with Gaullist officials. CA certainly did not have the manpower or resources to establish a more direct form of military rule, and the French would certainly have resisted this. Allied officials were also concerned with the political opinions of France's various regional populations towards any early recognition of de Gaulle, as one CA officer wrote, "The French are keenly alive to politics and we had to exercise care in political discussions ... While refusing to take part in politics or in political discussions, a Civil Affairs officer had to maintain an attitude of friendliness and sympathy. We were very careful about our political comments so that no misinterpretation could be taken."[52] Yet most French in northern France, including Normans, Bretons, and Alsatians, greeted the Allies with fervour, accepted the new French leadership, and were ecstatic to finally be rid of the shackles of German occupation. There was simply a cautious disconnect between those formulating policy back in England and the reality at the front. Within this complicated sociopolitical environment, the task of dealing with the French civilian population fell on the shoulders of the small, but dedicated, cadre of Civil Affairs officers, including those of the Canadian army and regardless of Allied policy tip-toeing around Gaullist recognition, the situation at the sharp end made cooperation with Gaullist officials the most prudent course of action.

Despite the jubilant mood severe fighting was still to come. The landings on 6 June saw the Allies force a bridgehead onto Norman soil, and soldiers were soon ashore and safely dug in. General Omar Bradley's First US Army, the western arm of 21st Army Group, made slow progress in the Norman bocage. At the same time, Lt General Sir Miles Dempsey's

Second British Army, the eastern arm of 21st Army Group, forced its way south with the objective of capturing Caen and the surrounding ridgelines that dominated the terrain. Progress was disappointingly slow. The Panzer Lehr 12th ss and 21st Panzer divisions repeatedly counterattacked, and, although they failed to push the eastern arm of 21st Army Group back to the beaches, they succeeded in pinning it down and stalling its advance. Temporarily part of Second British Army, 3rd Canadian Division engaged in a series of battles inflicting heavy German losses and beating back numerous German counterattacks. Caen remained in German hands and on 26 June Montgomery ordered Second British Army to capture it. Again, progress was slow, and it took several bloody and costly operations to reach the ancient city. The final assault was preceded by a major aerial bombardment that destroyed much of Caen. Nonetheless, an Anglo-Canadian contingent finally entered the city on 9 July. Clearing Caen and its surrounding area of German troops would take another twenty days.

The first Canadian CA officer to arrive in France was Col George P. Henderson who crossed with elements of Second British Army and arrived 8 June. The next day he was temporarily placed in command of II Canadian Corps CA (II Canadian Corps becoming operational on 9 June) and for the next ten days Henderson was the senior most Canadian CA officer in France. Brig. Wedd arrived on 18 June with one staff officer (Major J.P. Manion) and proceeded to set up at Amblie in anticipation of First Canadian Army becoming operational, which occurred on 23 July.[53] At that time, Henderson became Wedd's "colonel executive," effectively his second-in-command. Until FCA went operational; however, it would be Henderson and the men of II Canadian Corps CA who would face the first major test for Canadian Civil Affairs when they entered the dystopian-like city of Caen.

Caen: The Martyred City

Caen was the first major urban centre encountered by Canadian Civil Affairs and it presented the first significant challenges to the inexperienced organization. As Major Reid aptly put it, "No account of Civil Affairs in France would be complete without some reference to Caen which, being the first town to present any serious problems, tested many theories and taught many lessons which were to influence and guide the conduct of Civil Affairs throughout the entire campaign."[54] Anglo-Canadian patrols first walked the rubble strewn streets of the city on 9 July. Followed on their heels was an advance party of CA Detachment 201 led by Col Charles Usher, a fifty-two-year-old Scotsman who would become the senior CA officer for Caen. This advanced party was followed over the next few days by advance elements of Detachments 208, 209, and 219. On 11 July CA responsibility for Caen was officially given to II Canadian Corps (at that time part of Second British Army as First Canadian Army had yet to become operational). By 12 July, all four detachments were up to full strength (a total of sixty-four officers including several French officers acting as liaisons). These detachments went to work while fighting still raged in the city. The Orne River had by this point become the front line, splitting the city into an Anglo-Canadian occupied northern half and a German occupied southern half. Extensive street fighting continued.

Caen was a disaster zone. Approximately two-thirds of the historical city of William the Conqueror was completely demolished, much of it by Allied shelling and bombing. Roughly 25,000 people, of an original population of 60,000, still lived in the city and an estimated 13,000 of those were homeless. The Allies estimated there were between 2,500 and 3,000 civilian dead and almost 1,500 wounded after the ten days it took to clear the Germans from the city. As a Canadian Army report read, "The civilian authorities had provided an efficient service for clearing readily-available bodies out of ruins, but it was estimated that 600 bodies still remained buried under debris. These, however, were so deeply buried that they were not an immediate source of danger to health."[55] The streets were so choked with masonry and rubble that it was difficult for tanks to enter. There was no sanitation and the spectre of disease hung over the city like the clouds of ash and dust.[56] The water distribution system was heavily damaged, as was the electrical power system; the Allies were therefore unable to pump or bring in water or establish a working sewage system. Allied troops struggled to move supplies to areas in need because of debris piled up in the streets. The eastern end of town was completely cut off from the western end by a barrier of rubble and ruins.[57] CA officers estimated that roughly 20,000 to 25,000 people had to be fed in Caen during the first days of liberation.[58] Rations for 20,000 people were transported into town within twenty-four hours of the arrival of Civil Affairs, along with supplies of soap, antilouse powder, and other disinfectants.[59] The extensive amount of rubble in the streets and the on-going fighting made distribution of these supplies extremely difficult.

The temporary arrangements for Caen's displaced people were entirely unsanitary. An estimated 7,000 homeless civilians were crammed into the Lycee Malherbe, a large secondary school in the centre of the city. Another 1,500 were taking shelter in the eleventh-century Abbey de Saint-Etienne, which acted as both a makeshift hospital and shelter.[60] Surprisingly, the medical situation in Caen was not as bad as predicted: "the French services for looking after the wounded in the hospitals ... were working admirably when CA entered the town."[61] CAOs organized transports for civilian casualties to hospitals outside of the city in order to keep hospital beds within Caen empty for emergencies. CAOs also organized the distribution of II Canadian Corps medical supplies to local hospitals in order to help alleviate widespread medical supply shortages throughout the city. These early days were a chaotic scene of CAOs, military medical personnel, civilian doctors (sixty chose to remain in Caen despite the fierce fighting), and nurses all working closely together to help the wounded.

The primary objective for II Canadian Corps CA in Caen was to move the homeless population out of the city and away from the fighting as quickly as possible (Caen remained in the forward battle area for the next two weeks and was an important transportation hub for the remainder of the Normandy campaign). Large numbers of homeless civilians wandered aimlessly through Caen's broken streets while a smaller number were reported living in temporary shelters underground and in local cave systems. While fighting continued between the north and south bank of the Orne, civilians were evacuated to a number of CA-established refugee centres, primarily along the Caen–Bayeux highway, although some were also set up near Amblie. Civilians were initially transported in French lorries (requisitioned by CAOs), but when these were found to be unreliable, the army provided a company of eighteen lorries.[62] At first many Caen civilians refused to be evacuated. Only 250 were evacuated on 11 July with another 700 on 12 July. One of the more tragic events occurred on the night of 13 July when heavy German shelling during an evacuation of 830 civilians resulted in heavy casualties.[63] The next day saw a dramatic increase in the number of volunteers for evacuation, 1,950 were moved out of the city. Civilians remained in the refugee centres until being allowed to return to Caen while others were billeted in outlying towns and villages. Those civilians who had relatives and friends outside of the city were given passes to move freely to those destinations on foot and remain there until allowed back into Caen.[64] Walking on foot proved very dangerous: "The third [bomb] exploded on a tree at the end of the ditch. The shrapnel killed my 23 year old brother and fatally wounded four members of the same family, aged 9, 10, 15 and 16! The cries of the wounded sent everyone running for their lives. The smoke and smell of burning were unbearable."[65] Within four days an estimated 6,000 refugees had been evacuated from Caen, including 800 wounded and "many hundreds sick and infirm."[66] The refugee situation north of the Orne was finally stabilized by 16 July.

A second phase of civilian evacuation was initiated on 17 July coinciding with a major Anglo-Canadian military push towards the southern outskirts of Caen, Operation's Goodwood and Atlantic respectively. During this phase of evacuation heavy fighting embroiled the Orne River's southern bank and spread into the southern outskirts of the city. To remove civilians from the battle space CA established a refugee staging area on the north bank at the Lycée Malherbe that had been "completely cleared and disinfected after being vacated by its previous tenants."[67] Ten three-ton lorries were used to transport civilians to this staging area via one of three bridges erected by British Second Army engineers. Once at the staging area, CA established a security checkpoint and provided medical aid. The civilians ate and slept at the staging area and were then transported via British Second Army lorries to preestablished refugee centres north of the city. From these centres, the refugees were sent to various locations throughout the countryside. While hundreds of civilians were evacuated via this scheme, hundreds more requested to remain in what was left of their homes or shelters. If the local

CA officer deemed them to have enough food, water, and medical support they were generally left alone to wait out the battle.

Grottoes, caves, and cellars became temporary shelters for thousands of civilians. When CA officers entered the southwestern district of Fleury-sur-Orne they found "2000 persons living in the caves and quarries. They included 400 bedridden old people and 100 orphaned children."[68] Yvonne Mannevy emerged from one cave with 800 other Normans shortly after liberation:

> We couldn't bear to look around us. It was hell. Everything had been destroyed.
>
> The dead animals on the roads were bloated due to the early August heat. The corpses of soldiers were decomposing in the embankments and orchards. We returned to discover a pestilent odour of death ... I tried to avert my eyes but there were so many corpses on the ground that it was impossible. While this was happening, we crossed paths with a convoy of trucks with soldiers giving us the V sign and tossing us cigarettes, chewing gum and bars of chocolate. This was it; this surreal, spectacular combination of deliverance and death was the Liberation.[69]

Many of these people were stranded with little to no food or water. CA detachments organized the delivery of supplies to these hard to reach shelters. In one instance, the Germans fired mortars at a lorry carrying biscuits and disinfectant to a cave in Fleury-sur-Orne setting off an hour-long artillery duel. Because the fighting was still quite close to the caves of Fleury-sur-Orne most civilians were told to stay put, only the aged and infirm were evacuated. When the fighting finally moved on all the remaining civilians were evacuated.

Caen finally fell to the Allies on 20 July with the completion of Operations Goodwood and Atlantic. Three days later First Canadian Army, under General Harry Crerar, was made operational, as was First Canadian Army Civil Affairs under Brigadier Wedd. Shortly after, II Canadian Corps was then transferred from Second British Army to First Canadian Army bringing II Canadian Corps Civil Affairs under Wedd and First Canadian Army's jurisdiction.

Caen's inhabitants received the Allies with mixed emotions. Although generally happy to be liberated, the civilians were equally dismayed by the extensive bombing. Perhaps slightly naïve, one Canadian report read, "The morale of the population was good. Most [Caen] inhabitants do not understand the reason for severe Allied bombardment of the city. However, only among those who have lost immediate relatives does resentment occasionally appear."[70] A Canadian lance bombardier from 2nd Anti-Tank regiment wrote, "All the French I spoke to here were very nice and glad to see us, but I could tell they resented their buildings being torn down by shells and bombs."[71] Mr Dauré, Caen's new Gaullist prefect, agreed when he informed one CA officer that "the strength and efficacy of the bombardment made some people compare it to the well-known methods of the enemy."[72] Two leading religious officials lamented, stating, "We have suffered an undeserved fate. Apart from the grievous sufferings of the population, many old buildings and churches have been destroyed."[73] Yvonne Mannevy was a volunteer nurse working in Caen, "Everywhere I looked, there were caved-in houses, dead bodies on the ground and people screaming. That same morning those same people had been living peacefully in their houses; in the blink of an eye, the town had turned into a lunar landscape."[74] A 1946 report by Major Reid, Canadian CA historical officer, recognized this sacrifice for liberation: "Words fail to describe the anguish of Caen. It had indeed paid a fearful price for its liberation. However, the civilian morale was high."[75] The contemporaneous assessments of civilian morale seemed to be informed primarily by whether one was a civilian in Caen or not. Almost two decades later F.S.V. Donnison, in his British official history on Civil Affairs, wrote, "The inhabitants left were not alone in questioning whether such an obliterating bombardment had been necessary."[76] Despite the controversy over the destruction of their city, most reports suggest that the population was generally friendly to their liberators, as the region's prefect concluded, "There is not the slightest doubt that the people are delighted to be liberated."[77]

The primary focus of Canadian CA was to organize and control civilian movement so as to not interfere with ongoing First Canadian Army military operations. Officials envisioned a general plan to quickly and efficiently evacuate civilians and then to focus on the restoration of infrastructure. This proved to be a very difficult challenge. CA doctrine in practice was neither organized nor centralized. Operations in Caen were a patchwork series of localized decisions based on individual detachments and did not reflect a coordinated and centralized plan. Brigadier Wedd wrote, "Since this was the first attempt at large scale control of refugees in France, it is obvious that mistakes were inevitable."[78] Though regrettable, these operational mistakes proved valuable as they provided the men of Civil Affairs with an opportunity to learn significant lessons.

The scale of the problems encountered was emphasized in an after-action report published in August 1944. The report focused heavily on problems with refugee control, writing that "unless military necessity so required, do not make refugees of people who are perfectly willing to stay put."[79] CA officers tended to evacuate all persons living in designated city shelters, unnecessarily creating more refugees. But as the Caen report states, "Sleeping in a shelter does not make a refugee of a person."[80] Some shelters provided more than adequate protection, like the caves at Fleury-sur-Orne. Many were considered satisfactory, sanitary living quarters for the interim period. Yet certain CAOs considered anyone inhabiting a cave shelter to be a refugee and forced them to evacuate, which unnecessarily increased the traffic of refugees moving out of the city. This placed a significant strain on available transportation, risked clogging up roads that were to be used by military personnel, and added further pressure to the already overworked Field Security and Civil Affairs personnel overseeing the evacuations. Furthermore, refugees congested preset evacuation routes creating a traffic jam and slowing down the entire evacuation process. This exposed these large crowds to greater risk from enemy bombardment.

To prevent superfluous numbers of refugees, the report called for the establishment of a classification system. This would be based on the refugees' "state of homelessness, willingness to evacuate, and whether or not they [had] a definite destination in mind."[81] By using strict guidelines to classify civilians, Civil Affairs intended to prevent unnecessary evacuations and show that the Allies were willing to respect, as much as possible, the local inhabitants' wishes.

The report also identified problems with different detachments carrying out contradictory evacuation policies. Some detachments implemented a voluntary policy while others called for compulsory evacuation. There was an obvious problem with this inconsistency and it stressed the need for an overarching policy to be applied throughout the operational area. This meant that evacuations should be delayed until all detachments were thoroughly organized and in place. The urgent need to immediately remove civilians from Caen appeared to override any organized, official plan. This created a patchwork implementation of CA policy causing more confusion and chaos than was necessary.

Finally, the Caen report challenged the decentralized command structure that governed the movement of refugees. It recommended that one officer be placed in charge of the entire refugee operation with enough staff to delegate as he saw fit. Although SCAO Colonel Charles Usher of 201 Detachment technically commanded the Caen operation, each detachment commander was left to his own devices. Very little interdetachment communication was occurring and though Usher was quite hands-on in dealing with the myriad of problems throughout Caen he did not enforce a single policy towards refugees. This was a root cause of the operational inconsistencies between detachments. CA needed to "Place one single officer in charge of refugee work and move[ment] control. Do not override his authority, do not give him staff which he does not require, and let him delegate as much as possible of his work to local authorities."[82] This officer would also be in charge of obtaining from all detachments under his command a complete list of available accommodations in each detachment's operational area so as to maximize the efficient distribution of refugee groups. With a centralized officer armed with sufficient authority, staff, and information, refugee movement could be better facilitated and controlled.

Civil Affairs officers encountered another major problem only weeks after the Caen operation had been completed: unauthorized returning refugee traffic. In Caen, as well as in numerous other towns and villages throughout northern France, refugees began making their way back to their homes regardless of warnings and bulletins issued by military authorities. These waves of uncontrolled refugees seriously threatened military security, communication, and supply lines. Refugee traffic could interfere with the movement of military personnel and equipment. Rogue civilian groups were also a risk for starvation and disease, something that would place further humanitarian demands on Allied resources. CA officials feared that law and order in Caen would be jeopardized by the waves of refugees returning at will, before an adequate police force had been established.

Enemy agents using the refugee population as camouflage was also a concern. It was feared that these "fifth column" agents could easily move within these groups to sabotage or gather intelligence (though very few instances of sabotage or intelligence breaches were ever successfully proven), and any civilian returning home along military routes could plainly see Allied troop positions and equipment locations. One Canadian private expressed this concern while on guard duty at caves near Caen: "The caves were full of French civilians hiding from the Germans, but there were a few spies in them, women who were married to Germans and trying to get information."[83] Another story was relayed by Captain J.E.G. Labrosse. Captain Joseph Ernest Gaétan Labrosse was from a small French Canadian community in eastern Ontario. He graduated in pharmacy from the University of Montreal and later received his economics degree from the same university. When he joined the army in 1941, at the age of forty-three, he was running a successful pharmacy business in Montreal after spending time working for a pharmaceutical firm in New York. With ample civilian experience, and being too old to serve in a combat unit, he was thus a natural fit for Civil Affairs.[84] In 1944 Labrosse was temporarily serving with an American CA detachment when he relayed another tale about the concern over German sympathizers amongst the civilian population: "On my way back from church service an American officer was relating to me that a French woman had been caught smoking in the window of the hotel ... It was believed that by signalling with her cigarette she had given information to the Germans who were about one mile [1.6 kilometre] away on the top of a hill facing the hotel. She was arrested at once, court martialed and executed by an American squad."[85] Another report spoke of a Madeline Guillod of Camilly who was caught fraternizing with soldiers from

II Canadian Corps on a road barred to civilians. CA detained her and handed the case over to Field Security. The citizens of Camilly publicly accused her of being too friendly with German soldiers, an investigation by Canadian Field Security concluded that, "her interest in [troops] is only physical."[86] She was released.

Uncontrolled refugee movement posed a serious security issue. Canadian Field Security Sections (FSS) often commented on these issues; 15th Canadian Field Security Section, for instance, identified how "adherence to movement restrictions have already proven a problem"[87] and they placed the blame for lack of refugee control squarely on the shoulders of Civil Affairs: "This problem appears as much the fault of CA as anyone ... unless there can be some tie-up between CA, Provost, French authorities and CI [counter-intelligence] the whole 'restriction of movement' appears to be a farce."[88] CA officers hoped that predesignated routes for civilians to use when returning to their homes would solve the issue. Many civilians simply ignored these for better-known shortcuts. Officers then distributed posters and made personal appeals to the civilian population but there were not nearly enough military personnel to effectively cover all the areas of return. Many refugees continued to return home using whatever route they saw fit. Field security concerns became more serious and "in some cases [CA officers took] more drastic action against those who disregarded such instructions."[89]

Drastic action often meant detention and/or arrest. In the village of Cairon lived Eugiene Toroude. Both her parents had been killed in the early days of the war and her closest relative was an uncle in Thaon, who was a confirmed collaborator. In the summer of 1944 German shelling killed her uncle and Eugiene set off to Thaon on foot to bury him. On the road she was stopped and detained by CA for travelling along a military route while "showing more than average interest in troop movements by her questions to troops."[90] Though both soldiers of 3rd Canadian Infantry Division and a few locals reported her activity, a subsequent investigation concluded she was not a security threat. Nonetheless, she was ordered to report to the Mayor's office twice a week while in Thaon.[91]

Civilian refugees desperately wanted to return home, and tension emerged between them and the military personnel preventing their return. Many were forced to travel through fields adjacent to the main roads creating nomadic tent villages. Refugees carried with them "most of their worldly possessions. They came with huge wagons, all manner of carts, bicycles laden with bedding, clothes and bottles of cider. Many even attempted to bring cattle with them."[92] The lack of available transport further increased the problem. Almost all of the refugees were forced to walk, those lucky enough to have buggies or carts could only move at the slow pace of their foot-bound travelling companions. Although some Allied vehicles were made available to help in transporting civilians these were limited and only put further strain on military resources. As one officer noted, "The problem of transport, is, at the present time, the only serious one caused by refugee movement."[93] While Field Security would continue to be frustrated with the perceived chaos of returning refugees, Civil Affairs and II Canadian Corps reported that the flood of returning refugees "was restrained to a number which did not materially interfere with Army traffic."[94]

With Caen empty of most of its citizens, looting became a serious problem. Civil Affairs officers thus became responsible for establishing a semblance of law and order in order to deter would-be thieves. Their first step was to reinstate and arm the prewar gendarmerie (police) and deputize local French resistance forces. In Caen, this resulted in the establishment of a fairly effective French police force that would patrol the streets on a regular basis. This official presence proved strong enough to deter many locals from looting their neighbours; the real problem, however, was that many of the perpetrators were discovered to be Canadian soldiers. This posed complications for the French who were unsure of their jurisdictional ability to arrest Canadian soldiers. Not to mention Canadian soldiers were often better armed than the recently established French gendarmerie. Now, sometimes breaking the law was an innocent case of theft from the wreckage of a building, "The ash tray I sent you is plunder and is from the Church ... We blew the church all to pieces as it was an observation post for the enemy."[95] An officer with the Regiment de la Chaudiere recalled cases of food theft by his men,

> It was prohibited but they [Canadian soldiers] would steal eggs from chicken coops. It was a change for them. They were not sup-

posed to but I would look the other way and say, "don't get caught." One guy named Theriault, he came along one day with his steel helmet full of eggs and three or four bottles of wine in his arms. He ran into a Frenchwoman and she said "my god, have the Canadians come here to save us or to steal from us?"[96]

Sometimes officers did not look the other way, as was the case for one unlucky Canadian soldier who was caught by the gendarmerie, turned over to the Canadian army, and brought up on charges for stealing luggage from an abandoned house.[97] In another instance, two Canadian soldiers entered a wine warehouse "brandishing Sten guns and held up the manager for [two] kegs of wine."[98] The very next day, the same warehouse manager discovered three Canadian soldiers had broken in through the attic and attempted to take off with some of his prized barrels. In another more dangerous incident, "two drunken soldiers were found firing their Stens in one of the inhabited streets of Caen and terrifying the population."[99] Some reported cases went unsolved, like the safe stolen from the mayor's house in Mondeville (a suburb to the southeast of Caen) and 25,000 francs reportedly stolen from another house nearby. "Out of Bounds" and "Booby Trapped" signs placed throughout various areas of the city were used as deterrence, but both the military police (MP) and French law enforcement struggled to maintain law and order. In fact by August looting had become such a problem that strict movement controls were put in place on any military personnel entering Caen. Any soldier below the rank of a Lt Colonel could not enter the city without written authorization.[100]

In one more unusual case, a Canadian MP arrested a French civilian caught stealing, but because the Canadian MP could not speak French and the French jailer could not speak English, the civilian was held for a week before the jailer finally approached the appropriate military authorities to inquire about the charge against the civilian. The MP who had arrested the civilian had moved on with his unit without leaving any record of the arrest, and no one at headquarters could give the French jailer any answers. The civilian was consequently released.[101]

A major problem as to why Civil Affairs officers faced a chaotic law and order situation in the weeks following their takeover of Caen was the inability to get various organizations to cooperate with one another. One report accurately summed up the difficulties:

> [Canadian Division Provost] stated that they could not investigate such cases since their sole function in town was traffic control. A First Canadian Army SIS [Security Intelligence Section] and [Provost Section] were in town for a few days but could not begin to cope with the cases brought to their attention. [Lines of Communication] Claims and Hiring's had an office in town, and stated that they preferred to do their own investigation of such cases before the trail was sullied by other investigations.[102]

The British and Canadian military police did not have enough personnel to effectively prevent lawlessness and investigate every reported charge. While the French government was handing out severe penalties to civilian looters (up to twenty years hard labour if caught), some French officials and civilian leaders felt the Canadians were not enforcing the same justice to their own and that in some cases even turning a blind eye: "Some French people are so outraged that they are talking of shooting looters found on their premises. The absence of counterpart measures on our side appears to some [civilians] to reflect our own tepid attitude towards military looting."[103] On 3 August when II Canadian Corps CA officially handed over responsibility of Caen to Lines of Communication, issues of law and order still plagued the city.

Brig. Wedd was not pleased with the inability for Canadian Civil Affairs to solve the law and order situation in Caen and ordered new security practices put into place for future urban CA operations. He felt that the main issue was the limited size of both the military police and provost, and he received permission from Crerar to increase the size of both. Wedd also stated that new policy would require senior military police and senior local law enforcement officers to coordinate with Civil Affairs upon arrival in any new area. He ordered that a central complaints bureau be established, whereby civilians would have a direct channel to the military for filing grievances. Wedd also solved the jurisdictional issue between French police and Canadian soldiers when he sent out a directive "granting to French police the power of arresting soldiers, providing such soldiers [were] immediately turned over to MPS."[104]

Not only were new security directives issued after Caen but a new more effective policy was established for deploying CA detachments. One detachment would now be assigned to each division, and these would be integrated within each division's headquarters. Upon entering a town, these "spearhead" detachments provided immediate relief and addressed any pressing concerns. They were then relieved by static detachments that would remain in the area for longer periods to deal with larger issues. The spearhead detachments would then move forward with their respective divisions. Prior to this change in policy, there was no distinction between spearhead or static detachments. The first CA detachment to enter a town often had to cope with numerous short- and long-term issues and then just as quickly might be ordered out of town. This "first on the scene" approach meant that CA detachments often prioritized tasks based on their ability to quickly solve them before moving out, often at the expense of more complicated long-term problems.[105] Now a spearhead detachment could deal with short-term issues upon entering a town and then present a report to the incoming static detachment which would take over long-term responsibility for the place. From 24 August to 9 September, for instance, 225 Detachment, attached to 3rd Canadian Division, set up headquarters in nine different towns along 3rd Division's march through France submitting reports on each town it entered. Reports covered the reliability of local administrative officials, the status of the FFI (French Forces of the Interior) in the region, the quantity of food, clean water, and medical supplies, the refugee situation, the state of law and order, any captured German equipment, the condition of local infrastructure, and any other issues that the detachment commander felt necessary to pass on to the incoming static detachment.[106] A much fuller picture of each town and its surrounding region was thus available for incoming CA officers.

Wedd's reforms also improved communication between CAOS and their colleagues at corps and division HQ. Prior to the creation of spearhead detachments, detachment commanding officers (COs) often had to work with a variety of different HQs and thus different and unfamiliar combat officers in every region they entered. This meant that cooperation between CA detachments and combat headquarters was limited. With the new policy, however, each division got to know and to depend upon its own particular "spearhead" detachment. The members of the detachment understood and were able to deal with the problems and personalities in their respective areas or divisions.[107]

Caen provided a battlefield classroom for many of the Civil Affairs officers in II Canadian Corps. In coping with the large urban population of Caen it prepared these men for northwest Europe's large industrial cities. These men learned to use and coordinate available transportation networks, control mass refugee movements, maintain law and order, establish effective local civilian administration, provide access to food, medicine, and clean water, and cope with combat threats. By late July the experienced Civil Affairs staff of II Canadian Corps now answered directly to Brigadier Wedd and his CA staff at First Canadian Army headquarters and First Canadian Army Civil Affairs would need all that experience and more in order to minimize civilian disruptions to military operations during the brutal battle for the Falaise Gap in August and the channel ports to follow.

The Falaise Pocket

Even though Anglo-Canadian soldiers first entered Caen on 9 July, the last German holdouts in the southern sections of the city would not be pushed out until the 20th. In the following battle of Verrieres Ridge, British and Canadian soldiers engaged in a series of costly yet ultimately successful operations to clear the Germans from these dominating heights south of Caen. By the beginning of August German 7th Army began a retreat eastward to defensive positions along the Seine while the Allies sought to encircle and trap them near the city of Falaise. The Germans found themselves in a slowly closing Allied pocket with First Canadian Army driving in from the north, Second British Army pushing hard from the northwest and First and Third US Army closing the pocket from the west and south respectively. The retreating Germans had destroyed numerous villages and evicted the civilian population from their homes. Large numbers of refugees clogged the roads, fields, and woods in search of shelter, food, and safety. These large groups of destitute civilians threatened to impede First Canadian Army operations. II Canadian Corps spearheaded First Canadian Army's closing of the pocket through two key operations, Totalize (from 7 August to 10 August) and Tractable (14 August to 17 August) whereby the Canadians succeeded in capturing the city of Falaise. While this was occurring, II Canadian Corps CA ordered that civilians remain in place until the battle had moved on, a "stay put" policy as it was called. They were only allowed to return to their homes once both the SCAO of II Canadian Corps Col J.J. Hurley and General Simonds at II Canadian Corps headquarters agreed that such a return would not hinder military operations.

Yet even after the fall of Falaise on 17 August the encirclement was incomplete and vicious fighting continued as desperate Germans sought to escape the noose that had become the Falaise pocket. Corpses of both men and animals intermixed with countless destroyed vehicles painted a horrific "highway of death" and these obstacles seriously impeded travel along the local road network.

> There were 10,000 German dead in the area plus thousands of farm animals – the place was rife with rats. It was a very hot summer; everything was covered with maggots. You can't even imagine what kind of a scene it was; it was beyond compare. What they did, it was such a jumbled mess, they sent in bulldozers to clean the roads, shoved all the animals and humans in a heap and then set fire to them, which they had to do to get rid of the rats. It was terrible.[108]

At this point supply issues became a serious concern for FCA CA as the increasing distance from front to rear placed detachments that wished to provide the civil authorities with emergency Civil Affairs supplies in an impossible position.[109] The distances were too far and the roads were littered with obstacles. This was further compounded by the "stay put" policy. It was recognized that the civilians adhering to this policy be given sufficient food until they were allowed to return to what was left of their homes. Yet spearhead detachments of II Canadian Corps CA, responsible for distributing the food, could not get enough supplies to these civilians in need. The method by which spearhead detachments requisitioned and delivered supplies was by transporting the necessary amount via vehicle from a specifically designated Civil Affairs supply depot in the rear to the intended drop point near the front line. But this method was now wholly inadequate due to the long distance from the supply depot to the front line (roughly sixty kilometres of two-lane roads that were windy, pock-marked, and full of military traffic). Col Hurley was able to reach a temporary "friendly agreement" with the Royal Canadian Army Service Corps (RCASC), the Canadian branch responsible for logistics, and with the permission of Gen. Simonds, could draw upon supplies at any and all levels when required.[110] This was only a temporary situation though, as Simonds did not want to permanently divert any of his resources away from II Corps to II Corps CA. Col Hurley soon ordered that spearhead detachments carry with them a limited supply of rations drawn from CA supplies for emergency situations. This policy soon became standard for all spearhead detachments in First Canadian Army.

THE CHANNEL PORTS

After the closing of the Falaise pocket, First Canadian Army turned east as part of the Allied drive across the Seine towards the German frontier. First Canadian Army now operated on the left flank of 21st Army Group. General Bernard Montgomery, commander of 21st Army Group, surmised that capturing a series of channel ports could alleviate the logistical and supply problems plaguing his formation. He aimed to capture the port towns of Le Havre, Dieppe, Boulogne, Calais, and Dunkirk. In the *Official History of the Canadian Army in the Second World War*, C.P. Stacey argues the following: "Montgomery calculated that with the ports of Dieppe, Boulogne, Dunkirk, and Calais and some help from Le Havre, he could go to Berlin."[111] Montgomery's enthusiasm for capturing these ports was not just a product of Supreme Commander Eisenhower's strategic directive but also reflected his hope that these port cities-turned-supply depots could enable him to thrust into Germany across the plains of northern Europe.

As early as May '44 SHAEF planners had conceived a broad front strategy, whereby two army groups would move both north and south of the Ardennes forest to capture the Ruhr, Germany's industrial heartland, and eventually move towards Berlin. SHAEF planners felt that they could avoid the possibility of a head-to-head collision between the main Allied thrust and the main German defensive stand. A broad front would give the Allies a strong defensive position with room to manoeuvre in case of a German offensive. Although Eisenhower generally agreed with this strategy, by July 1944 Montgomery argued that the circumstances that "had now arisen – the Germans' disorganization resulting from their defeat in Normandy – offered an opportunity for a concentrated attack on a relatively narrow front."[112] Moreover, by September, there was no possible logistical way to carry out a broad assault by all available Allied forces; as Stacey writes, "There was simply not enough gasoline to be had at the front to move their vehicles."[113] Eisenhower recognized these logistical difficulties facing his forces and decided that Montgomery's forces should be given priority supplies and should clear the northern coast, liberate Belgium, and seize the Ruhr, while Bradley's US 12th Army Group, on Montgomery's right, supported them.

The logistical problems that began to surface in August 1944 were therefore anticipated. In his initial logistical plan, devised in the spring of 1943, General Sir Frederick Morgan, COSSAC's supreme allied commander (designate), recognized that the greatest Allied problem with a Normandy invasion would be building up and maintaining Allied supplies and troops following the landing. The Norman coast had several small ports, but even with Cherbourg and Le Havre captured intact, they would still not provide enough deepwater shipping for the invading Allied forces' logistical demands.[114] General Morgan suggested using artificial harbours, called "Mulberries," to sustain the continual flow of supplies. Two were built and assembled in Normandy in June 1944. The American Mulberry off Omaha beach was destroyed in the great storm of 19 June to 22 June, which left only the British artificial harbour at Arromanches operational. By late August 1944, this artificial harbour was receiving the vast majority of supplies intended to support the Allied forces pushing east. The harbour at Cherbourg, which the Germans had thoroughly destroyed in June 1944, was finally fully operational but had only just begun to receive supplies. By the end of August Allied forward elements were racing for the German border without assurances that they would have the necessary material support. A logistical crisis was in the making.[115]

With the Allied forces facing logistical difficulties, capturing French port installations became all the more important. General Crerar's First Canadian Army was given this important task and thus faced a series of coastal cities turned fortresses, Le Havre, Boulogne, Calais, and Dunkirk. Crerar recognized the importance of the Canadian objectives when he wrote, "It follows that speedy and victorious conclusion to the war now depends, fundamentally, upon the capture by First Cdn Army of the Channel ports which have now become so essential, if the administrative problem is to be solved."[116] The fortifications defending each city had been constructed and improved over several years of German occupation. Gaining control of these fortress towns meant brutal street fighting on a battlefield containing thousands of civilians.[117]

Civil Affairs's responsibility was thus preventing civilians from impeding military operations through mitigating collateral damage against the civilian population and even removing them from the battle space. This period was marked by a series of complex evacuation schemes that accompanied the battles for the port cities of Le Havre, Boulogne, Calais, and Dunkirk. CA also remained responsible for the provision of medical aid and supplies to civilians in need, the vetting of local civic leaders to ensure their reliability, the establishment of local police forces, and ensuring that both the mayor and police took responsibility for clearing roads being used for military purposes.[118] CA officers sought to quickly establish a central authority that would remind the civilians that they were now active partners in continuing the war effort. Yet many officers noted a general attitude that "the departure of the enemy from an area should permit an immediate return of that area to unheeded civilian life under pre-war conditions."[119] Sadly, for many civilians the reminder that they were still in a war zone came in the form of destruction and death. Once combat erupted in the battle space, Allied commanders almost always saw civilian safety as a secondary priority to obtaining the combat objective. Military operational necessity took precedence over any CA responsibility. This meant civilian casualties. When Caen was liberated, an estimated 2,500 to 3,000 civilians were killed. During the military operations to recover Le Havre by I British Corps, between 1,500 and 2,000 civilians perished in what one historian describes as "a week of air raids which, though militarily quite ineffective, destroyed most of the city."[120]

Le Havre

Le Havre was the first of the coastal cities to be liberated. From a strategic perspective, regaining Le Havre, France's largest channel port, was crucial to the logistical demands of the Allied war machine. By late August 1944, the Allies needed the city's harbour to supply their continuing advance across France. Ultimately, the Allies mounted a massive bombing campaign against the German garrison from 5 September to 10 September, dropping an estimated 9,000 tons of bombs on the city to soften German defences before General John Crocker's I British Corps assaulted the city on foot. Much like Caen, Le Havre was a disaster zone when Allied troops entered on 12 September 1944. "Havre is a dreadful sight," a British CA report concluded. "The whole of the area between the Boulevard de Strasbourg and the docks, comprising the business and residential quarters, is reduced to rubble ... It is generally agreed at Havre that this destruction was a terrible mistake."[121] Like at Caen, the destruction gained the Allies very little tactical advantage while creating hardship and death for the civilians awaiting liberation.[122] This mistake fell on the shoulders of First Canadian Army, who had called in the Royal Air Force to provide tactical air strikes on German positions throughout the city. Upon learning the extent of the damage, Air Marshal Arthur Harris, head of RAF bomber command, sent officers to investigate and "it was decided to limit the use of heavy bombers at Boulogne."[123] For future operations, RAF command arranged for an "RAF officer on the ground to communicate directly with the master bomber."[124] Bomber command felt that the use of their bombers for the attack on Le Havre was excessive and misplaced, and the relationship between First Canadian Army and the RAF was strained for the remainder of the war.[125]

The destruction in Le Havre was extensive. A SHAEF fortnightly report in late September explained that Le Havre was "relatively more damaged than any other city of France, [thus] the chief administrative problem [was] one of rehabilitation ... subject to assistance from Civil Affairs officers."[126] That same report stated that 82 per cent of the city was damaged while it estimated that 50,000 inhabitants remained in Le Havre (49,000 having already either voluntarily fled the city prior to the bombing or been evacuated by the Germans to the surrounding countryside).[127] Despite the high number of casualties, Allied authorities estimated that, "had the bombing occurred at any other time of the day or had the population not already been evacuated by the Germans from the immediate dock area, casualties would have been far higher."[128] The destruction was so significant that a census carried out in 1946 found that half the city's population was still homeless.

Civil Affairs faced difficulties physically and morally rehabilitating Le Havre owing to the local civilians' widespread resentment. One CA officer wrote, "This resentment [of Allied bombing] is more widespread and does not appear to be lessening ... It is a fact that the effect of the bombardment of the town of Havre has had an effect of great shock and caused general bitterness and resentment amongst the population."[129] Civil Affairs officers had to not only clear an immense amount of debris and provide shelter and supplies but also win back the hearts and minds of local civilians. This task would take time; CA officers, in conjunction with French officials, set about establishing shelters for the thousands of homeless, providing food, medical supplies, clothes, and bedding for anyone in need, increasing the ration quota by releasing German food stocks, and establishing clean water points. Meanwhile, engineer and pioneer personnel cleared debris. In Le Havre, much like in Caen, Civil Affairs found distributing supplies quite difficult owing to the mass destruction turning once accessible roadways into rubble strewn barriers.[130]

SHAEF sought to quickly transfer authority to French officials in order to limit Allied personnel's participation in local affairs and remove, as much as possible, the object of local resentment. As Lt Col Woolum, commander of 213 (C) Detachment in Le Havre, wrote, "It would be difficult to explain to the French that we had many towns more badly damaged. They feel particularly hurt that it was done by the Allies – and it is necessary to see the damage to appreciate it ... I would suggest that as far as military necessity permits, slightly generous consideration for the people of Le Havre should be shown."[131] Even though captured by First Canadian Army, SHAEF did not intend Le Havre to provide logistical support to Montgomery's 21st Army Group; instead, it would be used as a major port for Gen. Omar Bradley's 12th American Army Group. By the end of September Le Havre was inundated with American soldiers and they began immediately reconstructing the city, specifically its heavily damaged port facilities.[132]

SHAEF was concerned about the large numbers of civilian casualties at Caen and Le Havre, and it fell on the Canadians at Boulogne, Calais, and Dunkirk to find methods to avoid similar results.[133] Civil Affairs officers now had to better balance concerns over civilian casualties with the fact that combat objectives would still take operational priority. Ultimately, CA operations on the coast of France would have to successfully manoeuvre within this tight framework and limit civilian casualties while preventing civilians from impeding military operations.[134]

Boulogne

The liberation of the remainder of the port cities, Boulogne, Calais, and Dunkirk, fell to Gen. Simonds's II Canadian Corps. Boulogne was the first of the port cities to be liberated in what was labelled Operation Wellhit (17–22 September). Boulogne is one of France's oldest port cities and was once the primary port connecting Britain to the rest of the Roman Empire. Napoleon had intended to invade Britain by launching his Grande Armée from Boulogne. It has been fought over countless times by various nations and stands as a testament to the French people's endurance to the horrors of war. The city is surrounded on all sides by hilly terrain; in particular, Mont Lambert and the Herquelingue feature both stand at roughly 168 metres (550 feet) and dominate all the approaching ground. The city is a natural fortress, and for years, the Germans had been improving their defensive fortifications in and around it. These defensive positions boasted extremely well built concrete bunkers, which often contained several hundred men. Numerous smaller positions, consisting of twenty to thirty men, were built around artillery pieces and machine gun nests, which were further surrounded by barbed wire and vast mine fields. Boulogne was an impressive and daunting objective. Moreover, once the Canadians penetrated the outer defences, they had to fight through the streets, while the Germans used machine guns, snipers, and mortar teams to cover every narrow laneway and road.

Faced with these daunting conditions, Canadian Civil Affairs officers played an important role in caring for the civilians during the liberation of Boulogne. Between the two field detachments responsible for Boulogne, 219 Relief Detachment under Major Shelley and 225 Corps Detachment under Major Driver, and the CA staff at II Corps headquarters, roughly forty-five CAOs were involved in the Boulogne operation, commanded by Colonel J.J. Hurley, senior Civil Affairs officer for II Canadian Corps and future Canadian high commissioner to South Africa. At Boulogne CA successfully evacuated masses of civilians and reduced casualties, while cementing a doctrinal formula for future CA operations in urban areas. The success of Operation Wellhit directly resulted from the reforms implemented and lessons learned after the Caen operation.

On 9 September, Simonds issued a general operational directive to his division commanders that would heavily impact CA operations in the area. The directive tasked 2nd Canadian Infantry Division (CID) with occupying the coast from just east of Calais to Bruges to prevent any Germans from escaping Calais. Fourth Canadian Armoured Division (CAD) was ordered to "obtain bridgehead over Canal Du Ghent and try to rush a crossing over Canal Leopold. Bruges [needed] to be sealed off but [needed to] NOT be attacked for [the] time being as it [would] probably fall once [the] second canal line [was] turned."[135] Simonds directed General Dan Spry's 3rd CID to patrol and probe "for [the] purpose of reducing enemy held area and isolating gun positions preparatory to attack on BOULOGNE."[136] On 12 September, General Simonds met with General Spry to finalize plans for the assault on Boulogne.

At first, Civil Affairs officers sought to remove civilians living only within the city of Boulogne itself; however, the Allies suspected a serious security leak in the port city's outlying areas.[137] The war diary of the Stormont, Dundas, and Glengarry Highlanders reported, "We are to evacuate civilians ... Besides being in the way, it is felt the enemy may have planted some agents."[138] For security purposes, 3rd CID evacuated a belt some three to four miles (4.8 to 6.4 kilometres) deep encircling the city.[139] Lt Col Walker, executive staff officer for II Canadian Corps (essentially Hurley's second in command), in conjunction with Major Driver, 225 CA Detachment's CO, his second in command (2 IC), Captain de Mun, and Lt Col Ernest Cote, 3rd CID's quartermaster general, drew up the plans for Boulogne's evacuation. The two Canadian detachments involved in the evacuation, 225 CA Detachment and 219 Refugee (R) Detachment were to work with the French authorities, including neighbouring commune officials, the town of Montreuil-sur-Mer's mayor, as well as the French Forces of the Interior and the Secours National (a civilian organization intended to aid civilians during wartime), in order to clear the area occupied by Canadian forces on the eve of the assault.

The plan called for a general evacuation of the area between the Wimereux River to the north, the Boulogne Forest to the east, and the village of Ecault on the Outreau Peninsula to the south. This was a large area, and Civil Affairs established four major refugee collection points near significant villages and towns: in Bellebrune, to the northeast of Boulogne, in Wirwignes to the east, and two to the southeast near the small village of Zelique. Civil Affairs planners divided the evacuation area into Zones A and B; the northern boundary for Zone A was the Wimereux River, and its southern boundary was the Boulogne-Desvres road, running west to east through the city centre. Zone B incorporated the area south of the Boulogne-Desvres road all the way to the sea. CA personnel directed refugees from Zone A towards the collection points near Bellebrune and Wirwignes and refugees from Zone B towards the two collection points near Zelique. As one Canadian soldier noted, "Moving slowly their brightly coloured clothes in sharp contrast to their unhappy expressions, these people bore enormous burdens ... Few if any of these people realized that food, shelter and transport is to be provided for them."[140] From the collection points, CA personnel then transported refugees to the town of Montreuil (roughly forty kilometres south of Boulogne) via train and vehicles provided by the army. Once in Montreuil, French civilian authorities took control of the refugees and either accommodated them in Montreuil and its outlying communes or allowed them to stay with relatives elsewhere until the fighting moved on. Civil Affairs notified civilians of the evacuation scheme by distributing leaflets printed by 3rd CID. Deputy Assistant Adjutant General (DAAG) Major Keith of 3rd CID oversaw the leaflet production and distribution. Planes dropped these leaflets over German-occupied areas, or troops personally handed them out in Canadian-occupied areas.[141]

The evacuations in and around Boulogne occurred in two phases. In the first phase, Civil Affairs focused on evacuating the city's outlying areas, essentially the Canadian front lines. In the second, civilians were evacuated from within the city limits but only after German commander Lt General Ferdinand Heim arranged a temporary truce with the Canadians in early September.[142] This option for the garrison commander, to evacuate the city's residents, is one the Canadians dealt with several times along the coast. At every French port city, the German garrison commander allowed or at least considered evacuation of its urban occupants. At Boulogne, and later Dunkirk, the Germans allowed civilians to evacuate early in the combat phase, whereas in Calais they evacuated late in the battle. Canadian officers and French civilians then worked closely together to ensure the civilians were moved away from the battle space as quickly and efficiently as possible. As Lt Col Walker wrote optimistically, "It seems to me that there is every reason to think that this scheme should function easily and effectively. I think it is a first-rate example of the French looking after themselves and we [sic] assisting them."[143]

Although Canadian Civil Affairs intended to remove the majority of civilians from the battlefield, they recognized that many civilians would choose to remain in their homes. Prior to the truce, they feared that the Germans might even prevent the civilians from leaving the city in hopes that the large civilian presence would limit Canadian artillery and air strikes. Lt Col Coté, army adjutant and quartermaster general for 3rd CID, was reported to have been "very much concerned about the position of [civilians] in Boulogne and action to be taken to care for them on entry into the town. He felt that the reputation of the [division] depended in considerable measure on the way in which [civilians] were handled."[144] Therefore, a plan was devised to ensure that these civilians were cared for the minute the fighting passed them.

The plan relied on an accurate assessment of Boulogne in terms of three primary concerns: medical supplies, water, and food. With the help of II Canadian Corps French liaison officer Commander Mengin, CA officers knew that food in Boulogne was becoming scarcer every day, especially milk supplies for younger children. Medical supplies were limited, as the Germans were hoarding stocks and no new supplies could get in. The water situation was bordering on critical, as war damage to Boulogne and the outlying areas had contaminated most water sources. Coté felt that to be immediately effective the forward CA detachments needed to enter Boulogne "practically with the leading troops and be able to state to [civilian] authorities that feeding, water, [medical] care would be available the same day."[145] To ensure this Coté and the CA detachments entering Boulogne established a three-point plan addressing these three major concerns.

First, Coté ordered that 91,000 litres (20,000 gallons) of water be delivered in the first twelve hours after liberation, followed by 227,000 litres (50,000 gallons) every twenty-four hours after the initial supply. Recognizing the scope of the water delivery program Coté requested additional transport vehicles from II Canadian Corps to reinforce the divisional transport fleet intended to execute the scheme. Once the city was in Canadian hands, convoys of Canadian trucks carrying large vats of drinking water would then be rumbling through the cobbled streets of Boulogne with a CA officer often in the lead truck directing the distribution effort.

Second, Coté ordered enough rations for three days, drawn from the Civil Affairs supply depot, for the estimated remaining population. Due to the advanced state of undernourishment and the condition of the children in particular, Coté ordered that "the rations should contain considerable extra milk and soft foods."[146] Canadian soldiers alongside French medical teams and members of the Red Cross would distribute the rations by hand from a series of established central distribution points in various neighbourhoods throughout the city. Within several hours of liberation civilians could be seen lining up to receive their rations. After this three-day period, civilian supply channels from the countryside would then be established ending the need for military rations.

Finally, Coté ordered the shipment of medical supplies, primarily bandages, antitoxins (for diphtheria and typhoid), and anaesthetics, to Boulogne. Furthermore, Coté increased the number of trained medical personnel by bringing in an English Red Cross team and a French surgical unit to work alongside Canadian army medical teams. Though there were medical supply shortages within the city these were met by distribution of Civil Affairs supplies and equipment. Luckily, no serious epidemics were reported and enough hospital beds were available to care for the wounded civilians.[147]

Bringing up supplies was characterized by close cooperation between CA detachments and French government and nongovernment bodies. During active military operations 3rd Division HQ handled all supply requests, but once military operations moved forward, French regional authorities directly requested supplies from their superior civilian administrative bodies. After these requests were consolidated into bulk orders, the French would send their requests to supply officers at Civil Affairs Inland Depot (CAID) stores or further up the Canadian chain of command if the orders were larger. CA detachment officers advised local French officials on ordering supplies but were not directly involved in supply requests themselves. By September 1944, the French authorities had already "computed requirements for all supplies for the months of October and November."[148] Because of this system and the cooperation between French civilians and the Canadian military, there were no serious supply issues in Boulogne nor along the channel coast, though the lack of transportation was still "the limiting factor in the resumption of normal food distribution."[149] In an attempt to relieve this transport issue, "certain French transport companies [were] formed. These [were] equipped with British vehicles and [were] manned and maintained by French military personnel administered by the French Military Authorities."[150]

The battle for Boulogne lasted for five brutal days. The Canadians launched their assault on 17 September and it was not until 21 September that the final German defenders surrendered. Fighting for Boulogne was fierce, and the Germans, bolstered by thick concrete, barbed wire, minefields, and deadly artillery, contested every inch of ground. The Canadians extensively used medium and heavy artillery in the preliminary barrage on 17 September, but during the assault, they primarily used tanks, mortars, tactical air support from Typhoons, and flame-throwers to keep the Germans neutralized while the infantry rooted them out. In particular, Life Buoys (flame-throwing devices that could be carried by one man) and flame-throwing Churchill Crocodile tanks were used to great effect and caused havoc amongst the German ranks. The fear of being burnt alive seemed to scare many who "folded up very quickly in the face of [these] flame throwers."[151] In one instance, "Lieut. Porter, who was wounded ... was captured by the enemy and taken to an underground fortress near the cemetery. Through the night he undermined their morale by continual reference to [these] flame throwers and at first light the complete garrison brought him in [to Canadian headquarters] on a stretcher to negotiate surrender — a lot of them were drunk."[152] The roads into Boulogne were "impassable due to heavy bombing and enemy obstruction,"[153] so the Canadians used bulldozers and flail tanks to repair the roads and clear them of mines. After several key German defensive positions fell, particularly the citadel in Boulogne and the garrison at La Trésorerie, the Germans began to raise their white flags. "Prisoners [were] coming in so fast that the cage [was] not large enough to hold them and clerks, signalmen, etc., not on duty [were] pressed into service to guard them."[154] Once the Germans finally surrendered the defensive position of Le Portel, where the German garrison commander Lt General Heim held out, the battle for Boulogne was over.

The assault on Boulogne was not only a successful operation for Canadian combat troops but for the men of Civil Affairs as well. Civilian casualty rates were extremely low because CA detachments were able to provide basic needs immediately upon entering the town and were able to evacuate many civilians before combat started. In fact there were no reported civilian casualties once combat stopped. One unit's war diary reported,

> The Boulogne battle was against carefully sited and constructed fortifications, yet the division completed its tasks using only two

brigades and one armoured regt [regiment] ably supported by a force of arty [artillery]. The Boulogne garrison had only received one dose of heavy bombing. The general then compared this operation with the similar one at Le Havre at which 2 complete divisions were used.[155]

While the combat troops rested, Civil Affairs men worked tirelessly throughout Boulogne and the outlying areas. On 24 September, civilians and military personnel were given a rare treat: several officers from 214 Detachment organized a picture show in a captured German recreation room in the village of Audresselles. The movie was *Going My Way*, starring Bing Crosby.[156]

Calais

While 3rd CID troops assaulted Boulogne, the Canadians were already planning a similar assault on the large city of Calais (as part of the larger Operation Undergo 22 September to 1 October), the second port city to be liberated by II Canadian Corps. The strategy for Calais in dealing with the civilians was similar to the one used at Boulogne and speaks to the ability with which CA officers were able to implement similar practices in successive operations.

Like Boulogne, the Germans had spent four years converting Calais into an immensely strong fortress. A Royal Winnipeg Rifles report stated there was, "the presence of strong enemy forces in shell proof shelters, supported by arty [artillery] all throughout the area. All approaches to Calais from the SW [southwest] and South were flooded and bridges destroyed."[157] Lt Col Ludwig Schroeder, the garrison commander, had built new fortifications surrounding the city while integrating these into the original medieval fortifications. Minefields, artillery, and infantry positions dominated all the landward approaches. From the south and east, marshy ground and flooded areas restricted movement to a small easily defended causeway barely wide enough for one battalion. From the west, a series of strong defensive positions, such as the massive coastal batteries at Noires Mottes and along the Bellevue ridge near Vieux Coquelles, challenged any approaching enemy. Still more artillery, minefields, pillboxes, and bunkers protected the coastal route to the city, running into northern Calais and the coastal gun installations. The coastal gun installations were serious obstacles that contained strong garrisons ensconced in heavily fortified concrete bunkers. The guns themselves were Brobdingnagian in size as the diary for 7th Canadian Infantry Brigade attests: "Haringzelles contains a bty [battery] of 4 huge 38cm cross-channel guns, each encased in very thick concrete (some estimates give 18–20 feet thick) and surrounded by pill-boxes and outside that an outer ring of defence."[158] An "outer ring of defence" was traditionally barbed wire, minefields, slit trenches, and machine gun nests.

Calais was important for two reasons. Its port would provide logistical support to Montgomery's northern army group. As well, capturing Calais would eliminate the large German guns entrenched around the city and out towards Cap Gris Nez, a constant threat to shipping in the channel and even to the southern coast of England. Neutralizing these guns would also free up the approaches to Boulogne's port facilities, in one stroke giving Montgomery's supply lines unfettered access to two channel ports. Soldiers of 3rd CID, spearheaded by Brig. J.G. Spragge's 7th Canadian Infantry Brigade, attacked the city on 25 September. Attached to Spragge's division was 318 CA Detachment commanded by Major Alker. Once again, Canadians were fighting in an urban environment against a determined enemy. Division commander Gen. Daniel Spry commented, "To my amazement, they [the German garrison] did not want to talk surrender, but rather wished me to consider Calais an open town. To which my answer was 'All balls! I cannot consider it.'"[159]

The assault on Calais worried Civil Affairs officers because 20,000 civilians still remained in the city and as one war diarist for the Canadian Scottish wrote, "The civilian population, too, must be considered."[160] Much like they had done at Boulogne, Civil Affairs drew up operational plans to evacuate these civilians to the countryside. Unlike at Boulogne, the fighting commenced before the city could be evacuated. Canadian soldiers met "fierce resistance and ... the determined enemy had to be driven back house by house."[161] Calais had two times the population of Boulogne, and Lt Col Schroeder initially refused to allow the civilians to leave the city. Thus, for much of the military operation, scores of civilians were huddled in their houses, cellars, shelters, and trenches in the middle of an urban battlefield. It was not until near the end of September, when the German garrison seemed near defeat, that Schroeder allowed the civilians to leave the city. This was truly a tactical nightmare for Brig. Spragge when "surprise came to everyone. There was a 'sort of' truce in effect."[162] Lt Col Schroeder sent word to General Spry requesting that a twenty-four-hour truce begin on 28 September and as the CanScots war diarist sardonically points out, "He [Col Schroeder] [had become] very conscious of the 'suffering civilians' and asked for a truce to allow the civilians to be evacuated from the city. This seems to have been the first time that the enemy ... worried about the troubles of the civilians."[163]

Lt Col Schroeder's proposal benefited both sides; the Canadians regrouped and sent supplies to their forward elements, while the Germans readjusted their defences based on the now-exposed Canadian attack plan. As the war diarist for 7th Brigade states, "We were rather disappointed in this deal as it gave Schroeder time to change his guns around but there was nothing we could do about it for if we had rejected Schroeder's proposal and continued to shell the city it would have made very nice propaganda for the Germans."[164] The "nice propaganda" referred to being the killing of casualties by Allied shelling. By the morning of the 28th the frontline settled into an eerie calm as 7th Brigade prepared for a renewed assault the following day.

During this truce, Civil Affairs officers received nearly 15,000 French civilians and as one Canadian soldier recalled they "felt the fighting was going to get much heavier, they started to flee the town by the thousands. All roads leading out of Calais were clogged by these refugees and whatever belongings they could carry on their backs or roll along in carts, wagons and baby carriages. It was obviously not a time to be sending shells or engaging in machine gun fire back and forth."[165] Schroeder thought the evacuation would force the Canadians to redirect military resources towards civilian movement control and leave the Allies unprepared to resume hostilities. Brig. Spragge was reported to have been "more than slightly put out by the whole affair and cheerfully would have killed Schroeder if he could have got his hands on him."[166] Schroeder was obviously unaware of the Civil Affairs staff and their civilian partners' success in coordinating and evacuating large civilian populations.

During the truce Col Hurley was put in the unusual position of attending a meeting with none other than Lt Col Schroeder. It was here that Col Hurley gained the impression that the Germans would surrender Calais "after a sufficient show of resistance [had] been made to make their surrender appear an honourable one."[167] By nightfall of 29 September, all 7th Canadian Brigade forward elements had been fed and reequipped with supplies and ammunition. The brigade war diarist wrote, "And so ended this very unusual day with everyone on tenderhooks [sic] just longing to get at Gerries [sic] throat, and instead having to wait like good clean sportsmen until the referee said it was alright to go again. However, a bargains [sic] a bargain – and our word was always better than the Bosche's anyways."[168]

The Calais garrison surrendered on 30 September, just twelve hours after the conclusion of the truce, and immediately CA officers set to work. Though the food situation in Calais was not critical there was a shortage of clean water. Men from Major Alker's 318 Detachment led the way into Calais, quickly reestablishing a clean running water supply as well as bringing in vats of fresh water loaded into the backs of Canadian lorries. Electricity was reestablished later that afternoon while food and medical supplies were moved into the city and distributed by local French volunteer groups. In one of the more unusual incidences it was learned that a German generator had been found and auctioned off by French civilians to the proprietress of a brothel just south of the city in the commune of Guînes. Complaints were made to 225 CA Detachment responsible for the area. The officer commanding 225 Detachment, Major Cox, ordered the generator taken from the brothel and given over to a local hospital.[169]

Dunkirk

Dunkirk was the final port town along the coastal route of the Canadian advance. The soldiers from 2nd CID made several small-scale assaults into the town but found stiff resistance. As an operational objective,

Dunkirk was less significant than Calais and Boulogne, and the Canadians decided to surround the garrison and mask the city instead of wasting resources and lives in conducting another siege. In early September 1944, the Germans requested that Gen. Foulkes, commanding officer of 2nd CID, allow thousands of civilians to evacuate. In response to this, senior Canadian and British officers at 21st Army Group Headquarters debated the request. At a meeting on 21 September, while the attack for Calais was being planned, several officials strongly argued against the evacuation. Guy Simonds, and many others meeting at 21st Army Group HQ, believed that because the German garrison commander proposed the evacuation, it was more likely to benefit the Germans and be militarily disadvantageous to the Canadians. Both Simonds and Foulkes also opposed the evacuation on security grounds believing it would give German agents considerable opportunity to infiltrate Allied lines.[170] Senior operational planners at 21st Army Group were also sceptical about an evacuation as they were confident the city would fall in due course, "[the] saving in life by evacuation would perhaps not be great in light of the hazards of moving women and children to an emergency camp this time of year."[171] The Canadians also lacked transport; meaning evacuees would either be walking long distances or stuck in overcrowded emergency camps awaiting transportation. Yet as one report on the proceedings noted, "It was true that an appreciable saving of life would be effected and this humanitarian consideration must not be overlooked."[172] There would be combat to capture the city and this would place civilians in danger.

Pressure, however, was brought to bear by the French Red Cross and Simonds relented to the humanitarian implications of allowing an evacuation to occur. On 3 October, Civil Affairs warned the communes in Dunkirk's surrounding areas to prepare to receive refugees. On 5 October, now with operational experience at Caen, Boulogne, and Calais, II Canadian Corps CA officers began the evacuation.[173] Several refugee reception centres in the area were already operating, and these became the cornerstone of the evacuation program. Col George P. Henderson, First Canadian Army Civil Affairs's second-in-command, wrote, "These camps are org[anized] and operated by the FFI and French voluntary social workers ... I visited one at the railway station at Esquelbec and found it a model of cleanliness and good organization."[174] While most refugees left the city on foot, Civil Affairs transported the wounded, sick, and the elderly via ambulances. Civil Affairs also moved four trainloads of refugees out of the city towards Esquelbec and Lille. Once in the countryside, "all [supplies] were to be provided by the Sous-préfet from civ[ilian] resources. Communes in which refugees were to be dispersed accepted full responsibility for their maintenance."[175]

CA officers certainly did not conduct these operations alone and were helped immensely by local French authorities and volunteer groups. Continual praise was given to the French people's ability to provide for their citizens. Col Henderson wrote, "I should like to give credit to the Sous-préfet [of Dunkirk] for the way in which he org[anized] his resources and directed his personnel to carry out the plan outlined by CA."[176] Another report reads, "The French authorities have been most helpful in finding accommodation, providing communal feeding and arranging for medical care."[177] In most cases, Canadian Civil Affairs officers coordinated the various French organizations that were eager to help in every aspect of the evacuations. These organizations included the Red Cross, the FFI, Civil Defence, and various French civilian medical organizations. At Dunkirk, Civil Affairs officers brought together the various civilian organizations only twenty-four hours before the refugees started pouring out of the city.[178] In total, 20,000 civilians were evacuated. The Belgian army then masked Dunkirk for the remainder of the war, and the German garrison finally capitulated in May 1945.

Despite the claim by some that the clearing of the channel ports was a period marked by no outstanding Civil Affairs difficulties, First Canadian Army Civil Affairs in fact overcame significant obstacles in dealing with the continued presence of thousands of civilians directly in the path of First Canadian Army.[179] By the time Dunkirk had been successfully evacuated, II Canadian Corps CA had twelve detachments operational stretching along the French coast into Belgium. First Canadian Army CA as a whole had twenty-six detachments it could call upon (a total of approximately 250 men), five with I British Corps and the remainder operating within Lines of Communication (the rear echelon of First Canadian Army).

Resistance Groups

One of Civil Affairs's most interesting tasks while they were engaged on the coast was dealing with the French resistance groups operating in the area. Broadly speaking the French resistance was labelled as the French Forces of the Interior (FFI). In fact, the FFI was a semihomogeneous group composed of various resistance movements, such as the right wing Ceux de la Libération, the communist Front National, the left-wing groups Libération-Nord and Libération-Sud, and the Christian democratic movement Combat.[180] Alongside the FFI were the Maquis bands, which operated primarily in rural areas in southern France. They carried out a variety of guerrilla-style raids and provided safe haven for those fleeing conscript labour in Germany. Similar to the FFI, the Maquis were composed of a variety of political and social ideologies; however, most Maquisards belonged to close-knit groups less disposed to following an ideological objective than "charismatic leaders who were a law unto themselves and inspired fierce personal loyalty."[181] A concerted effort by de Gaulle and his subordinate, Jean Moulin, to organize the various resistance groups under the administrative control of the National Resistance Council (CNR) prior to invasion met with success.[182] The Maquis, which were far more regionalized and independent than their colleagues in the CNR, were a bit more difficult to centralize.[183] Nonetheless, by May 1944, the Allies incorporated the FFI and Maquis into the Allied chain of command. General Eisenhower at SHAEF relayed orders to General Marie-Pierre Koenig, who was nominally recognized as the French resistance commander.

On the ground, Canadian CA officers often enlisted the FFI to coordinate and distribute relief and help direct refugee traffic. Furthermore, these FFI men guarded German prisoners for the army, acted as local guides and auxiliary police (as in Caen), and even engaged in operations against small pockets of Germans that may have been bypassed by the main assault. The frequent interaction between Canadian CA officials and FFI men created a strong relationship with CA officers often assuming the role of pseudoliaisons between First Canadian Army and these paramilitary groups.

The fear of more radical political ideologies, particularly the communist influence, amongst FFI personnel could lead to complications for CAOs when dealing with them. In one instance, a group claiming to be members of the French navy arrived at Lt Col Coté's headquarters to say that they were ordered by a French resistance leader (an unknown major) to seize a German weapons cache stored in Calais. The Pas de Calais prefect, a Gaullist appointee, expressed grave concern to Commander Mengin (French liaison officer to II Can Corps CA) about who exactly might be receiving these weapons and specifically requested that they not fall into the hands of certain "civilians and in particular into the hands of the FFI."[184] Mengin expressed these concerns to Lt Col Coté who solved this minor crisis by ordering the French sailors home, cordoning off the town from the FFI and effectively destroying the weapons cache.[185]

Problems also arose due to the "over-zealous activities" of resistance groups.[186] "Quite a few sights took the boys eyes," one Canadian CA officer noted with concern, "especially a woman collaborator who was being paraded through the streets with her hair shaven off and a swastika painted on her forehead."[187] Upon liberation, many previously hidden resistance groups emerged well armed and organized and began arresting known or suspected collaborationists. The chaos that would later be seen with Belgian and Dutch resistance groups was avoided as the French authorities, with help from Civil Affairs legal experts, quickly set about finding a solution to the growing numbers of arrested suspects. In many cases, the French established "a special commission, of two judges and one police officer" specifically designed to investigate accusations towards suspected collaborationists by resistance groups and authorize "the release, internment or trial of the accused."[188] Thus, the French quickly vetted arrested suspects, which prevented build up in local or make-shift prisons and set a legal precedent for arresting and detaining suspected collaborators.

Generally speaking the French resistance was quite cooperative. Problems with resistance groups in France never reached the level that they would later in Belgium. Resistance members were all well armed, organized, and, as a First Canadian Army report states, "most willing to cooperate in any matter on which their assistance [had] been requested."[189] Recruited as local police (gendarmes), and armed and backed by First Canadian Army and Free French authority, they were incorporated fairly easily and provided a reliable source of manpower. As one Canadian report in late September stated, "In France, the state of law and order is generally satisfactory."[190] Furthermore, First Canadian Army kept these resistance groups busy and unified in their objective to aid the Allied war effort against the Germans and "the discipline of the majority of the FFI and the Maquis [was] excellent."[191]

TRIED AND TESTED

Northern France was the first real test for II Canadian Corps CA. For both the military and civilian population, the work of CA played a role in the transition from German occupation to liberation and then to civilian rule by a Free French government. However, more importantly CA facilitated the ongoing military operations of First Canadian Army as it broke out of Normandy and then moved eastwards. This transition to French civilian rule further meant that the new French government could provide military support to the western Allies. Interestingly, this transition had not actually been formalized doctrinally by CA planners (at 21st Army Group or SHAEF) in any sort of detail before 1944. The assumption was that the localized efforts culminating in the transition to French civil authority would simply mirror the larger handover by Allied officials to French civilian government. The system would, it was believed, essentially work itself out.

After the experience in northern France, Brigadier Wedd set about clarifying the process of transition from military to civilian authority while ensuring that this transition did not impede military operations. To do so he outlined some specific administrative improvements that were to be made. He outlined a broad, yet logical, process by which government control was slowly handed over to civilian administrators at each level of command. This transitional process began at the division level (the battalion level saw complete military control of an occupied area) where some local civilian authority, town and village mayors for instance, would be reestablished based on the assessment of the local

CA detachment commander. The corps level would see some greater coordination of the civilian authority with the military on a broader area level, so regional administrators and prefectures of departments and provinces. As First Canadian Army moved on, army headquarters would negotiate the handover of responsibility for larger areas to specific civilian administrative bodies. Once a region passed to the responsibility of Lines of Communication (the part of First Canadian Army's chain of command responsible for keeping up supplies, reinforcements, and transportation networks) these civilian administrative bodies would now cooperate on a fairly close basis with Lines of Communication HQ. This was, as Wedd put it, "The final phase of military supervision or control."[192] When an area was no longer required for L of C purposes, the territory was then given over to complete civilian control.[193]

Wedd was particularly concerned with clarifying this process in regards to responsibility for refugees, for it was refugee populations he felt posed the greatest threat to military operations. Though CA had performed admirably in regards to refugee aid and control there was still some confusion as to what point these civilians were handed over to an autonomous civilian administration. Wedd stated, "to some extent the military must retain responsibility for conditions in the receiving communities."[194] He identified potential problems if civilian administrators failed to care for incoming refugees. For instance, if food and shelter were not made sufficiently available refugees could "again become a military problem when they wander away in search of more congenial surroundings."[195] In the interests of public health and public safety, both crucial to maintaining law and order behind the front lines, Wedd emphasized that the sick and injured had to be cared for. He further stressed the importance of maintaining sanitary conditions amongst the civilians in order to "safeguard fraternizing troops."[196] On one hand Wedd recognized that it was in this "hinterland of responsibility that CA must pave the way towards a smooth and rapid turnover of authority to the civilian administration" yet also feared that "communities which have learned to accept assistance will fall back into an apathy which may well cause a resurgence of problems to again burden the military authorities."[197]

Wedd advocated for closer cooperation between Civil Affairs and the French authorities to solve this potential administrative paradox.

Closer cooperation would allow CA to train and prepare civilian administrative bodies for eventual full takeover while also ensuring that civilian administrators completely understood the importance of refugee care to First Canadian Army. Wedd called for greater census data to be taken by local French authorities: this included the numbers of refugees in any given area, any medical requirements as well as food, water, and shelter needs. With this information Wedd argued that CA could better supervise (and promote) the establishment of local facilities run by local refugee committees. This "hands-off" approach would, in Wedd's opinion, facilitate a smoother transition to civilian authority at the local level.[198]

First Canadian Army Civil Affairs in northern France successfully demonstrated that support for civilian populations meant support for Allied military operations. This is particularly highlighted in the successful evacuations of the coastal towns. Civil Affairs prevented civilian movement from hampering military operations, much to the chagrin of men such as Col Schroeder, and various civilian agencies cooperated with Civil Affairs to limit the drain on military resources. They evacuated nearly 7,000 out of a population of 8,000 people in the immediate township of Boulogne and the inhabitants of the security belt surrounding the town. In Calais, Civil Affairs moved an estimated 15,000 civilians from the city to the surrounding countryside and in Dunkirk, 20,000 civilians. By keeping the population levels within the urban centres to a minimum, CA detachments were able to rapidly and effectively assist those civilians who remained inside the town once it was liberated. Furthermore, civilian casualties at Boulogne, Calais, and Dunkirk were significantly lower than at Caen and Le Havre. As one report stated, "Although fresh reports of concentrations of refugees are being received, mainly from the Channel coast … no special problems have arisen and the French authorities appear to have the matter well in hand."[199] Boulogne became an effective doctrinal template for future evacuation operations, marking the beginning of a string of First Canadian Army Civil Affairs successes. Yet, the relationship between civilian and soldier became further complicated in Belgium, where Canadian Civil Affairs were headed next. They would be required to build on the lessons learned in northern France while continuing to learn and develop "on the job."

CHAPTER THREE

Death from Above in Belgium

"Never believe any war will be smooth and easy, or that anyone who embarks on the strange voyage can measure the tides and hurricanes he will encounter."
– Winston Churchill

At first glance the task of Canadian Civil Affairs in Antwerp seemed to be entirely opposite to that in northern France. Whereas at Caen and other French urban centres the men of CA sought to remove civilians from the battle space, in Antwerp their ultimate purpose was to keep civilians in the city, working the docks and keeping alive the crucial supply centre that was Antwerp's port. Antwerp thus posed a unique challenge for Canadian Civil Affairs. How does an organization keep a civilian population from leaving a city that is under direct constant attack? The key was morale. If the morale of Antwerp's civilian population could be maintained, this could in turn prevent a mass exodus from the city and a subsequent loss of labour for the all-important harbour. Antwerp's port was a crucial component to the Allied logistical plan, and it needed to be fully operational as soon as possible. Between October 1944 and March 1945 German V-1s and V-2s struck Belgian soil nearly 5,200 times causing almost 32,000 casualties. Eight hundred of these rocket attacks landed in the city of Antwerp during this campaign causing 9,390 casualties.[1] These attacks put the city into a siege-like state. FCA CA took responsibility for Antwerp's fledgling Civil Defence system in order to mitigate the damages from V-weapons and maintain the morale of the civilian population. The successful resurrection of

Antwerp's Civil Defence by CA helped to limit the physical and moral effects of the constant attacks on Antwerp's population, thus sustaining one of the Allies' most important port cities.

STRATEGIC PICTURE, SEPTEMBER 1944

Antwerp was one of the most important objectives for 21st Army Group. After the breakout from Normandy in August, its supply lines became more and more strained as it rapidly moved eastward increasing the distance from its supply bases along the Norman coast. Montgomery's formation needed to continue to capture port installations in order to support its continued push through Belgium, into the Netherlands, and eventually into Germany. Although northern France had several good ports, including Le Havre and Boulogne, Belgium's port of Antwerp was the second largest in Europe at the time, and its facilities were crucial for Montgomery's drive across northern Europe. First Canadian Army was given the responsibility of making sure Antwerp's ports were running. To do this, FCA needed to first clear the approaches to Antwerp via the Scheldt Estuary and then keep the city and its labour force functioning.

Most of Belgium was liberated fairly quickly. The American First Army pushed hard towards the towns along the Meuse Valley, while British Second Army captured Brussels and moved quickly into Antwerp in early September 1944. First Canadian Army units not involved in clearing northern France's channel ports, 4th Canadian Armoured Division (CAD), and 1st Polish Armoured Division (PAD) maintained momentum along the western flank by capturing Bruges and Ghent on 9 September 1944. By mid-September, most of the country was free from German occupiers (a portion of eastern Belgium would not be fully liberated until February 1945), and Belgium's citizens took to the streets to celebrate. The Allies' speed and efficiency during Antwerp's recapture, with help from a proactive Belgian resistance, meant that the port installations were taken relatively intact. Canadian troops were still forced to fight the Germans for months in the seaward approaches to Antwerp, known as the Scheldt Estuary, in order to allow the Allies to safely use its superb facilities. Once these approaches were cleared in early November 1944, the port was ready to receive the full brunt of Allied shipping.[2]

PREWAR BELGIUM

The prewar situation in Belgium played a role in complicating CA efforts in the country. Belgium is essentially divided into two primary cultural groups: the French-speaking Walloons and the Flemings, who speak a hybridized Dutch language of Germanic origin known as Flemish. These two groups had always lived side by side in some form of political entity. As far back as the early sixteenth century, the Spanish Hapsburgs ruled over what was then known as the Spanish Netherlands, including the provinces of modern-day Belgium. Napoleon's armies annexed this territory in the early nineteenth century and brought it under French rule, infusing the territory with revolutionary ideas. Then, the 1815 Treaty of Vienna united the Walloon and Flemish provinces with the Kingdom of the Netherlands. In 1830 Walloon and Flemish-speaking Belgians united, successfully rebelled against King William I of the Netherlands, and, with the 1839 Treaty of London, created the modern Belgian state.

By the turn of the century, this Belgian state was a complex socioeconomic entity. The richer industrial and economically prosperous southern and eastern provinces were predominantly French speaking while the rural and somewhat poorer regions of the north and the west were predominantly Flemish speaking. Traditional stereotypes cast the Flemish as rural and relatively traditionalist with strong loyalties to the Catholic Church, while the Walloon population was seen as typically having bourgeois attitudes towards church and state and a more modern approach to industry and society. Not only was there a prevalent cultural divide but also long-standing commercial and economic rivalries between the great cities of Antwerp, Ghent, Bruges, Brussels, and Liege. During the early twentieth century, industrialization further stratified Belgian society as the divide between the relatively wealthy middle and upper classes and the numerically superior working class continued to grow.

During the First World War, Germany's aggressive and violent occupation, as well as the Belgian military's stubborn defence of their country, engendered strong feelings of Belgian nationalism amongst both Walloons and Flemish.[3] The Germans tried to foster Flemish nationalism through propaganda campaigns in an attempt to divide Belgian society and encourage an alliance between the Flemish people and the German army. Instead, the draconian German occupation policy acted to unify the Walloon and Flemish cultural groups, who were once again looking to throw off the yoke of foreign rule. During the interwar period, a new power-sharing political system developed, with prominent Walloons and Flemings holding important political offices.[4]

Nonetheless, by the 1930s various dissident political groups began to voice displeasure with the system. These groups reflected the cultural, political, and economic divisions that abounded in Belgian society. Socialist and communist political organizations echoed the working class's growing despair. The Catholic Block, a conservative political party, fought for a return to traditional Belgian politics, once dominated by the Catholic Church. Flemish and Walloon nationalist parties competed for a variety of objectives ranging from greater autonomy to outright separation. The Germans would exploit this.

The Wehrmacht oversaw most of the period of occupation in Belgium, which officially began on 30 May 1940. This was in fact quite unique as most German occupied countries experienced some form of a civil–military hybrid administration. General Alexander Von Falkenhausen was the military commander in charge of the country while his deputy Eggert Reeder oversaw the day-to-day administration. While Falkenhausen was a long time Wehrmacht officer with a conservative political background and Reeder was in fact a member of the SS, both men resisted jurisdictional incursions by Heinrich Himmler who sought to establish SS dominance over Belgium.[5] By late 1941 they were also fending off opponents in Berlin who argued for a civilian administration like that in the Netherlands. At the same time both administrators sought to take advantage of divisions amongst the Flemish and Walloon populations to broaden support for the Nazi regime. Léon Degrelle's Rexist Movement, representing nationalistic Walloon interests, and Staf de Clercq's Flemish National Union (VNV), which stood for

Flemish separatism, helped the Germans acquire allies from within Belgian society during their occupation. The Nazis were particularly focused on gaining the support of Flemish Belgians, who were seen as ethnic cousins to the German people. Through the VNV they carried out an official "policy of encouraging Flemish separatism."[6] In the initial weeks after the occupation, Flemish prisoners of war were being released in greater numbers than their Walloon counterparts. Himmler actively recruited the Flemish into his personal Dutch-Flemish SS force, SS Standarte West. Over the four years of the occupation Reeder appointed numerous Flemish collaborators, many of them drawn from the VNV, to administrative positions throughout the province. Hitler even expressed his wish for the administration to favour the Flemish over the Walloons.[7]

Widespread collaboration and support proved difficult for the Nazis. Although the ideals of a national socialist state appealed to certain Flemish and Walloon groups, strong Catholic ties made the majority of Belgians wary of German fascism and its penchant towards militarism, and none could forget how the Germans destroyed Flanders in the previous war. As well, Nazi infighting hurt efforts to gain Belgian support. Himmler's continual challenges to the military regime, including supporting rival Flemish and Walloon groups, particularly hurt Nazi efforts at gaining widespread support and eventually resulted in the military administration being replaced by a pro-SS civilian one in July 1944, similar to one in the Netherlands. This administration would barely have time to assert itself, however, as Allied soldiers entered the country in early September 1944.

As early as February 1944, G-5 SHAEF had issued Civil Affairs handbooks detailing the political, social, and economic issues affecting the various countries that the Allies were to liberate. These Civil Affairs handbooks would act as "ready reference source books containing the basic factual information needed for planning and policy making."[8] The B handbook on Belgium, written with approval from Belgian authorities, contained a wide variety of information about the country prior to the war and what to expect from it as a result of German occupation. Some of the topics included geographical and social backgrounds on the Walloon and Fleming populations: "The latter are primarily of

Dutch stock, while the former, who speak a French dialect, are descended from a branch of the Celtic race."[9] The handbook further included missives on government finance, natural resources, agriculture, public health and sanitation, education, public safety, and industry and commerce. It also contained rather terse comments on the country's internal divisions. For instance, in assessing the social divisions within Belgian society it stated, "The Walloons tend, with little justification, to regard themselves as superior to the Flemings."[10]

LIBERATED BELGIUM

The initial Belgian reaction to liberation was euphoric, but this feeling would not last. The continued presence of Allied soldiers coupled with the Allied authority's control over the day-to-day lives of the Belgian people created tension amongst a civilian population that had, for the second time in less than thirty years, cast off the chains of German oppression. Even while much of Belgium was celebrating their liberation, "currents of discontent were gaining significant force beneath the waves of admiration."[11]

The Allies imposed fairly strict security measures, which frustrated many Belgian civilians. This included everything from bans on photography to control of inter-Belgian communication and movement. The billeting of large numbers of Allied soldiers throughout the country quickly began to wear on the civilian population. The Allies struggled to import essential supplies such as coal, food, medicine, petrol, and rubber, and it took months before they achieved adequate levels of such supplies. Belgian civilians' daily rations were below the optimal 2,000 calories per day. Combatting lawlessness in the form of the black market, theft, and corruption created a constant pressure on military resources. While at the same time the continual delays and problems encountered by the Belgian government in creating an effective legal system prevented, in many cases, the execution of justice.

While the broad objectives for Civil Affairs remained the same as in France more specific instructions were sent out in regards to the power vested in Civil Affairs while in Belgium, it read

A. An agreement has been entered into with the Belgian government which provides that in areas affected by military operations it is necessary to contemplate a first or military phase during which the Supreme Commander must de facto exercise supreme responsibility and authority to the full extent necessitated by the military situation.
B. It is not intended, however, that Military Government will be established in liberated Belgium and civil administration will normally be operated by the Belgian government.
C. If at any time or in any locality the Belgian authorities do not render the assistance necessary to enable the Supreme Commander to accomplish his mission then such executive action as the military situation may require is authorized.
D. As soon as, and to such extent as, in the opinion of the Supreme Commander, the military situation permits the resumption by the Belgian Government of their responsibility for the civil administration he will notify the appropriate representative of the Belgian Government accordingly. The Belgian Government will thereupon, and to that extent, resume such exercise of responsibility.[12]

The initial responsibility for Canadian CA was the area liberated by 4th CAD and 1st PAD in West Flanders. Civil Affairs established three static detachments in the towns of Ypres, Ostend, and Bruges, and numerous other spearhead detachments worked around these three centres. This early period posed some difficulties in developing an effective centralized CA policy "as the number [of detachments] available for the immense territory now to be covered was totally inadequate."[13] Civil administration was decentralized and dislocated, pockets of Germans continued to resist, and the Allies had no functioning method to communicate between towns as "the only satisfactory method of passing orders to detachments was by using Staff officers on liaison duties."[14]

Things improved in mid-September 1944 when First Canadian Army took over responsibility for the northwest section of Belgium, including the city of Antwerp, and by the end of that month, all First Canadian Army unit headquarters were established in the country. The jurisdiction for First Canadian Army Civil Affairs's expanded to cover most of northern Belgium. This included nineteen CA detachments throughout the provinces of West and East Flanders, whose capitals were Bruges and Ghent respectively, as well as the city and province of Antwerp, the city of Turnhout, and the surrounding countryside. In early October, the northern coast of France including Ostend port, along with the arrondissement of Le Havre, Montreuil, St Omer, Boulogne, and Dunkirk, passed from CA First Canadian Army to CA Lines of Communication (L of C), which cleared First Canadian Army Civil Affairs to focus squarely on Belgium.

Initial Concerns

Belgium would eventually suffer the trials and tribulations of a country at war, but CA officers and the population at large had few problems during the first days of liberation. Operational tasks during this phase of rapid advance and minimal destruction were confined to assuring that suitable civil administration was set up and functioning at all places.[15] Belgium's initial situation was not as dire compared to France and what would later be seen in the Netherlands. Civil Affairs did not immediately need to supply food nor evacuate civilians from battle zones. Setting up a working civilian administration was far less chaotic. In general, the day-to-day tasks that characterized the early days of liberation went relatively smoothly. Because of this, combined with minimal physical war damage as compared to other countries, the population took a somewhat relaxed attitude towards preparing for the continuation of the war. Regarding his first impression, one Canadian officer wrote, "Materially Belgium appears to have suffered very little from the war. It is doubtful whether the people fully realize how fortunate they have been compared with other European countries."[16] The civilians' relaxed attitude caused some early tension between CA officers and their civilian counterparts.

Belgian authorities appeared to Civil Affairs as hesitant and even unwilling to assume full control of their own civil administration. The country's ineffective political leadership further exacerbated this problem. As a Civil Affairs report noted, "Belgium's reaction to CA was rather different to that of France where resolute representatives of a provisional government felt themselves capable ... of putting their house in order. The Belgians tended to the other hand. There was confusion and indecision in all administrations and a large body of public opinion was anxious to see some form of allied military government established."[17] Hubert Pierlot, a Walloon, was the recognized leader of the Belgian government-in-exile, but his government took its time establishing itself in Brussels; because of this delay provincial and municipal government workers were hesitant to make decisions without first consulting the new government, which created further delays in decision making. Due to this administrative dislocation, the Belgian authorities failed to fully comprehend the essential needs of the Belgian people and the indigenous resources available to them.[18]

The hesitancy for provincial and municipal government workers to make decisions was also a result of Pierlot's vague and often unclear policy initiatives. Simply put, the Pierlot government failed to offer any effective leadership in these early days. As one CA report read, the Pierlot government "did not bring with it the resolute leadership and strong action which the situation required."[19] Two major problems created this ineffective administrative situation. The sudden transition from an occupied country to a liberated one partly concealed the gross dislocation "which the civil machinery had suffered from the removal of German control and the flight of many Regional officials."[20] Secondly, unlike in France, most collaborationist officials that had fled had their vacant positions filled by "inexperienced men."[21] Brigadier Wedd repeatedly asked for Pierlot's administration to take greater action and was not pleased with the response, "When a nation which [has] been subjugated for years suddenly regains its freedom it is inevitable that certain elements should react with an irresponsible and excited exuberance. When that happens it is the duty of the government to exercise proper control. In Belgium, the government failed in this duty."[22] Ralph Allen, correspondent for the *Globe and Mail* in Belgium, wrote on the growing concerns over Pierlot's government, "Restiveness increases daily. Last week 2,000 unemployed paraded in Brussels ... This week 3,000 women demonstrated to show their dissatisfaction ... Whatever Monsieur Pierlot's fate, maybe it is already largely out of his hands."[23] To further add to the political disconnect, the Belgian people, like the French and the Dutch, had shifted in their political outlook to a more left-leaning stance. Pierlot was a Catholic right-winger, and the policies of the socialist opposition, led by Achille Van Acker, had gained strong support amongst the Belgian people.[24] Pierlot's government was, simply put, out of touch and his administration was to be short-lived.

The Belgian government's ineffective control changed the entire Canadian Civil Affairs mission. Operational policy was initially to provide immediate and short-term relief while the indigenous administration righted itself. Instead, Civil Affairs became engaged in long-term commitments (a pattern that would repeat itself in the Netherlands); as the war dragged on through the autumn and into the winter, Belgium became an essential rear area for Allied armies pushing into the German frontier and the southern Netherlands. In December, during the massive German counterattack known as the Battle of the Bulge, Belgium became a combat zone as well.

A food crisis then compounded the stress of the Belgian people. Although much of the country was spared the destruction that France endured, the vital canals and bridges linking the nation's supply network suffered German demolition squads and Allied bombardment. In addition, the Belgian government had dissolved the Nazi regime's department responsible for Belgian food distribution but had failed to establish any sort of successor. The absence of any organization responsible for food distribution as well as Belgian's damaged supply lines created a nationwide food crisis by the late autumn of 1944. Pierlot's administration was blamed, and this did nothing to alleviate the government's continuing woes. Civil Affairs officers were also blamed, although unfairly. The Belgians expected their liberators to bring with them endless amounts of food and provisions. Instead, access to Allied supplies in Belgium dwindled and Allied supply lines became stretched extremely thin as they pressed the Germans into the Netherlands. CA detachments struggled to bring relief to the Belgian people and by December 1944 they were unable to increase the daily caloric intake of the average Belgian to higher than it had been under German occupation; the civilian population was discontent and found scapegoats in their liberators as well as the Pierlot administration. The early days of celebration and high expectations of the Allies, therefore, soon gave way to immense frustration and the cold reality that things were not improving.

Resistance Groups in Belgium

The machinations of the various resistance groups reflected a growing tension and lack of confidence in the Pierlot government. Resistance groups in all the liberated countries presented difficulties for military personnel and primarily those of the Civil Affairs branch, who often found themselves the liaisons between these groups and Allied forces. In Belgium, however, Canadian CAOs dealt with some of the most fractious and noncooperative resistance groups of any liberated country. Reporter Robert Eunson writing for the *Globe and Mail* in Belgium wrote, "A former Brussels newspaper reporter [Fernand Demany] who heads the resistance movement in Belgium is challenging the leadership of Premier Hubert Pierlot ... Chief of these is his charge that the government has been wholly ineffective in dealing with collaborators and is even friendly with them [and that] the resistance in Belgium opposed any government coming back from exile to take over a country in which resistance members lived and fought during the occupation."[25] One CA report put it bluntly: "The resistance groups are active, armed and vindictive."[26] The primary Belgian resistance groups were the Front de l'Indépendance, La Légion Belge, La Garde Blanche, Les Mousquetaires, and the Front National de la Liberté. These resistance networks were politically motivated and often directly opposed to one another. This was quite different than the situation in France where resistance groups were relatively united in their fight against German troops and generally cooperated with the Allies to rebuild their heavily war-damaged country. Belgium's swift liberation resulted in a restless and less than unified spirit amongst the various resistance groups.[27] These groups were politically divided and lacked any sort of umbrella organization to unite them. Generally, participants in the Belgian resistance movement were amateurs. They were ill equipped to fight the Germans in open warfare and lacked any training in the subtleties of guerrilla combat. As one historian of Belgian resistance groups writes, these men "often showed themselves to be woefully ineffectual" and were nothing more than a "motley crew."[28] Disorganization and the unruly nature of most groups caused CAOs and the Belgian government significant problems in reasserting law and order.

Belgian resistance groups began causing trouble by arresting and punishing suspected collaborationists. In some cases, the resistance arrested or punished rival faction members under the pretence of persecuting collaborationists. To further complicate matters, "the terms of the agreement between the Belgian Government in London and the Governments of the United States and Great Britain [had] not been published or sufficiently circulated. The text of the Belgian law against 'collaboration' [had] not been seen by anyone."[29] This meant plenty of room for interpretation. In one instance, two Belgian civilians sought safety with Major Van Dyke, the public safety officer for 619 Detachment in St Nicholas, after they had been badly beaten up for working with the Germans during the occupation. Major Van Dyke reported that a female friend of the two was also in hiding after half her hair had "been cut off and the other half fairly well torn out" for sleeping with a German.[30] Major Grier, First Canadian Army CA public safety staff officer, visited a prison in Termonde that housed 1,500 inmates. Many of these inmates had only recently been arrested and had yet to stand trial. No one running the prison had any clear idea how to prosecute the prisoners; there was no legal precedent. Subsequently, Grier wrote, "It is becoming more and more urgent to obtain the text of the law on collaboration."[31]

Without any centralized authority, many groups took to enforcing their own particular brand of vigilante justice. Various resistance groups exploited the breakdown of law and order by purging suspected collaborationists, settling old scores with political rivals, and engaging in a variety of other illegal activities including arson, theft, murder, and general brigandage. A First Canadian Army HQ report from November 1944 expressed concern that certain groups within the resistance movement remained a potential threat to military operations especially because the Belgian gendarmerie were "depleted in numbers and arms were lacking."[32] Many late recruits to resistance organizations, nicknamed the "September Resistance," had joined only prior to liberation and in light of the impending German retreat. These were some of the most ill disciplined of all resistance members. In one instance, four supposed members arrived at the headquarters of II Canadian Corps with their leader reported as wearing "a bastard sort of officers uniform" and informed Lt Col Walker that they had been told their petrol and supply needs would be looked after by the Canadians.[33] Walker curtly informed them otherwise and they left. As the war diarist wrote, "They were a most unpleasant gp [group] and might have come straight out of a Hollywood gangster picture."[34]

An incident in September 1944 highlighted how Canadian CAOs would intervene on behalf of the Belgian civil authority when resistance groups posed serious challenges to stability. Ypres's mayor, or burgomaster, encountered trouble while attempting to establish proper control over three different resistance groups operating in the historic city. These armed and organized groups arrested numerous rival faction members and alleged collaborationists. Furthermore, some group members began seizing the cars and property of those deemed collaborationists. Essentially, armed gangs calling themselves "resistance" roamed the streets. The local police force, which had only recently been organized, was unarmed and, besides directing traffic, could play no role in establishing order. Ypres was disintegrating into districts controlled by armed factions, and although the burgomaster attempted to restore proper authority, the various factions continually ignored his appeal for cooperation. Thus, he was forced to call on the Canadian Army for help. Shortly after this request, Colonel J.J. Hurley, SCAO II Canadian Corps, arrived at Ypres and "took the law into his own hands."[35] He first ordered his men to collect all weapons held by unauthorized persons. Groups of five to ten armed Canadian soldiers drove lorries out into the various districts to personally collect the weapons from the various armed factions. Subsequently, Hurley held a meeting with the various faction leaders explicitly stating that the burgomaster was the only recognized Allied authority in Ypres and that the various factions were to either place themselves at the burgomaster's disposition and help him in every way possible or be removed from any positions of authority. As the war diary reported, "these orders seemed to settle the matter."[36]

Similar unrest existed in Roulers where reports of a communist riot and tension amongst various resistance groups led to an intervention by Major Grier, the SCAO in Roulers, along with his head of security,

Captain Morrison, and Lt Marchant of 306 CA Detachment. After initial investigation by the team it was discovered that the new town burgomaster, having been removed by the Germans in 1941 and having held his current appointment for only one week, was unable to exert any control over the troublesome groups. As well, the "Gendarmie [sic] [were] attempting to control all the armed factions in the city, but the job [was] almost impossible for them. Owing to unemployment, unrest [was] increasing in the city."[37] After the Canadian officials discussed matters with the burgomaster, Grier asked him to call a meeting of the various faction leaders. As Hurley did in Ypres, Major Grier emphasized at this meeting that the Allies recognized the burgomaster as the only authority in Roulers; Grier offered a veiled threat to those resistance leaders who might be considering resisting the burgomaster's attempts to establish law and order. Grier left Lt Marchant to deal with any aftermath from this meeting, but Marchant did not file any further incident reports. Lt Marchant did, however, comment on the general political situation in Belgium, stating that Roulers's drama "was no worse than it was in the whole of Belgium. Most of the male population [was] now armed and certain gps [groups], especially the Communists and Armée Belge, [were] very active. All political parties in Belgium [were] trying to take advantage of the sit [situation] to secure power and to prevent their competitors getting ahead. Communications with the capital [were] bad and directives [lacked] in vigour or authority."[38] Lt Col Sheppard, commanding 320 P Detachment in Ghent, echoed these concerns when he reported that the situation in East Flanders was, "very delicate and capable of producing a most unpleasant situation."[39] Interestingly, when these concerns were illuminated to First Canadian Army CA they were deemed "alarmist" in nature and FCA CA had supreme confidence that "the government recently installed in Brussels would prove strong and popular and would get an increasingly firm grip on the situation."[40] This confidence was shown to be misplaced.

Regardless of the impression at FCA HQ, II Canadian Corps detachment commanders often intervened to prevent resistance-initiated violence from escalating. In Ecloo, a Belgian soldier on guard duty tried to stop a car full of partisans, essentially the combat element of the resistance. After challenging the group and receiving no response, the guard opened fire, killing one of the partisans. Later that night, the group returned with more than one hundred supporters bent on revenge. Major Norton, commander of 629 CA Detachment in Ecloo and the man who had ordered the Belgian soldier to stand guard in the first place, "held a meeting ... at which partisan leaders were present, and dressed them down fully."[41] He emphasized that he supported the guard for doing his duty and threatened severe action on any civilians who retaliated or independently acted because of this incident. His threats worked and no retaliation was sought.

Part of the problem with widespread lawlessness was rooted in the fact that the gendarmerie, the government-recognized police force, was not fully armed, and resistance groups completely outmanned and outgunned them. As one historian succinctly wrote, "The Belgian state entirely lacked the means to impose its will on the Resistance."[42] In October 1944, SHAEF estimated the resistance had 85,000 fighters while there were just more than 8,000 national gendarmerie members and approximately 12,000 local police.[43] Belgian authorities continually assured senior Canadian officers that they were working to properly equip local police forces and that "speedy enrolment into the Belgian army should provide sufficient control for the younger and more irresponsible elements."[44] Not until early October did the equipment problems begin to be ameliorated and local police forces begin to exercise proper local authority. The Allies had to intervene to help the Belgian government disarm many of the resistance groups, an order issued by Pierlot on 13 November. Twelve days later, Communist resistance groups organized a mass protest outside of the Belgian parliament buildings in response to forced disarmament. The crowd attempted to force its way into the square facing the parliament building. While Allied soldiers and tanks looked on, the gendarmerie opened fire wounding thirty-five of the protestors. While this event could certainly have triggered more protests and challenges to Belgian authority, the presence of Allied military personnel limited any blowback. While this event was another damaging blow to Pierlot's authority, there was in the aftermath widespread acceptance of the disarmament order. By early December 30,000 weapons had been handed in to the government. Concurrently, the Belgian army's recruitment drive also helped reduce the power of the resistance groups as it successfully drew the youngest and most active elements from the various resistance groups, 40,000 young men were recruited by the end of 1944. Finally Civil Affairs officers' active involvement in dealing with unruly activity aided the Belgian government tremendously, and by the end of the year, almost all mention of resistance group problems ceased in the war diaries.

The Black Market

Canadian CA officers also faced a thriving and troublesome Belgian black market. During the German occupation, the Allies encouraged the Belgian people to develop and maintain a black market as a form of economic resistance to German occupation. Upon liberation the black market then became an impediment to the recovery of the Belgian economy. Supply and commodity costs had to deflate, and this was near impossible with a thriving illegal market dictating the prices of goods. To quell this illegal industry, Pierlot's government standardized commodity prices. Belgian authorities issued a series of monetary decrees introducing new legal tender into circulation and made the previous tender, primarily used on the black market, illegal. Each family was allowed to take in a maximum of 2,000 francs of old tender to trade for new tender. This drastically curbed black market spending and, in some cases, massively reduced black market accumulated wealth. To further combat black marketeering, CA officers recommended that the Belgian government import substantial supply quantities. A deal was reached with the Allies in November 1944 whereby the Belgian government would start receiving regular supplies from Britain.[45]

CA officers further recommended that the Belgian government force agricultural producers to release hoarded foodstuffs. This, in combination with the regular supplies from Britain, would essentially flood the market with goods. Once the market was saturated with goods, the need for the black market would be nullified. The Pierlot administration balked at implementing this final recommendation. The government refused to force agriculturalists to release their surplus foodstuffs, possibly for fear of alienating voters in the rural areas. The Belgian government was not prepared to take this final necessary action and, as a result, the black market continued.[46]

Canadian soldiers also contributed to a thriving black market. Many saw it as an opportunity to make some extra money and the influx of significant Allied military goods into Belgium gave them the collateral to carry this out. Allied foodstuffs were particularly desired and fetched high prices while blankets, shoes, coats, and other clothing accessories found their way into Belgian back-alley shops. A Canadian soldier could receive 300 francs in return for an ordinary driver's leather jacket while selling a gallon of petrol could net him 250 francs. Soldiers could also ascertain sexual services through the sale or bartering of war department material. Some of the most frequent recipients of war goods were in fact Belgian prostitutes who accepted items in exchange for sexual services and then were able to sell the goods on the black market themselves.[47] Captain Labrosse, now serving with Detachment 103 as part of Second British Army CA, took part in a raid on one of these "bawdy houses" and wrote, "The women had made nice winter coats out of our blankets, and warm dresses or coats for their children. Battle dress suits were found repaired and dyed and used as civilian suits."[48] The temptation for soldiers to sell or exchange military supplies was quite strong, and many a young man succumbed to it. One Canadian private in an interview years later spoke about the theft of military goods for sale on the black market, "I shouldn't say steal, scrounge, scrounge means it doesn't belong to anybody so it might as well belong to you."[49] One American GI justified the temptation, "We each had a ration card that allowed us to buy a carton of American-made cigarettes per week for fifty cents a carton … It seemed like such a simple way to make some fast spending money … They paid us 20 dollars a carton."[50] Canadian soldiers, like their American counterparts, would sell everything from rations to bars of soap to clothing in order to turn a quick profit.[51] The black market also offered an opportunity to purchase items as Major Harold Gonder of the Cameron Highlanders noted, "Almost anything in the way of food could be had on the black market, which was a flourishing business."[52] Sometimes Canadian equipment would simply disappear. Major Ronald Ferrie of the Canadian Signal Corps recalled how he parked his jeep outside of his billet's house while he went in for a coffee. Ten minutes later he returned to discover that his jeep was gone. Canadian policy stipulated that all vehicles had to remain guarded by military personnel or rendered inoperable. Ferrie did neither and thus had to face a board of inquiry as to the whereabouts of his jeep, the board suspicious that Ferrie had in fact sold it off to black market dealers. The jeep was never recovered and Ferrie let off with a reprimand, "I should have been given more than just a chastisement," he recalled, "but that's all I got for it."[53] The suspicion directed towards Ferrie hints at the fact that senior Canadian officials were aware that Canadian soldiers were complicit in allowing military equipment to end up on the black market. In fact, II Canadian Corps HQ sought to enlist the help of the Belgian gendarmerie to stem this problem when it issued an order in October, "Mil personnel may be arrested by the Belg Gendarmerie, but that they must be handed over to the Army for trial."[54] Of course a more stable economic and political structure would reduce the attraction (and at times need) of black market activity, but, while instability remained, many in Belgium, including Canadian soldiers, were utilizing the black market.

A systemic problem with soldiers' pay was also to blame for Canadian participation in black market activity. A Canadian private would earn about $40 Canadian a month; overseas he would be paid the equivalent in the British pound (so approximately 9 pounds a month). The exchange rate was 176 Belgium francs to the pound, so a Canadian would be earning the equivalent of roughly 1,584 Belgium francs a month. A kilogram of butter in economically unstable Belgium could cost up to 600 francs. This meant for a Canadian private to purchase a kilogram of butter in Belgium he would spend approximately 3 pound 40, just over one-third of his monthly salary. Soldiers' salary coupled with this exchange rate of 176 francs to the pound limited the spending power of Canadian soldiers, while the black market offered them a way to augment their income through the illegal sale of war department material.[55]

Petrol shortages also contributed to black market activity. During the final months of 1944, petrol supply issues continued to plague the Belgian government; consequently, black market activity continued and public dissatisfaction with the Pierlot administration grew. Fundamentally, the Pierlot administrators failed to adequately coordinate or communicate with provincial and municipal authorities; in fact, municipal officials often relied on Civil Affairs officers for any information on government plans to distribute the valuable liquid. A fortnightly report stated, "When the latter [CA officers] are also unable to inform them, there follows a loss of confidence in certainly the civil and possibly also in the military administration."[56] A mid-October shipment of POL (petrol, oil, and lubricants) provides a glimpse of the ineffectiveness of distribution. 21st Army Group delivered this shipment to the Belgian government who in turn added it to the national stocks (meaning property of the central Belgian government). Adding it to national stocks meant that the Belgian government would not distribute the shipment to local levels even though local authorities were "living from hand to mouth and their plans [were] hampered by lack of knowledge about the immediate future."[57] Local authorities throughout Belgium were aware of this vast shipment and questioned civil and military officials on its eventual local distribution. Many Belgian officials and Canadian CA officers were aware of this bulk POL shipment, and those at the municipal level could not understand why it was not distributed locally nor could local detachment commanders give them adequate answers.

Shortages in coal further contributed to black marketeering and growing dissatisfaction with the Belgian administration. Distribution problems were not nearly as acute as the ones the Netherlands would see later, but the Belgian government was still unable to adequately raise coal levels until the Canadian military became involved. Coal should not have been a problem, as Belgium was extremely rich in coal and possessed a well-developed system of mines that were left undamaged by the retreating Germans.[58] By mid-October 1944 production had dipped to roughly 500,000 tons per month, compared to 1.6 million tonnes during the German occupation and 2.4 million tonnes pre-1940.[59] By this point, most Belgian civilians could only purchase coal on the black market, a bucket of cheap coal costing somewhere between 25 and 50 francs.[60] A combination of limited transportation methods, labour shortages, and labour unrest continued to exacerbate the coal distribution problem.[61] Theft also became a concern. Coal cars were often plundered at night, often with the guards and local authorities all either complicit in the theft or turning a blind eye to it. As Capt. Labrosse pointed out, "Local police did not pay much attention to the complaints, claiming they were quite unable to cope with the situation."[62] In one instance Civil Affairs officers actually carried out the arrest of a mayor, two aldermen, and a prominent civilian in a small Belgian town when it was discovered that they had stolen fifty tons of coal from a recently arrived shipment.[63]

The situation became so serious that by November 1944 Civil Affairs was forced to take control of coal distribution within the country, essentially militarizing the coal distribution network. This meant coal shipments were guarded by Canadian military personnel, and the entire distribution network was run by Civil Affairs.[64] Each coal convoy was placed under the command of either an officer or a noncommissioned officer from the local CA detachment. Once a coal shipment had arrived at the intended destination it was weighed to confirm the amount was the same as when shipped. This weighing procedure was overseen by the CA officer in charge of the coal shipment. Once completed, a receipt was then signed by local civilian officials confirming the tonnage amount, this receipt was then kept by the officer in command. Local distribution to the general public followed, each member of the public receiving coal had to sign a receipt confirming they had been given their allotted amount.[65] This "militarization" policy worked; by the end of January 1945 coal production was climbing to near prewar levels and black market purchases of coal were significantly reduced. The coal network would stay under the authority of Civil Affairs till almost the end of the war.

Supply problems, black market activity, and the failure to exercise administrative control all added to the public's growing disappointment in the Pierlot government. Public sentiment became so negative that the First Canadian Army Civil Affairs war diary reported that there existed "widespread expressions of the wish that the Allied Authorities would establish a form of military government."[66] Historian Peter Schrijvers tempers this contentious statement slightly: "The people wanted instead a government which would act with the collective resolve that they associated with the Allied powers."[67] Pierlot's administration failed to become this type of government. Elections were finally held in February

1945 and the left-leaning Flemish-born Achiel Van Acker replaced Pierlot. Acker's administration, which lasted until 1951, oversaw Belgian's transition to a social-welfare state.[68]

ANTWERP

Although most Belgians suffered a great deal during the period of German occupation, the people of Antwerp experienced a uniquely harrowing postliberation period; one marked by constant V-1 flying bombs and V-2 rocket attacks. It would fall to the men of FCA CA to deal with the threats from these new weapons because, as one *Globe and Mail* article stated, "As far as Antwerp is concerned, that is now a Canadian town and any Canuck gets a good welcome in the crowded downtown streets."[69] Yet some within Canadian Civil Affairs felt that the people of Antwerp treated liberation as the end of their war, not as the beginning of their fight alongside the Allies for the duration of the war. One CA report on Antwerp stated, "Despite the fact that bombs were falling, it was no easy task to persuade the Belgians that although they were liberated, the war was not over."[70] The attitude of Antwerp's civilian population was a constant frustration to the men of First Canadian Army Civil Affairs. Yet, SHAEF considered the opening of Antwerp's port facilities absolute priority for 21st Army Group. Eisenhower saw Antwerp as the crucial logistic base for his "broad front" push towards Germany. Montgomery saw Antwerp as the key to his "narrow thrust" deep into the heart of the Ruhr. Regardless of their competing strategic visions, both understood the vital importance of the city and its port as key to the continued Allied advance. To ensure the port facilities functioned, Antwerp's labour force had to remain in the city. With bombs constantly falling from the sky, keeping Antwerp's dockworkers from fleeing to the safety of the countryside would not be easy. This difficult task became the primary objective of FCA CA and from the fall of 1944 to the spring of 1945 it engaged in one of the largest civil defence operations of the entire war.[71]

Preparing Civil Defence

The Allies found it difficult to use traditional defensive methods against the German V-weapons. These "V" or "vengeance" weapons were essentially jet propelled rockets, inaccurate but deadly when they managed to hit anything. Anti-aircraft weapons were somewhat effective against V-1s, but the more accurate V-2s travelled three to four times faster than the sound of speed and were virtually undetectable until they had hit. All that could really be done against the V-2s was to reinforce passive defence measures.[72] In view of the strategic importance of Antwerp's port, Antwerp's civil defence focused primarily on maintaining the morale of the population to avoid large-scale evacuation of essential personnel required for operation of the port.[73] Back in London, for instance, factory production noticeably declined because of a marked exodus of people to the countryside.[74] The Allies feared that a similar labour decline would occur in Antwerp's port if a CA-led civil defence was incapable of making civilians feel protected. Roughly 15,000 civilian labourers who worked on the docks lived throughout the city and the arrondissement (the suburbs and countryside). This dispersion meant that no single, direct hit from a rocket could catastrophically inflict large-scale casualties on the work force; it also meant that any effective civil defence had to cover a much larger area.

When FCA Civil Affairs officers began organizing a cohesive civil defence plan, they encountered several serious obstacles. Antwerp city authorities and the authorities of the surrounding villages, including Merxem, Deurne, Borgerhout, Berchem, and Hoboken, were not cooperating with each other. Under the German occupation they had been forced to work as an agglomeration and upon liberation there was an immediate desire to revert to the former parochial system.[75] Although today these towns have been swallowed up by the growing metropolis of Antwerp and are essentially suburban districts, in 1944 they were separated by countryside but still vulnerable to rocket attacks. Canadian CA officers had to coordinate civil defence measures with these outlying villages by reamalgamating them.

Before the Allies liberated Antwerp, the city's civil defence system was almost nonexistent; under occupation, the Germans' only serious effort in some sort of civil defence consisted of the construction of bomb shelters. Passive air defence and reconstruction teams had either fallen into a state of decrepitude or were nonexistent. The main organization for passive air defence, the PLB (Passieve Lucht-Bescherming) atrophied while under German control, developing numerous operational weaknesses both internally and externally; operational control was not centralized, the PLB chaotically responded to incidents, and were unorganized on-site. PLB staff had inadequate training, transportation, and equipment, disaster response teams were inefficient and undermanned, and the organization rarely communicated or cooperated with other elements of urban disaster response, such as fire or medical emergency response teams. Upon liberation, Civil Affairs found the organization grossly ill prepared for the task it was to face. The head of the PLB was even found guilty of collaboration and removed, while the deputy head, Cadet Goemens, was under investigation for collaboration (he was cleared prior to taking charge of the organization). Regardless of its serious flaws, the PLB did provide an embryo for CAOs to build an effective civil defence organization around.

Even an effective emergency response system would struggle with the fact that Antwerp, by the autumn of 1944, was a leave centre for thousands of Allied troops. These large numbers of unorganized Allied soldiers invariably appeared at all incidents and, along with the PLB, Flemish Red Cross and Belgian Red Cross, Belgian police, resistance groups, fire brigades, and medical teams, all responding to rocket attacks, meant absolute mayhem at any site.[76] Civil Affairs officers had to forge some sort of organized response within this chaos.

In the first few months of the attacks, Lt Col Henry Barnes, CO of 325 Detachment, was tasked with organizing the various administrative elements into a cohesive centralized unit. Although civil defence was both a national and military concern, regional authorities struggled to retain their control, limiting any initial centralized cooperation across jurisdictions. In October and November 1944, Barnes chaired two meetings to impress upon the various participants how this had to change. Consisting of CA officers, municipal authorities, and representatives from the PLB, Barnes stressed that a unified command structure was the only effective way forward. He also was emphatic that the Allies desired a rapid centralization of the civil defence force.[77] At first, various burgomasters were hesitant to cooperate, primarily because they suspected Cadet Goemens, now acting head of the PLB, of collaboration. It was not until a second meeting in November that the wheels of cooperation began to turn (helped by the fact that Goemens was cleared of any suspicion), and both the PLB and municipal authorities began taking steps to enact Barnes's recommendation.

By the end of November, Barnes's leadership had helped create a basic organisational scheme that included personnel from Civil Affairs along with various Antwerp relief agencies, including the police, medical representatives, the Antwerp Fire Service, the gendarmerie, and the Belgian Red Cross and Flemish Red Cross. It established reporting and communication methods within the civil defence organization and between various agencies, on-site protocol for response teams, permanent PLB positions, incident and first-aid post locations, and casualty reporting. This scheme was the "fundamental basis on which the CD [civil defence] organization was built. It was amended and improved as time passed and in the light of experience gained."[78]

That same month, this loose committee of CA officers, burgomasters, and representatives from various relief agencies appointed Major Van Cappellen, the head of the Antwerp Fire Service, as director of the PLB, and Cadet Goemens continued as deputy, providing some "institutional experience."[79] Certain Belgians within the committee still suspected Goemens of collaboration and were unwilling to support his appointment to director.[80] Van Cappellen's appointment allowed for more detailed planning and better cooperation due to his connections with the city's relief services and the full support of the committee. Along with Van Cappellen, Col Charles Sillevaerts of the Belgian army was appointed to the position of general commissioner for civil defence, essentially becoming responsible for the civil defence budget. In December, Civil Affairs established the position of high commissioner for the protection of the civilian population and appointed a local politician, Mr Andre Vaes. These men, in conjunction with Barnes, essentially made up the leadership for Antwerp's civil defence.

The PLB's central headquarters was wholly inadequate for the large task at hand. The PLB had very few staff, and there was relatively no communication between control and other emergency response services. Positioned in a small basement room at the city's central fire station, it had only two phone lines available for operational control: one connected to the observation post (OP) in the cathedral tower and the other to emergency services. The room itself had no incident boards, maps, or charting procedures. In theory, when the observation post notified the PLB of a rocket-bomb attack, the PLB would order out the necessary emergency teams, including fire defence, ambulance, military, and police services. In practice, none of this happened. Barnes and his men realized quite quickly the pitiful state of PLB headquarters: the minimally trained staff, obsolete communications equipment, and lack of any general operational infrastructure. For Barnes, this was a problem "whose solution was more urgent than the provision of equipment or the increase in personnel."[81] First, they had to find an appropriate facility for the control centre but they weren't successful until February 1945. In the meantime, they doubled the size of the current control centre to accommodate incident boards, maps, and more staff. They installed two more phone lines and established a backup line to the OP. Barnes appointed incident control officers, who were trained and put in charge of establishing incident posts and coordinating temporary first-aid shelters at attack sites. CA provided the police with crowd-control training, but civilians' and off-duty military personnel's eagerness to help continued to disrupt efficient response operations.

When in February the control centre was activated in its newer, larger location, it had six phone lines and an additional four private lines to three OPs and to Allied PAD (Passive Air Defence), which also provided an early warning system for the PLB. Its staff complement was twenty-four line operators who worked in shifts to cover twenty-four hours a day. Barnes decided to move the main observation post from the cathedral to the roof of Europe's first skyscraper, the Boerentoren building.[82] As well, they established new OPs in Berchem and Merxem ensuring ample warning from any direction to accurately plot the course of incoming rockets.

Barnes and his men continued to face staff shortages while trying to create a fully functioning PLB. Under Barnes' supervision, the PLB began a serious recruitment program in early October, which doubled the organization's size to roughly 1,400 personnel divided into nine companies. At first, PLB leaders were hesitant to allow female personnel. This attitude quickly changed. Barnes and others explained to the PLB the successful work performed by women in Britain. Reluctantly, the PLB began enrolling women. These women quickly proved their value and their numbers increased rapidly.[83] To accommodate the staff increase, the PLB opened nine more stations (for a total of fifteen) and created a new combined headquarters and training facility.

The PLB's recruiting objective was to create a wartime organization of 1,600 personnel, but the PLB struggled to reach this goal. Various problems affected recruitment. The port authority and various military work projects offered higher wages, and, especially during the early stages of PLB recruiting, it was difficult to prevent workers from switching jobs. Representatives from the PLB, supported by Barnes, complained about this problem to the government. In response, the Ministry of Labour and the port authority agreed that the port authority would not hire men or women who left the PLB.[84] PLB workers continued to angrily compare their pay with that of port workers, which resulted in two short-term strikes. In response, Barnes convinced the organization to introduce an incident pay of ten francs an hour on top of the monthly wage to help ameliorate the discontent.

The PLB also suffered from a serious lack of equipment and supplies; they desperately needed vehicles, heavy rescue equipment, tires, petrol, floodlights, and a variety of other miscellaneous equipment. Civil Affairs soon contracted most of the Belgian firms that built heavy equipment and established a spare equipment and parts pool; any items that could not be made by Belgian firms were leased by the military to the PLB. Slowly but surely, the PLB collected equipment such as heavy jacks, compressors, and oxyacetylene cutters in sufficient numbers, and by early February 1945 the PLB's heavy equipment shortage was solved.

The PLB's endemic vehicle shortage was made good by the delivery of more than twenty Canadian army trucks designed for moving light and heavy rescue equipment and various vehicles that could be converted into ambulances. The PLB continually struggled with their fleet's low-quality rubber tires, although they attempted to combat this problem by requisitioning tires from local salvage depots. In one instance,

PLB officials and Civil Affairs officers attempted to track down rubber tires from three different tire sources throughout Ghent and Bruges, but as the II Canadian Corps CA war diary explains, "all three garages had no supply of either tubes or tires in decent shape."[85] Barnes was able to secure the delivery of more than fifty bicycles from First Canadian Army to the PLB, a delivery that solved the messenger transportation problem.

The PLB was constantly concerned with acquiring petrol for their vehicle fleet, and their attempts at securing a comfortable amount were continually frustrated by government red tape. Civil Affairs personnel used military channels to provide the PLB with a temporary supply to keep the fleet going until the supply question had been worked out with the government. With help from CA officers and local ingenuity, the PLB slowly acquired other equipment, such as loud speakers, floodlights, generator sets, uniforms, boots, helmets, shovels, and picks.

Training was another problematic area that concerned both PLB officials and their CA advisors. With so many new civilian recruits joining the organization, it was imperative that they be brought up to functional standards. More than just the PLB recruits needed training; senior PLB officers, senior police officials, heavy rescue personnel, female personnel, Belgian Red Cross and Flemish Red Cross members, and utility services personnel all required different forms of instruction as well. Training consisted of disaster response, crowd and traffic control, effective cooperation with other services, communications between various response teams, as well as developing early warning systems. One Civil Affairs report optimistically stated that although "training imparts technical knowledge, it also provides the basis for discipline and co-ordination of effort. These were notably lacking in the early operations of Antwerp Civil Defence."[86]

The PLB's initial obstacle to effective training was the shortage of suitable instructors. Two CA officers were responsible for the training program but could hardly be expected to provide adequate instruction for the quickly growing organization. Persistent rocket attacks continually interrupted training, although at the same time these attacks provided valuable real-time experience for PLB recruits. Belgian civil defence instructors, trained in the UK, arrived in November and helped alleviate some of the pressure on the CA officers. As Lt Col Barnes pointed out, "Training paid a big dividend. Incident control, operational control, and work on the job at the end of March was efficient and speedy."[87] Barnes noted that the early days of PLB training set the precedent for a national Belgian civil defence school. This school was established in Brussels and officially inaugurated in the last weeks of April 1945, shortly before the end of the V-attacks.

Ancillary Services

The Antwerp Fire Service was the only area of civil defence that did not pose a significant problem for Barnes and his team. The fire brigades in the city, throughout the arrondissement, and in the port were well equipped. In fact, "during the occupation, the fire stations had been centres of underground resistance and before the liberation the staff had successfully prevented the removal of fire equipment by the Germans."[88] Interestingly, fire was surprisingly rare during the V-attacks. Fuel, coal, and gas shortages in Antwerp actually limited the combustibility of the city. For instance, in six months only two major fires were reported from V-attacks.[89] Because of this the fire brigade was able to provide its experienced and trained men and equipment in support of other ancillary services.

The police service, on the other hand, suffered greatly from lack of personnel and transportation. During the occupation, the Germans were suspicious of the police force and removed many of them, failing to replace the lost personnel. Upon liberation, low wages within the municipal police force and the high demand (and pay) for policing at military installations and the ports hurt recruiting efforts by local police. The police, or gendarmerie, played an integral part in incident response, and their inadequacy seriously affected this important component of civil defence operations. At incident sites, police were expected to cordon off the area to prevent the access of unauthorized personnel, maintain public order, collect casualty statistics, and identify the location of trapped victims. Until more police were trained and the force itself became better prepared, CA officers and a small number of trained Belgian civil defence officers carried out these duties.[90]

Lack of personnel and transportation also hampered medical services. One report lamented that, "Because of civilian casualties resulting from flying bombs ... the hospitals of Antwerp city and province are becoming filled up and the available civilian ambulances inadequate in number."[91] The Belgian Red Cross and the Flemish Red Cross, the fire brigade, public hospitals, and the PLB provided ambulances, but as Barnes reiterated, "The numbers of ambulances were simply inadequate."[92] CA officers requisitioned military ambulances whenever possible, and this helped alleviate some strain until November, when shipments from Belgian channels and the British Red Cross helped to almost double ambulance numbers. Nonetheless, a shortage of ambulance availability still plagued civil defence operations well into 1945.

Shortages of available hospital beds were also a constant concern. In January 1945, PLB High Commissioner Vaes solved the inadequate bed space problem when he ordered that all public hospitals be centralized under his authority. Prior to this order, hospitals ran on a parochial system, which often meant certain hospitals were overwhelmed by casualties while others had empty beds. The centralization of the hospital system allowed the PLB to distribute casualties evenly, and hospitals had to report on their number of empty beds so casualties could be delivered accordingly.

Interestingly, public utilities ran surprisingly well during the rocket and bomb attacks. The PLB enlarged the utility crews as required, but crews still faced the typical transportation and repair equipment shortages; these were overcome by borrowing vehicles and equipment from various military and civic channels. The utility companies kept the water supply constant, provided continuous but restricted gas service, ensured tram routes worked (although trams were delayed during attacks), and quickly repaired telephone lines. Antwerp suffered an electrical outage only once, when the Merxem Electric Plant was directly hit, the "Schelle station carried the combined load until the new section at Merxem could be cleared, repaired, and put back into service."[93] Although both plants suffered near misses, and various transformers and switching stations were damaged, the overall effect was negligible.

Civil Defence in Action

V-weapon attacks were merely "area" attacks. The weapons' guidance systems were primitive, so accuracy was almost nonexistent. Michael Neufeld, in his seminal work on the V-weapons, points out that "inaccuracy was one of the main reasons why German missiles were so ineffective. The V-2 could barely hit a giant city with any certainty; the V-1 was even worse."[94] This was no consolation to those directly affected by strikes, though. The missiles still caused heavy damage as both the V-1 and V-2 packed about one ton of high explosives.

During the attack period, from the fall of 1944 to the spring of 1945, 722 V-weapons caused casualties and/or damage to buildings. As early as October 1944, the Belgian Red Cross estimated that the average casualty figures per rocket attack were twelve killed and twenty wounded. That month a rocket struck Bontemantelstraat in old Antwerp and destroyed nearly forty buildings. This serious attack became a debris-clearing nightmare for the response teams, whose efforts took several days. The PLB estimated seventy-one dead and seventy-eight seriously injured. Another serious strike occurred on 27 November at the Frankrijklei-Keserlei-Teniersplaate intersection near the modern-day Vlaamse Opera House. A V-2 hit Antwerp's busiest intersection during lunch hour and killed more than 200 people: "dead and injured were scattered around, lying in about 1 foot of water caused by flooding from a large water main which had been fractured by the bomb."[95] Although the scene was horrifying, "the fires were rapidly extinguished and with a concentration of civilian and military ambulance and trucks the injured and dead were removed within an hour ... and within two hours the crossing was cleared and traffic resumed."[96] This was a remarkable civil defence achievement in the face of such a terrible attack.

It was in mid-December that the frequency of attacks hit its zenith. On 9 December 1944, a V-weapon struck the Agence Maritime building, which was being used by the Belgian Military Court, and destroyed the building's first four floors but left the upper floors intact. The impact scattered collaborationist files and records all over the street, and the police were frantic in recovering as much as possible during the clean up. Seven days later a V-2 hit the Rex Cinema resulting in the highest number of killed and wounded out of any single attack. Approximately 1,200 people had packed into the theatre for a Saturday afternoon performance when the rocket struck. The roof collapsed and two walls were completely demolished. Those spectators seated in the balcony were completely cut off from the ground floor and had to climb down ladders provided by the fire brigade. More than 500 people were killed; roughly half were civilians and half were military personnel. After this attack, and on Lt Col Barnes's recommendation, Antwerp authorities forbade the gathering of more than one hundred people in a single place at the same time.

On 6 January 1945, a V-1 hit the Boerentoren skyscraper, where the main PLB observation post was located, between its fourth and fifth floors. Although damage to the building itself was slight and casualties few, several older buildings in the area collapsed due to the concussion. To the PLB's chagrin, the observation post was not even aware of where the bomb had exploded and actually "telephoned the main control for information."[97]

Flying bomb and rocket attacks were terrifying and could cause heavy damage if the right type of target was struck, but from a strategic perspective this German campaign was a failure.[98] Nevertheless, 8,333 civilians were killed during this campaign, which went "uninterrupted for 175 days at an average of nearly 35 rockets or bombs per day."[99] Although the dock area was struck only 302 times, 5,960 bombs and rockets hit the 900 square kilometres (351 square miles) of Greater Antwerp. Only 65 per cent of all launches hit within Greater Antwerp. Roy Irons, noted author on the topic of V-weapons, states, "The accuracy achieved by the 'V' weapons against Antwerp was greater than that achieved against London, but was still poor."[100]

Relief and Response

The V-weapons' overall inaccuracy was little comfort to those who faced the horror of a successful strike, and a significant element of civil defence involved postincident welfare for those directly affected by the attacks. Reports show that as late as October 1944 "no organisation existed in Antwerp for the welfare and care of persons bombed out of their home."[101] Before the Belgian government established a centralized welfare organization, during the early months of the V-campaign, civilians whose homes had been bombed were forced to go to three separate offices for clothing, food, money, and accommodation. Several organizations were involved in postincident welfare, including the Commission of Public Relief, the Belgian Red Cross, the National Help Committee, Social Services, and the Infant Welfare Service. These varying services worked independently though, so the system was chaotic. It fell to Major J.J. Opray, relief officer for 325 Detachment, and Captain J.S. Patterson, SHAEF advisor on postraid issues to Belgian authorities, to find a viable solution to this disorganization. At Opray and Patterson's insistence, the Belgian government centralized the responsibility for relief and rehabilitation and appointed Mr R. Avermaete as the director of public assistance. By mid-December, Avermaete and his new coordinating committee administered all the groups involved in postraid relief.[102]

Avermaete and his committee faced a serious problem in the lack of rest centres or temporary shelters for displaced citizens of greater Antwerp. By December 1944, three primary rest centres in central Antwerp held more than 400 people in total. These were designed to act only as very temporary accommodations until local or out-of-town billeting could be found. Avermaete and his committee, supported by Civil Affairs officers, requisitioned school facilities to increase the number of rest centres, and by March 1945 they had established twenty-three, which were able to accommodate well over 3,000 people in total.[103] The experience of various CAOs in establishing rest centres in France was advantageous here. They spearheaded the search for suitable locations and quickly organized fully staffed and fully functioning rest centres. Local CA detachment members always led these centres, and often former school personnel staffed them with assistance from Belgian, Flemish, and British Red Cross teams.[104]

The rest centre authorities had varying success gathering the necessary supplies: beds, mattresses, and pillows were abundant while blankets were much more difficult to obtain. CA officers found cooking equipment, often borrowed from army stocks, and helped established kitchens in ten rest centres. These kitchens also delivered two meals per day to those centres without cooking facilities. New and used clothing was shipped over from England for the destitute, while furniture salvage teams labelled and stored furniture recovered from bombed homes. The rest centres were the key to the entire relief effort as they gave civil defence authorities time to organize those whom the attacks had left indigent.

Finding suitable accommodations for displaced Antwerpians proved to be a complicated process. Once relief authorities collected those displaced by the attacks at rest centres, gave them a meal, and registered them with the proper authorities, the Ministry of Public Works and the Ministry of Public Health attempted to find suitable billets. "These functions overlapped to a certain extent and caused some regrettable delays in the taking of decisive action," a British postwar report concluded, "little progress was made until, with pressure from CA, a Billeting Officer was appointed in January."[105] This billeting officer required various burgomasters to cooperate and exercise their right to request and obtain suitable billets; because numerous burgomasters had close relationships with local populations, they were hesitant to exercise this right. With pressure from Major Opray, the billeting officer conducted a survey of possible billets and presented it to the eight commune burgomasters outside Antwerp to ensure adequate accommodation for those who still remained in rest centres. Unfortunately, this process was complicated by the fact that thousands of civilians had privately evacuated their homes to move to outlying towns or villages, taking up much needed space. Safety concerns became so acute that in December relief organizations voluntarily evacuated more than 6,000 children from Antwerp to safe areas.[106]

Debris Removal and Repairs

Out of all the tasks overseen by the PLB it was the debris removal and repair teams that fought a losing battle, trying to clear detritus from the streets and initiate repairs as more bombs continued to drop. In the early days of the attacks, the labour force committed to these tasks was grossly understaffed and also lacked transportation. At the end of November 1944, only 350 men and thirty lorries of varying quality were available to clear debris.[107] Workers struggled to clear the brick, timber, and glass that piled up with every strike. Because windows often shattered at ranges of one kilometre (1,000 yards) from the bombsite, glass was frequently broken in places a significant distance from where the bomb actually struck. This resulted in cleanup areas being scattered throughout the city.

In December, Lt Col Barnes recognized the need for a vast increase in equipment and manpower and led the creation of a provincial coordination committee. Although Belgian officials, including the city engineer and the city architect, nominally headed this committee, Major A.J. Dunn (Civil Affairs Staff Officer II Technical) was sent from II Canadian Corps HQ to supervise it. This committee began recruiting manpower and obtaining equipment from a variety of civil and military sources specifically for clearing debris and completing repairs. By January 1945, the committee had found the necessary equipment. One method by which the committee was able to make up the bulk of the equipment shortage was in striking a deal with the British Ministry of Home Security to borrow one hundred lorries and three cranes. By early April, Major Dunn's force reached an impressive size of 2,000 men, 220 lorries, and ten cranes.[108]

The repair teams faced a far more difficult challenge then their colleagues in debris clearance. Repair crews lacked equipment and supplies in almost every category, from roofing tiles to cardboard, and most labourers were unskilled. In mid-December, 3,500 homes awaited repairs and 2,000 buildings were scheduled for demolition. Orders were placed for materials, but they did not appear in usable quantities until late in January; meanwhile, damage was increasing and only forty houses had been repaired.[109] Red tape delayed funding for the repairs, but after being pressured by Lt Col Barnes, the Belgian government authorized High Commissioner Vaes to delegate funds without having to go through the standard government channels (in this case approval from the Ministry of Public Works). Vaes also appointed various officials to oversee building demolition, debris removal, property repair, and control and supervision of reconstruction material distribution. By circumventing the red tape, Vaes certainly helped the reconstruction effort though he was fighting a losing battle. While the bombing was sustained, the number of houses being damaged would always exceed those being repaired.[110] One week after the bombing attacks ceased, crews had yet to repair more than 3,000 houses; 540 men faced this enormous job, having already repaired more than 800 houses.

The Suburbs

Although the Germans targeted the city of Antwerp, the inaccurate V-1 and V-2 rockets affected Antwerp's communes almost as severely due to errant targeting. In fact, Civil Affairs officers wrote that the inhabitants of the outlying communes suffered proportionately worse than those in Antwerp, added to which was an almost complete lack of civil defence, medical, and postraid services such as existed in the city.[111]

In 1944, Antwerp's arrondissement included more than fifty communes. It was roughly 1,000 square kilometres (391 square miles) and stretched from the Dutch border in the north to the town of Boom in the south, and from the River Scheldt in the west to the town of Oostmalle in the east. Organizing civil defence in the communes was an extremely difficult and tiresome task for Civil Affairs officers and local officials. Like with the PLB, Civil Affairs had a difficult time recruiting labour for civil defence teams. Large numbers of civilians already worked for the ports and received better pay than offered by civil defence. Civil defence teams in the communes were often small or nonexistent. In some communes, Boy Scouts and volunteer fire brigades carried out the tasks. Their equipment consisted of the most basic items required (namely, picks, spades, and shovels), and like every element of civil defence, they lacked transportation.

A lack of effective leadership in the communes hurt CD operations. As well, the commune burgomasters were often hesitant to enforce their authority for fear of angering and alienating locals. For instance, as civil defence teams were continually short on transportation, burgomasters were under pressure to requisition vehicles from locals, with whom they were either friendly or at least knew in some capacity. Often burgomasters were simply uncomfortable forcibly requisitioning vehicles from these families and residents whom they had known for a long time. This, for obvious reasons, made the process more difficult.[112] By December CA officers were becoming exasperated with the recalcitrant burgomasters: "It was evident ... that the majority of burgomasters failed to take sufficiently serious their responsibilities for the defence of their communes."[113]

Some things, like communication issues, could not be helped. Officials in the communes and the city struggled to communicate with one another due to extensive damage to telecommunication infrastructure. What limited telephone lines were available were shared with the military, causing frequent disruptions to service, and these lines were continually damaged by bomb attacks.

At II Canadian Corps headquarters, Civil Affairs officers sought to devise a way to motivate the burgomasters. At the insistence of CA, PLB Director Major Van Cappellen organized two meetings of the commune burgomasters to be held in January 1945. With full attendance Cappellen outlined the burgomasters' civil defence responsibilities and asked for them all to adhere to these requirements. At the end of the month, he sent Baron Van der Straeten, a PLB representative, and Major Charles Berry, a Civil Affairs staff officer at II Canadian Corps headquarters specializing in civil defence and fire prevention, to report on the state of the communes' civil defence. Throughout February and March, these two officials submitted reports on the various communes and made recommendations that, slowly but surely, became implemented. Each commune sent men to the Antwerp PLB school for training and instruction so that they could provide leadership in their respective communities.

In the communes, as in Antwerp, fire was not a major problem; however, fire equipment was often so obsolete that the city and First Canadian Army had to supply newer machinery. For instance, the Wommelgham commune received a modern British pump to replace the secondhand pump that the town had purchased in 1870. In March 1945, the PLB created a "quick reaction team" of Antwerp PLB firefighters to aid any commune in immediate need and equipped the team with modern British medium pumps (the most common firefighting pump in London) and appropriate transportation.

Belgian, Flemish, and British Red Cross teams provided medical services in the suburbs, but as in the city, they lacked available ambulances. Emergency personnel often requisitioned vehicles on the spot to transport casualties, but some "of the more isolated communes had often to stop a lorry on the main road in order to send a stretcher case to hospital."[114] In Aertselaer, south of Antwerp, medical personnel even relied on horse-drawn vehicles.[115] Relief teams used Canadian military ambulances when available, and in March, ten more ambulances and a fifty-bed field hospital arrived with units from the British Red Cross and St John's Civil Relief. Nonetheless, during the V-attack period, commune relief workers continued to have difficulty evacuating casualties because of the ambulance shortage.

After the attacks ceased, the lack of resources and the city's demands put further strain on the ability for the communes to provide immediate care for those left homeless; specifically, the dissemination of building materials, furniture, blankets, and clothing became an issue. The retreating Germans heavily looted certain communes, and the combat had inflicted serious material damage. The civilians in these areas suffered greatly during the winter and early spring months of 1945. Often, relief officials could not distribute available building materials to needy communes due to the lack of vehicles needed to transport the material. People continued to live in the cellars of their own, ruined, completely uninhabitable houses, usually in unhygienic conditions, "because they had a strong sense of possession and wanted to hold on to what little remained."[116] Fortunately, rest centres were not generally needed in the communes because generous neighbours billeted those displaced by the destruction, and in many areas, many children and some women were evacuated to safe zones.

AN IMMENSE AND FRUSTRATING TASK

Organizing Antwerp and its communes' civil defence force was a highly complicated and challenging operation for Canadian Civil Affairs. As Lt Col Barnes wrote, "Uninterrupted bombing and the stress of operational work during six months obscured to some degree the realisation that progress was being made all the time."[117] From anti-aircraft defence, to incident response, to postraid welfare, all facets of civil defence were impaired by organizational challenges, political tensions, and social upheaval. Without the dedicated and experienced support of CA detachments, the fight against the V-weapons would have been much more difficult. A letter from Major Van Cappellen to Detachment 325 highlighted Civil Affairs's achievements in Antwerp:

> Now that the Civil Defence has fulfilled its task and that its demobilization must be arranged for, I feel it my duty to express to you and to your staff, on behalf of CD members and especially in my own name, my sincerest thoughts of appreciation and thankfulness for the great assistance and valuable advice, which you have so willingly given to the PLB during the difficult months of the Antwerp bombing. I fully realize that it is mainly due to your great efforts, to your help and to your previous experience that it has been possible to develop the PLB into a solid organization and that thousands of civilian casualties could be rescued alive.[118]

The CA report on Antwerp civil defence concluded, "The local authorities ... found their feet again, assisted and guided by Civil Affairs officers."[119] During these six months in 1944 and 1945, II Canadian Corps Civil Affairs maintained the population's morale and achieved their ultimate goal of preventing a mass movement of manpower away from the ports; one could say that Antwerp's fight against the V-weapons was a victory.

The fight for Antwerp's Civil Defence coincided with a serious administrative challenge to First Canadian Army Civil Affairs resulting in a restructuring of the branch's administration. This administrative shuffle, though, stemmed from one key source, General Bernard Montgomery wanting to shed 21st Army Group's responsibility for Civil Affairs. In a letter dated 17 November 1944 Montgomery recommended that Civil Affairs in France, Belgium, and southern Netherlands pass to the jurisdiction of each country's respective SHAEF Mission by 30 November of that same year (SHAEF Mission being the final civilian administrative body collaborating with SHAEF before total handover to autonomous civilian control).[120] Frankly, Montgomery had long held a disdain for Civil Affairs, which he saw as steeped in the legacy of the failed AMGOT. As well, operationally Montgomery's focus was now on Germany, and he felt that operational responsibility for both France and Belgium was fading while his formation was not concerned with the Netherlands "north of the present river line [that being the Waal River]."[121] With the crossing into Germany seemingly near, a greater focus on Military Government as opposed to Civil Affairs was needed. Montgomery used this reasoning as a convenient excuse to attempt to rid 21st Army Group of its CA responsibility. He argued that his headquarters should not "be called upon to deal simultaneously with two such dissimilar functions (CA and MG) in relation to the civil population."[122] This request was received with some shock by SHAEF, the DCA and certainly by CA commanders within Second British Army CA and First Canadian Army CA. SHAEF responded with a clear indication that this was not possible: "It is doubtful if the time has arrived when this change of responsibility can be effected – in any event it could NOT be achieved by 30 November."[123]

Montgomery was obviously not satisfied with this response. CA planners at G-5 SHAEF sought to placate him with a detailed clarification of how and when 21st Army Group could shed its responsibility for the civil administration. A detailed outline of the transition from military to civilian authority had actually yet to be clarified amongst SHAEF and CA planners at G-5 and Montgomery's pressure led to this taking place. Generally speaking, the advance across France had resulted in a fairly organic transition to civilian authority once the military rapidly moved on after August of 1944. With the concentrated military buildup in Belgium and southern Netherlands, the notion that rear areas would naturally transition to civilian authority once the military moved on no longer held water. While civilian authority was being, and in some cases already had been, totally reestablished in France, there was very little presence of any civilian authority in Belgium and the Netherlands because the two countries were part of the forward operating areas of First Canadian Army and Second British Army. Until such time that the countries were not in the forward operating areas, military authority reigned supreme. Although Montgomery was speaking from a place of disdain for Civil Affairs, he also recognized the current front line facing Civil Affairs and was unsure of how an efficient transition to civilian authority could take place.

A SHAEF meeting on 30 November hoped to solve all the confusion. From it came a far clearer distinction about how a military to civilian transition would take place. Each country would be divided into "Forward Zones" and "Zones of Interior." Forward Zones included everything within the boundary of the army, including Lines of Communication. Whatever fell within 21st Army Group's Forward Zone was the responsibility of the commander. This meant that Civil Affairs would operate within this zone as part of 21st Army Group's administrative structure (i.e. as part of First Canadian Army and Second British Army respectively). Once a region became designated an interior zone it now fell under the jurisdiction of that country's SHAEF Mission (so in this case SHAEF Mission Belgium and SHAEF Mission Netherlands respectively). Here, all responsibility for "civil administration within the zone of interior will be so far as possible matters for the national authorities."[124] At this point an increasing amount of civilian participation and control would begin taking place in preparation for eventual complete civilian administrative takeover. The only point at which Civil Affairs would operate within interior zones was when it became "necessary to support civil affairs activities in Forward Areas ... to alleviate distress or maintain law and order which might hinder military operations ... required by special policy decisions issued by the appropriate SHAEF Mission or SHAEF."[125] Essentially, military commanders no longer had to be concerned with civil administration once it had passed to the interior zone. For Montgomery, this meant he had to remain responsible for Civil Affairs as long as the territory occupied by his 21st Army Group remained part of his forward zone.

While this broader strategic discussion occurred at 21st Army Group HQ and while Canadian Civil Affairs struggled with Antwerp's civil defence, the "front line" of combatant–noncombatant interaction was taking on a whole new dimension to the north, in a small portion of liberated Holland. The most complex and extended Civil Affairs mission of the entire war was underway and both I and II Canadian Corps Civil Affairs, working together in the same theatre for the first time, were going to use every bit of experience and every resource available to prevent a serious humanitarian disaster.

CHAPTER FOUR

To Free or Feed the Netherlands

"There never was a good war, or a bad peace."
– Benjamin Franklin

The liberation of the Netherlands was the most complex and prolonged Canadian Civil Affairs effort of the entire war and can be considered the pinnacle of achievement by Canadian CA in northwest Europe. What was predicted to be a speedy liberation, like that in Belgium, turned into a drawn-out affair which created serious administrative problems for both the new Dutch government and Civil Affairs. In particular, coal distribution, refugee movement and control, as well as the supply of food all became serious challenges. Most alarming was that by the autumn of 1944 malnutrition was rampant throughout the country and the average daily caloric intake continued to plummet. Acute mass starvation became a serious possibility. First Canadian Army would marshal all of its Civil Affairs expertise and experience to bring relief to the Dutch and prevent a catastrophic humanitarian disaster.[1]

THE STRATEGIC PICTURE

First Canadian Army faced a stagnant front in the autumn of 1944. Operation Market Garden, launched in September, had failed to secure a crossing into Germany but had created a narrow salient whose tip centred on Nijmegen. Over the course of the next two months the Canadians expanded this salient, eventually occupying a large portion of the country south of the Waal River. First Canadian Army then began operations to open Antwerp and liberate the area of the Scheldt Estuary, including the Breskens Pocket south of the river, the Islands of Walcheren and South Beveland, and the landward approaches to the latter. By November 1944, the provinces of Zeeland and portions of Brabant were free, but the vast remainder of the Netherlands north of the river remained in German hands. This territory included major Dutch administrative and population centres, approximately three times as many civilians as in the liberated south.

The Allies then turned their attention to securing logistical support for the final thrust of the war. In March of 1945, after the Canadians had fought a series of gruelling battles to free up the western bank of the Rhine, the Allies crossed the border into Germany. On 22 March, 12th US Army Group crossed at Remagen, and a day later, during Operation Plunder, 21st British Army Group crossed at Rees, Xanten, and Rheinberg.[2]

With Allied forces across the Rhine, Field Marshall Montgomery, commanding 21st Army Group, sought to liberate the remainder of the Netherlands. He planned to push on towards the Elbe River to gain possession of the plains of northern Germany and to attempt a rapid advance on Berlin. Supreme Allied Commander General Dwight Eisenhower vetoed this advance; Montgomery would have to be content with the plains of northern Germany and the Elbe River. While one British and two American armies pushed into the German fatherland north of the Ruhr, First Canadian Army was given the relatively inglorious task of driving north and west into the Netherlands. Although this directive lacked the media-grabbing headlines that the advance into Germany held, it was a crucial element of 21st Army Group's northern advance. The Canadians were ordered to open up a critical supply route north through Arnhem, ridding the Dutch of their German occupiers, and finally clearing the German coastal belt towards the Elbe.

On 2 April, this final operation to liberate the Netherlands began. First Canadian Army moved northward with British Second Army, under Lt General Miles Dempsey, advancing along their right in a northeasterly direction towards Hamburg (see Figure 9). Protecting the whole of 21st Army Group's right flank was 12th US Army Group containing General William Simpson's US Ninth Army and General Courtney Hodges's US First Army. While continuing to defend 21st Army Group's right flank, Simpson's Ninth Army pushed across Germany towards the city of Magdeburg. On Simpson's right, Hodges's First Army continued its advance past Leipzig towards the Elbe River.

As early as the winter of 1944, reports came down from SHAEF that the Dutch population was facing a severe food crisis and that acute starvation was imminent. To accomplish the humanitarian and operational objectives of his task, General Crerar understood that it was important for his army to establish control over the key communication and transportation centres of Nijmegen, Arnhem, Zutphen, and Hengelo. To establish this control, Crerar ordered General Simonds's II Canadian Corps to cross the Isjell River and attack Deventer from the east. After completing this objective, Simonds thrust into northeast Holland to prepare for an advance into Germany along its northern coast. Here his corps faced heavy fighting against stubborn German defenders bent on protecting the northern approaches into Germany. General Foulkes's I Canadian Corps, recently arrived from Italy, forced a crossing of the Lower Rhine near Arnhem, securing Simonds's left flank, and then swung west to liberate northwest Holland, the most densely populated area of the country. Combat intensity was relatively low for I Canadian Corps though the supply and relief effort that faced the men of I Canadian Corps Civil Affairs was to be one of their most complicated and difficult tasks of the entire war.

DUTCH, GERMAN, AND ALLIED ADMINISTRATIONS

To understand why Civil Affairs faced such a daunting task in the Netherlands, one must understand how the Dutch civil government worked prior to the four-year German occupation and how it changed under German control.

The Netherlands is one of the oldest parliamentary democracies in the world. Parliament is composed of two bodies: the upper and lower chamber. The lower chamber, whose members are elected for four-year terms, amends, proposes, and enacts legislation while the upper body, elected for six-year terms, can only approve or veto bills being passed. In 1940, just prior to the German invasion, the Netherlands was divided into eleven provinces, each with its own elected legislative body.[3] A Queen's commissioner was appointed for six years as the liaison between the provincial and central government. The provinces exercised a significant degree of regional autonomy. Each was in turn divided into communes run by a crown-appointed burgomaster for six years and an alderman elected by the people of that commune for a period of four years.

When the Germans occupied the Netherlands in late May 1940 they maintained the basic structure but subjugated all semblance of democracy and benevolence. A National Socialist civilian administration was installed, headed by Dr Arthur Seyss-Inquart, former Austrian chancellor and one of the key figures in turning Austria into a province of the Third Reich. Nazi officials of Dutch nationality were appointed to most of the senior positions in both the central and provincial levels of government. At the municipal level, officials were approved and appointed by Seyss-Inquart and his cronies. Any Dutch resistance was hunted ruthlessly by both the German military and Dutch collaborators, nearly 2,000 Dutch resisters were killed during the war.[4]

As much as possible, Seyss-Inquart attempted to limit drastic changes to the traditional Dutch administration. For instance, a significant number of preinvasion officials in lower echelon positions were given the choice to continue their employment under the new administration, and many accepted. Over the course of the occupation, all officials found to be disloyal to the new state were removed and all elective bodies were disbanded, and "[w]hile leaving most departments intact, the Germans gradually introduced authoritarian principles into the government machinery."[5] This forced most government officials to flee the country, creating a Dutch government-in-exile in London. In 1944, when the Allies entered the Netherlands, the government administration had undergone four years of Nazi control and many, if not all, of the anti-Nazi officials were imprisoned, exiled, in hiding, or dead. Almost every major official still working within the country was considered a Nazi sympathizer or collaborator and had to be removed.

As they had in France and Belgium, the Allies sought to limit the time Civil Affairs controlled the machinery of the government. At the same time Allied officials were forced to tread lightly for fear of presenting the Allied military government as another military occupation. Yet, the Dutch political apparatus was in shambles when the Allies arrived. Dutch members of the government-in-exile that arrived with the Allies were completely dislocated from the country's civil administration. Any bureaucrat or politician that had remained in the country was suspected of collaboration. This, coupled with the lengthy and difficult liberation process, stalled Allied attempts to create an efficient, centralized governing body that relied as little as possible on Civil Affairs support.

Establishing an effective government quickly became even more difficult due to problems in anticipating German moves. Civil Affairs planned the relief and rehabilitation of the Netherlands in 1944–45 on the assumption, incorrect as it turned out, that the Germans would retreat quite rapidly implementing a scorched earth policy as they withdrew. Civil Affairs planners at G-5 SHAEF believed that after overcoming the initial issues of supplying immediate relief, they would primarily need to rehabilitate and reestablish a self-sustaining supply infrastructure throughout the country. Essentially being guided by the same broad objectives that had defined experiences in France and Belgium. The primary objective was initially to minimize the length of time that the military was directly responsible for the various civilian and administrative demands. During this opening phase of Allied military control, complete authority was to rest with SHAEF and SHAEF-designated officials. This phase was intended to give the Dutch civil administration time to organize itself and provide professional guidance on the various problems afflicting a country so recently liberated. Once the civil machinery was running effectively, Civil Affairs officers could move on to their next objective. Plans, however, had to change. The Germans did not withdraw rapidly, instead putting up a stubborn resistance especially in western Holland. This proved a serious obstacle to establishing an efficient Dutch civil administration and lengthened the period that SHAEF remained in control of the country.

The civilian organization that was intended to help transition the Netherlands into a fully functioning civilian-led government was the

Netherlands Military Administration (NMA). Anticipating the problems associated with a nation controlled by Nazis for four years, the Dutch government-in-exile in conjunction with SHAEF established the NMA in early 1944 to act as an interim government. The organization was essentially composed of the "forward echelon of [the Dutch] Government" living in exile in London.[6] It was designed to operate as the governing body until a fully functioning Dutch government, under Prime Minister Pieter Gerbrandy, was established. The NMA was charged with continually liaising with the Allied forces situated in the Netherlands, "[advising] the Supreme Commander and [representing] the wishes of the Netherlands Government."[7] Its commander, French Brigadier General Franck Jules Leon Cazanove, essentially divided liberated Holland into military districts, each run by a Dutch military officer. Each officer and his civilian administrative staff worked closely with First Canadian Army CA advisors to prepare for the eventual handover to a civilian government.

An administrative body, SHAEF Mission (Netherlands), was also created to act as the "channel of communication in all matters between 21st Army Group and the Netherlands Government."[8] This body, headed by SHAEF Major General John Clark, advised the NMA and liaised between the NMA, 21st Army Group, and SHAEF.

Despite Allied preparation and hopes, the anticipated rapid liberation of the country never occurred. Not only did the Germans refuse to retreat in the wake of the Allied forces advancing from southern Holland but they also fought stubbornly and showed no intention of abandoning the Netherlands. This problem seriously affected the efficiency of the complicated administrative relationship between First Canadian Army Civil Affairs, the NMA, SHAEF Mission (Netherlands), 21st Army Group, and SHAEF. The original plans by SHAEF and the Dutch government-in-exile had to evolve quickly.

The Allied situation in the Netherlands was further complicated by the complete breakdown of local administration coupled with the NMA's failure to function properly from the outset. In the initial days of its operation, the NMA lacked enough essential personnel to take over at the provincial and municipal levels, leaving administrative gaps in crucial areas. In Zeeland and Brabant, local officials were completely nonexistent as many had collaborated with the Germans and fled, fearing for their safety. As a result, in the liberated areas there was a complete absence of civil administrative personnel, machinery, and even records. The NMA did not quickly or effectively fill this void. While the organization occupied itself with the planning of large-scale relief efforts, it ignored this integral element of an effective civil administration and was frankly unsuitable for the tasks it was called upon to perform.[9]

Furthermore, because of the loss of operational momentum at the River Waal, the headquarters for both SHAEF Mission (Netherlands) and the NMA remained in Brussels, where the organizations were limited to planning and had little influence on the Dutch government or the situation on the ground. Brigadier W.B. Wedd, senior civil affairs officer for First Canadian Army, repeatedly requested that "arrangements be made to move forward a strong advance element of both bodies not only to control local officials but to also strengthen the position of provisional government."[10] This recommendation was not acted on until early April 1945, when both bodies moved from Brussels to set up headquarters in Breda and finally began to be integrated into the broader Dutch political apparatus. In fact, at this point NMA officials and Civil Affairs officers were stationed in the same headquarters and barracks facilitating a far more effective, close working relationship.[11] Until that point, however, the onus for supporting the fledgling Dutch government and its civilian population-in-need lay almost entirely with First Canadian Army and its subordinate formations I and II Canadian Corps.[12]

The essential problem for Wedd and FCA CA faced was how to keep the liberated area functioning, in terms of the political system but also in terms of the day-to-day existence of Dutch civilians, with a minimum call on military resources.[13] The first step in approaching this massive problem was organization. The Netherlands was divided into four zones of relief. Area A was the liberated area south of the River Waal and provided a stable base from which Civil Affairs operations could be carried out while CA officers continued local rehabilitation efforts. For the moment, the other three relief areas were under German occupation. The IJssel River was the boundary between Area B and Area C; Area C was located east of the river and Area B was located west of the river. Area B was further divided into two sub-zones along the Hilversum–Utrecht–Tiel line with B-1 west of the line and B-2 east.

First Canadian Army CA officers were well aware that the Netherlands was going to present a "series of formidable problems for CA and at best great hardship [would] be suffered."[14] In the early days of liberation even Brig. Cazanove admitted "that conditions in Holland were much worse than in Belgium." He predicted that the country's rehabilitation would face serious obstacles primarily as the "food and coal stocks had reached an emergency level."[15] The reality of the situation was much more complex and several major problems distinguished the Dutch relief effort as one of the most complicated Civil Affairs tasks of the entire war.

PROBLEMS WITH CIVIL ADMINISTRATION

One of the main issues that Civil Affairs faced in the Netherlands were the problems associated with establishing an effective Dutch civil administration. This meant that First Canadian Army Civil Affairs was forced to rely upon significant amounts of military resources in helping to prop one up. This allocation of resources went well beyond the original mandate, which envisioned a complete German withdrawal followed by a short period of CA support to facilitate the establishment of a functioning and effective civilian administration. By October 1944 SHAEF had revised the CA plan for the Netherlands recognizing that the administration in place was simply unable to cope with the responsibilities of governing the partially liberated country without extensive support from Civil Affairs.[16]

One of the first complications in forming a functioning Dutch administration was that, after four years of German occupation, Nazi sympathizers had been placed throughout all levels of government.[17] This meant that when the Canadians first entered the Netherlands, they faced a Dutch administration that was suffering from personnel shortages due to officials fleeing the country. For example, the 500–member Directorate of Police, which administered the entire force throughout the Netherlands, lost one-fifth of its personnel immediately upon liberation: more than one hundred personnel "deserted with the Germans, 22 [were] suspended pending investigation and a further 10 [were] arrested and charged with collaboration."[18] Similar personnel depletions occurred throughout the liberated territories.

First Canadian Army CA expected initial administrative problems, of course, but significant tension arose due to the inability and unwillingness of civilian officials to take charge. Brigadier Wedd continually lamented what he called the necessary "prodding" of civil administrators months after the front line stabilized.[19] At times, the war diaries read as if CA officers were playing the role of babysitters rather than advisors. Shortly after liberation, for instance, Wedd wrote that the administration seemed to have had "an acute attack of amnesia regarding med sups [medical supplies] which they had during the war, [and have] even [forgotten] the presence of factories manufacturing such supplies."[20] He noted that civil officials continually "demonstrated that they were still unable to stand on their own feet and in the supervision and control of their efforts much [remained] to be done."[21] This tone of frustration and doubt about the Dutch administration permeated Wedd's reports until the end of the war.

The Allied headquarters either misunderstood the situation or chose to ignore it. A SHAEF document written in December 1944 reads, "Good co-operation is reported to exist between Civil Affairs staff and Dutch administrative authorities in liberated areas. No serious problems have arisen."[22] On the contrary, Wedd's report from that very same month notes that there were "considerable administrative problems particularly in the matter of close co-operation among civilian authorities."[23]

In late January, as general conditions in the Netherlands improved, so too did the perceived effectiveness of the Dutch administration. Wedd clearly attributed this to the work of his Civil Affairs branch, "a great deal of the improvement [was] due to the great amount of direct assistance that the CA organization [was] able to offer."[24] He saw the improved situation more a reflection of the great work of Civil Affairs rather than indicating any improvement in the local administration.[25] Even into February Brigadier Wedd was concerned about the ability of the civil authorities to carry out operations independent of Civil Affairs when he wrote "It is still evident ... that the civil administration needs continued prodding ... Administrative arrangements need speeding up."[26] Various organizations within the Dutch administration were simply unable to act independently of the military. Although the NMA slowly assumed responsibility for the food distribution networks, for instance, Civil Affairs officers were required to oversee every phase of the operation as well as provide the staff necessary to coordinate all transportation of goods.

The civil administration failed to work effectively partly because many Dutch civilians viewed the NMA as an émigré government. These civilians, who had remained in the country during occupation and sought to play an important part in the new administration, found it difficult to reconcile with those who had lived outside the country during Nazi rule and had now arrived to run it. Brigadier Wedd addressed this tension in a report to Brigadier Thomas Robbins, deputy chief Civil Affairs officer (DCCAO) of 21st Army Group. Wedd, echoing his sentiments towards Belgian civilians, felt that Dutch civilians were ignorant about the extent of war damage in England, the sacrifices and hard work of the UK's civilian population, as well as the operational necessity of evacuations and billeting in order to make room for incoming forces. Wedd felt that the civilian population assumed that liberation would mean a quick return to normality, not a continuation of struggle to end the war, and that "the difficulties of re-establishing normal conditions [were] not appreciated by the people."[27] To further help in galvanizing public support Wedd's report to Robbins called for the establishment of a publicity program. This would be directed towards the Dutch with the objective of reconciling the public that had remained in the Netherlands with the officials that had fled. Wedd certainly blamed part of the administrative chaos on both local authorities and those newly arrived and their inability to cooperate.[28] In early 1945, under the supervision of Civil Affairs and the Dutch administration, a newspaper was printed in both English and Dutch reporting on the Allies' rehabilitation efforts. Aimed at civilians, this propaganda campaign alleviated some "suspicion and jealousy between local officials who [had] remained in [the Netherlands] during the occupation and those who [had] now come out from the UK with the Netherlands Military Administration."[29]

The Dutch Resistance

Tensions between the Dutch resistance and the NMA further complicated the situation. As early as September 1944, Prince Bernhard attempted to organize the Dutch resistance under the umbrella group of the Dutch Forces of the Interior (DFI). Hoping that a centralized resistance could be better integrated into the Allied war effort. The three most active resistance groups, the Order Service (OD), the Council of Resistance (RVV), and the National Action Group (LKP), were consolidated under this DFI designation. Complete unification of the resistance was never achieved, many of the smaller resistance cells were never incorporated, but with the largest groups unified under the DFI designation fairly strong political liaison and cooperation with Civil Affairs and the larger Allied effort was effectively achieved.[30]

Tension continued, however, between the leaders of the various resistance groups and NMA Dutch officials returning from England. One Canadian report blamed this tension squarely on the shoulders of the arriving government officials "who perhaps are not always fully aware of the local situation at the time."[31] Particular hostility was directed at NMA officials who had spent most of the war outside of the Netherlands and were now being given administrative positions. This, for instance, led to a perception of greater leniency towards Dutch collaborators by NMA representatives. Many leaders of the Dutch resistance felt that since they were the ones who had spent the war within the country, they were most qualified to decide whether someone was a collaborator or not. But NMA officials were very reluctant to let the resistance deal with collaborators without official government involvement. For many NMA officials, it was difficult to distinguish between valid accusations of collaboration and ones made by various resistance groups for political gain. For instance, communist resistance groups accused political rivals of collaboration in an attempt to remove the opposition.[32] Wedd explained to Dutch officials that this same problem was overcome in Belgium with the creation of three-man juries to deliberate on charges of collaboration. Dutch officials, seeking to avoid collaborator complications, jumped at this recommendation and quickly established local commissions of three appointed officials, including a representative from the resistance, to review every charge of collaboration and treason brought against someone.[33] This certainly ameliorated some of the tension.

The second major factor contributing to friction between the resistance and Dutch officials was the appointment of important administrative positions. Leaders of the resistance felt that their members should be appointed over civilians. The NMA, on the other hand, desired that only those qualified should be given positions in the new Dutch civil administration and did not believe priority should be given to any one group in particular.[34] Through meditation between the resistance and the NMA, facilitated by Canadian CA, a solution was arrived upon whereby prominent leaders of the resistance would be steadily incorporated into administrative positions.[35]

Problems with the NMA would persist, however. Brigadier Wedd, the Dutch civilian population, and representatives of the resistance became increasingly frustrated with the NMA's lack of effectiveness.[36] Major Reid wrote, "the organization was reluctant to assume its proper responsibilities and, to a large extent, [was] ill-equipped for the tasks which it was called to perform."[37] It seemed that only time would heal the gap and help develop a properly coordinated, efficient, and cooperative civil administration involving all Dutch civilians.

Any situation whereby fractious and hostile resistance groups impeded the efforts for an effective civilian administration to function was ultimately avoided. Unlike in Belgium, where various resistance groups threatened internal stability, Dutch officials and resistance groups attempted to cooperate.[38] The committees overseeing the trials of accused collaborationists were quite successful in convicting these individuals, thus mollifying some of the resistance groups' concerns. With the ardent support of the Allied military, many resistance members were eventually drafted into the army, so a large segment of armed and politically active agitators were removed. On the advice of Civil Affairs, many senior members of the resistance were given suitable posts in the new Dutch administration, which seemed to placate the resistance leadership. The relatively organized and centralized nature of the Dutch resistance under Prince Bernhardt made some cooperation possible. All these conciliatory and administrative efforts allowed for a remarkably quick transition for the resistance to go from challengers to the German-friendly Dutch state to participatory members in the new Allied-friendly one.

COAL SHORTAGES

The ineffectiveness of the new Dutch administration forced FCA CA to take complete control of one of the most important resources in the country: coal. Coal, to put it bluntly, was the controlling issue at the time. It was the basis of the economic life of the Netherlands. Coal distribution was supposed to be the purveyance of the Dutch government, but the Dutch government was unable to cope with the immense task and therefore one of the most important elements of CA work was getting coal to the people.[39] Coal fired the stoves and furnaces of Dutch homes, factories, and businesses; it provided fuel for cooking and for generating electricity to power everything from streetlights to drainage pumps in the low-lying areas of the Netherlands. In essence, the Dutch people's survival depended on their access to the valuable rock. The peacetime requirement for coal in the Netherlands was approximately eighteen million tons per year. Traditionally, three-quarters of the coal used in the Netherlands was mined in South Limburg, and the rest was imported from Germany and Wales. During the German occupation, the Limburg mines' production was severely reduced and imports to the Netherlands ceased.

When the Canadians first entered the Netherlands, the coal supply was already dangerously low and the manpower and transportation needed to move this commodity was severely lacking; one of Canadian Civil Affairs's first tasks was to help reestablish a functioning coal distribution network that would be overseen by civilian authorities. In Area A, for instance, initial reserve supplies of coal were exhausted quickly, and Civil Affairs officers, more often than not, found themselves taking the lead in acquiring it from new sources. Compounding this problem, between October 1944 and March 1945, the military consumed 15 to 25 per cent of the coal mined in the country, adding further strain to public consumption.[40] In late October 1944, when II Canadian Corps took over from XXX British Corps in the area around Nijmegen, the mines were found essentially undamaged. This was a short-lived victory as they also discovered that the existing coal supply would soon be exhausted. One report claimed that "[t]he supply of fat coal for gas production at Breda and Tilburg [would] be exhausted by 1 December."[41] Coal was a constant concern for Civil Affairs officers of II Canadian Corps, as shown in the war diary for the month of December. Almost every day there was an entry about an attempt to acquire coal. In one entry, it was reported that repeated appeals were made to XXX Corps, under the command of Second British Army, to replace 500 tons of coal removed from a barge originally intended for civilian distribution: "The coal is urgently needed for civilian requirements and the question of good faith is involved."[42]

Circumstances were complicated further because the mandate of Canadian CA detachments was to provide only immediate and short-term relief. The delay in NMA officials arriving at the "sharp end" meant that CA detachments remained far longer than was anticipated. Consequently, the CA operations were plagued for months by insufficient communication and cooperation from the NMA and provincial and municipal levels of government. This compounded situation was at its worst in December 1944 and January 1945. Colonel Hurley, senior civil affairs officer II Canadian Corps, agonized over this situation, "If stocks are exhausted by 17 January 1945, it will mean no electricity, no gas, no coal for civilian home consumption, industries will shortly have to stop and it is feared that the general health condition will suffer."[43]

Transportation issues hampered efforts to get coal to the Dutch. Normally, coal would have been transported by railway or barge. The barges could carry approximately 3,000–5,000 tons a day using the vast canal network throughout the Netherlands; the Germans, however, had destroyed many of the canal locks. This destruction seriously disrupted barge traffic. The alternative route, Holland's railway network, was in better shape than the canals, but the manpower needed for mining as well as loading and unloading the coal was in short supply.[44] With the daily caloric intake so low, it was difficult for workers to put in full days of difficult manual labour.

Military resources, both in vehicles and personnel, had to be used to mitigate distribution problems until Dutch infrastructure could facilitate the steady movement of coal. In the province of North Brabant, then under the command of I British Corps attached to First Canadian Army, it was necessary to "divert transport urgently needed for food distribution to undertake transportation of coal from centres having more than two week's supply to others where stocks were completely exhausted."[45] The absence of any sort of train network schedule further hindered coal transportation: "[W]e have had difficulty in obtaining a programme of coal trains ... [W]e can obtain no advanced notice of arrivals ... It is obviously difficult to prepare for the onward distribution under such circumstances."[46] The high price of coal on the black market made acquiring, distributing, and protecting it an exhaustive enterprise, and many times coal trains arrived missing large portions of their loads. CA officers continually battled corrupt officials and black market retailers for control over the precious commodity.[47]

CA officials became increasingly frustrated with the coal situation. In early January 1945, Brigadier Wedd expressed his annoyance when he wrote, "The problem of how to obtain deliveries of coal for the liberated Netherlands remains unsolved and unsatisfactory ... [T]his has produced a most unfavourable result in the minds and attitudes of the civ [civilian] population."[48] Recognizing the severity of the situation, he requested the distribution of coal be placed entirely under CA control and coordinated through military channels until the civil administration was able to carry out the duties on a fully functional level. This militarization of coal distribution was put into effect at the beginning of January. As Wedd reported, "Deliveries of coal in the last week of January were greater than those of the first three weeks put together ... [T]he unloading of coal wagons has shown considerable improvement under continued pressure from this HQ."[49] Within the first two weeks coal deliveries rose from 9,020 tons in the last week of January to 34,990 tons the first week of February.[50] Nationwide repairs to railway lines and bridges, as well as continued military control of the coal transportation network, resulted in the tonnage of delivered coal rising steadily for the remainder of the war.

REFUGEES AND DISPLACED PERSONS

First Canadian Army faced another complex problem upon entering the Netherlands in the autumn of 1944: refugees. Winter was fast approaching and the Dutch government, much to the annoyance of CA officials, had failed to establish any sort of functioning administration to help evacuate civilians or care for refugees and displaced persons (what would become the Civilian Evacuation Bureau and the Netherlands Military Repatriation Commission respectively). The administration of these vulnerable and destitute civilians was largely left to Canadian Civil Affairs. The influx of large numbers of refugees and military personnel into Area A, the only liberated portion of the country, placed even greater pressure on CA to find appropriate accommodations for armed forces and displaced civilians alike. This was of course magnified by endemic transportation problems as well as flooding in large tracts of the countryside.

A primary concern for Civil Affairs officers was controlling the movement of refugees in order to prevent it from clogging up main roads and impeding the military from moving from one objective to the next. Further difficulties would almost certainly arise were civilian populations to be left to fend for themselves without military aid. A lack of food, medicine, and shelter could easily spawn breakouts of disease and general lawlessness, which would not only impede military operations but also limit the population's helpfulness in providing tangible support for the conduct of the war. With a stagnant front line and a crowded Area A growing more populous by the day Dutch civilians were faced with innumerable problems including finding adequate shelter and food while also often trying to avoid exchanges of fire between Canadian and German soldiers. The only serious option for Civil Affairs was evacuation of civilians from the forward areas that posed the most extreme threat in this regard. These evacuations presented serious logistical problems. They stretched the already small amount of transport resources available to CA as well as rapidly reduced available accommodations. The evacuations brought with them many additional problems such as "the disposal of livestock, the care of household effects, of valuables and civic, legal and church records."[51]

Compounding refugee evacuation confusion, the civilian bureau that was supposed to be playing a significant role in coordinating refugee movement was in a state of near collapse. The Civilian Evacuation Bureau or Bureau Afvoer Burgerbevolking (CEB) was run by officials in The Hague. The Hague was still in German hands. The CEB could not form or function as an effective centralized administration from its position behind German lines. The Netherlands Military Repatriation Commission, in charge of the return of displaced Dutch civilians, was also not functioning and "considerable assistance [had to] be provided from military sources in order to attain the degree of preparedness necessary to cope with [refugee] situations."[52]

In December 1944, representatives from the SHAEF Mission (Netherlands), the NMA, and First Canadian Army Civil Affairs decided that establishing a new location for the centralized CEB authority was crucial to the military and civilian needs of the liberated Netherlands; consequently, in January 1945, this body was established in Nijmegen. This was a major step forward in terms of the CEB establishing operational effectiveness. By February 1945, the Civilian Evacuation Bureau was finally ready to begin its work "almost entirely as a result of the persevering efforts of this [CA First Canadian Army] fmn [formation]."[53] Between October 1944 and January 1945, an estimated 30,000 Dutch civilians were evacuated from dangerous forward areas such as Nijmegen and along the River Waal, particularly from Betuwe Island situated on the Waal just north of Nijmegen. This successful, albeit large, evacuation resulted in serious congestion in the major southern towns, such as Eindhoven, Breda, and Tillburg. Undernourished children were of particular concern, and CA oversaw large evacuations of Dutch children to Belgium, the United Kingdom, and even Switzerland.[54]

The presence of Allied soldiers also compounded refugee issues. The concerted military buildup in the small area of the Netherlands occupied by Allied troops compounded the refugee issue as accommodations needed to be found for these soldiers. As more and more troops came into the area in preparation for future operations north of the River Waal, accommodations became increasingly scarce. The cold and extremely wet autumn and winter in the Dutch lowlands made the issue of finding adequate accommodations even more pressing. British,

Canadian, and American young men found themselves living with civilian families. In some cases, civilian homes were requisitioned entirely for military use, and the families were moved.[55]

Procuring accommodation for the thousands of Dutch refugees from various areas was a frustrating task; one CA officer wrote, "The Israelites had a much easier problem to solve when ordered by the Egyptians to make bricks without straw. The difficult, CA have learnt to do at once, the impossible, though it admittedly takes a little longer, has as usual also been achieved."[56] In Meppel, accommodations were so limited that 225 CA Detachment was forced to use a German bicycle factory owned by Esso. This was a three-story building that could accommodate upwards of 1,000 people though significant amounts of broken glass and debris had to be cleared from its floors before it could be used.[57] Due to the limited space within the country, relocation was very rarely local. The entire process of finding adequate settlement areas and overseeing dispersal was based around a series of refugee transit camps. Large groups of refugees were moved from their homes first to corps transit camps and then on to army transit camps. They were then placed in nearby Dutch villages or sent to Belgium when suitable accommodations were unavailable.

The refugee problem was further complicated by military operations against the Germans. Buildings in most major towns were severely damaged due to months of fighting, and large tracts of land had been flooded by the Germans for defensive purposes and in some cases by the Allies to neutralize German defensive positions. Refugee movement in the province of Zeeland, which included Walcheren Island and South Beveland, posed a unique Civil Affairs problem. Since September 1944, Canadian troops had met vicious resistance from German defenders fighting desperately to prevent the Canadian capture of the Scheldt Estuary, which would open up access from the sea to Antwerp's shipping lanes. With dogged determination, Canadian troops pushed the Germans all the way back to the small island of Walcheren. Although today the island is actually part of the Beveland peninsula, in 1944 only a tiny causeway linked Walcheren with South Beveland. A coordinated assault between British commandos and Canadian troops was devised to capture this last German stronghold.

To neutralize much of the German artillery and infantry positions, senior officials, including Montgomery, Crerar, and Simonds, decided to breach the dykes of Walcheren Island by air bombardment. Numerous sorties were flown by Lancasters, and on 3 October 1944 the dykes were breached and the ocean poured in, flooding Walcheren Island. This flooding resulted in the rapid capture of the island but subsequently posed a serious Civil Affairs problem. Scared, cold, and hungry refugees huddled on what little high ground remained. Entire villages were underwater, and one CA detachment reported that "[m]any people were rescued by DUKWs and all the belongings they could bring were carried along with them. As the water flooded almost every house to the second story people were living in many places with their livestock in the same house."[58] One officer wrote, "The refugee situation is difficult ... Tilburg is being used as a reception area for evacuees from flooded districts but the position is becoming acute ... Possible future evacuations are from Walcheren and from the West Bank of the Maas River ... [I]t has been found necessary to find accommodation areas outside the Netherlands."[59] Luckily, an evacuation scheme had already been devised.

In early October, at the same time that First Canadian Army began the battle for the Scheldt Estuary, a large meeting was held between senior CA officials in Axel at II Canadian Corps headquarters to discuss predicted refugee movement during operations in Zeeland province, known to the Canadians as the Breskens Pocket. Brigadier Wedd, SCAO First Canadian Army; Col Hurley, SCAO II Canadian Corps; Brig. Cazanove, head of NMA; and numerous other Canadian, British, and Dutch officers involved in the refugee problem were present at this meeting. It was here that the general outline of a two-stage refugee plan was formed.

In stage one, civilians were evacuated from the towns in the southwestern area of Zeeland province, during Operation Switchback from 6 October to 3 November. These civilians would be allowed to return once military operations ceased. For those refugees in the western half of the Breskens Pocket, a principal east–west route was established. It ran through Belgian territory from Maldigem to a collection centre in Sas Van Gent in Dutch territory. Refugees were "accommodated from two to eight hrs [hours] in this collection centre and then evac [evacuated] to Axel and areas prepared for their reception."[60] For civilians in the eastern half of the Breskens Pocket, a north–south route was established via secondary roads to the collection centre in Axel. While 3rd Canadian Infantry Division attacked German positions within the pocket, its two CA detachments, 614 commanded by Major R.S.N. Clarke and 225 commanded by Major T. Driver, worked together to carry out the evacuation operation. The former oversaw the main east–west route and the latter, the north–south movement.[61]

When military operations moved north to Walcheren Island and the Beveland peninsula in late October 1944, reception areas for evacuated civilians also moved north, this time into the southeastern region of Zeeland province.[62] The plan called for the use of assault craft to move refugees from the battle area to the south bank of Scheldt River.[63] A strange scene thus ensued whereby landing craft would depart the south bank loaded with soldiers equipped and prepared for battle only to return with destitute civilians fleeing from the carnage on the north bank. Absorption areas were established in southeast Zeeland for approximately 10,000 refugees. In the Belgian arrondissements of St Nicholas and Termonde, accommodations for 5,000 refugees were set up, and further reserve absorption areas throughout western Flanders were established to accommodate approximately 10,000 more refugees.[64]

Walcheren Island posed some of the most serious challenges for CA officers in charge of civilian evacuations. Roughly 80 per cent of Walcheren Island was flooded and thousands of civilians had been forced to flee to higher ground. As one Canadian officer wrote, "one could see miles and miles of submerged land with here and there the roof of a church, a steeple or a large building emerging from the water."[65] Though some found dry ground in a few of the lucky villages that remained above the flood line, the majority of the island's population took shelter in the island's main city of Middleburg. Middleburg's population rose from 18,000 to 42,000 people. It had no electricity, no sewage system, no gas, and levels of fresh water and food were becoming dangerously low. The primary water distribution system in Middleburg had shut down since the flooding began in early October and most civilians were forced to drink rainwater.[66]

First Canadian Army and II Canadian Corps CA detachments tackled the various tasks with vigour. While the primary objective was to evacuate civilians as quickly as possible, numerous other tasks occupied the men: building and administering refugee camps, reestablishing infrastructure, providing medical aid, fixing Middleburg's sewage system, restoring electricity and gas, and repairing the island's fresh water supply system. These improvements all helped alleviate the strain on the civilian population while preventing serious outbreaks of disease.

Captain J.E.G. Labrosse, with 103 Relief Detachment of Second British Army CA, helped build a special transit camp for Walcheren refugees in Enghien, Belgium. This was no small task. The detachment consisted of a variety of officers in charge of administration, quartermaster duties, accommodations, marshalling, sanitation, movement, medical arrangements, registration, safety, public health and welfare (Labrosse's responsibility), the medical team, as well as fifteen other ranks, and a transport company consisting of seven lorries for moving goods and people.[67] Further assisting in the operation of this relief camp were two Belgian and two Dutch liaison officers, a British hygiene team, fifteen military police, fifteen Dutch and Belgian nurses and nurses-aides, ten cooks, two dozen wardens, and 130 various other personnel. Within one week, 103 Relief Detachment was able to find a suitable location and construct the transit camp to accommodate an average of 500 refugees per day. A former freight car factory towering over an abandoned convent and elementary school became the site for the transit camp. A pioneer party converted the buildings into a liveable space by constructing latrines and furniture and establishing working kitchens, running water, and electricity. Once the refugees arrived, they were registered, deloused and "taken to their respective billets for a hot meal and a good sleep."[68] After this, refugees were moved by convoy and billeted amongst the rural population of Belgium, where they were to stay until conditions in their own country improved enough to allow them to return.

The evacuation of the village of Vernraij in late October 1944 by Major J.S. Miles's 224 Detachment, attached to II Canadian Corps CA, exemplifies the efforts of both military and civilian officials in moving civilians away from forward areas. On 27 October the inhabitants were ordered to proceed on foot in small parties organized and controlled by local police. The civilians were told they were only allowed to bring "1 mattress, 2 blankets, 1 set of cutlery, perambulator and baby food," and each person was told to wear as much warm clothing as possible.[69] About 750 civilians per day were permitted to leave the village to travel to a rendezvous two kilometres west of the town, where they met transport provided by the military and some civilian agencies. Civil Affairs officers coordinated refugee transportation using empty army trucks heading to the rear to resupply; in essence this was an organized hitchhiking scheme. Schedules were almost nonexistent, and reception centres could rarely predict when refugees were going to arrive. The evacuation concluded on 31 October with more than 3,200 civilians moved without a single casualty.

The month of November would prove to be the busiest in terms of refugee control with Canadian Civil Affairs responsible for moving nearly 25,000 people.[70] An example of a large-scale operation during this time can be seen in the evacuation of the civilian population living on the island of Betuwe. II Canadian Corps was gravely concerned about the enemy flooding the island, which would seriously threaten its 14,000 inhabitants and most likely result in mass uncontrolled refugee movement. The Canadians feared that panic-stricken inhabitants would stream across the Nijmegen bridge, the only one connecting the island with the southern shore, seriously impeding and possibly preventing operational movement to and from that sector. On 15 November 1944, to circumvent this possibility, Brigadier N.E. Rodger, chief of staff II Canadian Corps, ordered Col Hurley to organize an evacuation of the island. The people of Betuwe initially protested this forced evacuation. This resentment gave way to gratitude and the protests to praise when, on the last day of the planned evacuation, the enemy breached the dykes holding back the River Rhine and the island was submerged.[71] At this point the Betuwe civilians begrudgingly obliged the polite but firm Canadian soldiers organizing the evacuation.

On 17 November refugees gathered at prearranged collection points organized by Civil Affairs officers recently arrived on the island. The Royal Canadian Army Service Corps provided vehicles to transport the civilians off the island and onto the southern shore of the River Waal to a corps refugee transit camp located in a monastery on the outskirts of

Nijmegen. Refugees first went through a screening process intended to identify spies or Nazi sympathizers moving amongst the civilians. They were then given a medical examination, some food, and a bed for the night. The camp was operated by 218 Detachment along with a variety of personnel including civilian doctors and nurses, members of the Friends Ambulance Unit (a volunteer Quaker organization), Dutch Boy Scouts (used for traffic control), and the Netherlands women's service (Vrouen Hulp Korps).

Finding local accommodations were a challenge. Initially, billets in the Nijmegen area were found for a small number of the refugees. These quickly filled up, and the rest were driven to a refugee reception camp at Tillburg. Upon the refugees' arrival, civilian officials from the NMA organized billets for them in and around the area of Tillburg and Breda. Due to very limited space, less than half of the 14,000 refugees could be billeted. After a night in the camp, several thousand refugees were transported via rail to Ath, Belgium, roughly 190 kilometres (118 miles) south-southwest of Tillburg. 21st Army Group supplied transportation from Ath to a reception centre at Geraardsbergen, twenty kilometres north of Ath, where Belgian authorities then took over the billeting process. By the end of this long evacuation process many of the civilians found themselves almost 300 kilometres from their homes. Life in the camps was not easy, but Canadian soldiers did their best to alleviate some of the strain. In a camp set up nine kilometres southwest of Nijmegen, operated by 302 Detachment, an ice cream cart was brought in and a Punch and Judy show was organized for the children. The adults had to suffice with the musical overtures of a Royal Artillery Band.[72]

Animals also became an evacuation concern. Before the civilian population had even settled into their temporary accommodations they began to demand a full evacuation of the island's livestock.[73] Although seen as a slightly unnecessary strain on available resources, Civil Affairs obliged carrying out one of the more unique cattle drives in modern history. Incredibly, they were able to save 98 per cent of the livestock as well as a significant amount of food and fodder by transporting it south to dry pastures via military vehicles.[74]

Sometimes evacuations were much smaller, as in the case of a tiny village found in the forward area in April 1945 by 4 Company 2nd Belgian Fusiliers. The village was so small that its name is omitted from the records. The Belgian company sent a request for a civilian evacuation to headquarters 1st Canadian Armoured Brigade, who forwarded this request to headquarters I Canadian Corps Civil Affairs, who arranged "for immediate evacuation by 302 (A) Detachment."[75] Twenty-seven civilians were evacuated by lorry.

By April 1945, Civil Affairs planners were faced with a now familiar challenge: the return of refugees and displaced persons to their homes. At this point First Canadian Army carried operational responsibility for essentially all of the Netherlands north of the River Waal. This included responsibility for relief and rehabilitation in the provinces of North and South Holland, Utrecht, Gelderland, Overijssel, Drenthe, Groningen, and Friesland. Initially, during combat phases, the military maintained strict control of road movement to prevent any large-scale return. Once areas became liberated and the fighting moved on, there was a natural inclination to allow civilians to return. In many cases they had no homes to return to as the fighting had destroyed their towns and villages. CA officers were unwilling to allow large groups of civilians to leave their present accommodations, either in billets or refugee camps, to return to cities, towns, and villages without adequate shelter, food, and services. CA officers knew that in time, the returning refugees would be in need of further aid. "Obviously there is little purpose in allowing people to return from refugee centres to ruined homes with no water, light, heat or fuel for cooking," the CA weekly report from I Canadian Corps observed.[76] Civilians from Arnhem, for instance, were permitted to return only after establishing their "proof of residence, and further proof that the house [had] a roof on and [was] still habitable."[77] After the German capitulation in early May it became more and more difficult to control the migration of not only civilians from within the Netherlands but also of those from outside the country. By the end of May all security restrictions on movement previously imposed by I and II Canadian Corps were lifted. Lt Colonel Lord Tweedsmuir, Canadian battalion commander, wrote, "It is interesting to note that for the first time in 5 years [the Dutch] control movement in their own country."[78]

RELIEF SUPPLIES

In October, both the United States and Great Britain had been convinced by the Dutch government-in-exile that SHAEF would need to take responsibility for the relief of the Dutch people.[79] It was to be a relief effort heretofore never attempted in size and scale. Major Reid outlines the reasons why it was necessary to provide relief on a scale in the Netherlands not seen in France or Belgium:

> A. Rations for the past year had been insufficient in comparison with those of the French and Belgians, the daily calorific value of the Netherlands ration being only half of that for German nationals.
> B. There was a railway and boat strike in the Netherlands which had been called for by the Netherlands Government at the time of the Arnhem air landings. As a result of this strike, the Germans refused to import or transport food for civilians and reserve stocks were being rapidly depleted.
> C. Inundations covering 500,000 acres [roughly 200,000 hectares] had destroyed crops and stocks which would otherwise have been available to assist in providing food.[80]

Yet during the battle to liberate the Netherlands, the Allies encountered serious obstacles distributing relief supplies to the civilian population. There was little transport outside of military vehicles and very little reliable manpower due to the weakened state of so many starving Dutch. As well, the civilian administration was almost wholly ineffective. In some cases, city officials were even "reluctant to distribute to the general public for fear that a greater emergency might follow and that no further stocks would be available to meet it."[81] Officials throughout the country charged with distributing relief supplies were plagued by this phobia of a greater future emergency. This fear precipitated tension between the military and civilian relief planners.

Prior to the Allied invasion of the Netherlands, First Canadian Army stocked supplies at both army and corps supply depots with plans to distribute them through local authorities once a region was liberated.

Additionally, First Canadian Army Civil Affairs planned for spearhead detachments of four or five men to carry large quantities of hard rations to distribute to areas considered in most need. Unfortunately, this system, which had been fairly successful in both France and Belgium, did not work in the Netherlands. This was because the shortage of relief supplies was greater than expected and the stagnant front line limited in-theatre operational mobility.

The reality of the Netherlands's military and humanitarian situation forced a revision of standard relief doctrine. The Allies could not simply use up the reserve stocks as they had in previous countries because First Canadian Army was going to occupy the Netherlands for an unknown length of time. By the autumn of 1944, First Canadian Army had, in many ways, become an army of occupation in Area A while still engaging in on-going military operations against a powerful enemy in northern areas of the country. This army of occupation had to establish a continual supply line to alleviate distress in Area A, which contained over a million and a half Dutch civilians, and at the same time had to use the same supply system to build up relief material for the eventual liberation and relief of the remainder of the country.

The supply system in the Allied-occupied zone was supported by a series of supply depots. These inland depots were set up in advance and designed specifically to speed up the movement of supplies throughout the distribution network. Supplies arriving to the continent intended for 21st Army Group were collected at an inland depot. Control of the depots varied. While many fell under the jurisdiction of First Canadian Army, some, like the largest depot at Breda, fell under the control of SHAEF Mission (Netherlands). Other depots fell under the jurisdiction of Lines of Communication. The administrative body in charge at these inland depots became responsible for the breaking up of these stocks and the redistribution to civilian-controlled depots often at the village or town level. At its disposal SHAEF Mission (Netherlands) had a variety of transport columns driven by differing nationalities, including British, Dutch, and French, and one transport company from the Royal Canadian Army Service Corps on loan from First Canadian Army. Regardless of who was responsible for the depot, within the area controlled by First

Canadian Army, it was Canadian Civil Affairs officers who oversaw the transportation of the goods, guarded the supply depots from civilian looters, and aided in the administrative work until local civilians could manage on their own.

Slowly, the transition from military to civilian oversight of the supply chain was completed. By December 1944, a Rijksbureau (bureaucratic administration) was formed under the NMA's command. This organization would oversee the distribution of supplies in Area A from a newly established civilian depot at Breda. At the end of December another inland civilian depot was established at Roosendaal, completely staffed by civilians but overseen by an FCA Civil Affairs officer. By February 1945 a third depot had been set up at Tilburg, and by March full authority for inland distribution passed to the NMA.[82]

The supply channels worked in the following way. A local civilian official would make a request for supplies and petrol to, for example, the Rijksbureau. After approval, this request would be forwarded to the Civil Affairs staff of II Canadian Corps, who would then forward it to CA First Canadian Army. A more detailed request identifying a distribution timetable as well as available transport resources would then be sent to the Civil Affairs staff at 21st Army Group. 21st Army Group CA would approve the request and supplies would be sent forward to a supply depot, where the local Civil Affairs detachment in conjunction with staff from SHAEF Mission (Netherlands) would oversee the distribution to civilian depots. At this point in the supply line, the military officially handed over responsibility to the civilian authorities, although Civil Affairs officers were also imbedded within the NMA to oversee efficient distribution.

FOOD SHORTAGES

The difficulties that the Allies faced in establishing an efficient distribution network exacerbated the food shortage in the Netherlands. It was here that the men of FCA Civil Affairs faced one of their most significant challenges in all of northwest Europe.

Under the Germans, the Dutch starved. The daily caloric intake for Dutch civilians was the lowest compared to French and Belgian nationals under the same regime. As one survivor noted, "We ate all of whatever apple, potato, cabbage, or carrot we could manage to obtain, taking any rot in stride ... The garbage man had long ago stopped making rounds because nobody had any garbage any more. There were few things that could not either be eaten or burned."[83] Another civilian noted how their weekly rations were reduced to "one loaf of bread, six pounds [2.72 kilograms] of sugar beets, and two ounces of skim milk powder."[84] Another recalled the following: "In the Christmas week our rations went down to three and a half pieces of bread and two potatoes a day. After butter and margarine, sugar had now disappeared too, and only children got a little bit of skim milk."[85]

The situation was exacerbated when railway and boat workers went on strike in September 1944 during Operation Market Garden. Though coordinated with the Allied timetable for Market Garden this strike severely disrupted the flow of supplies to the rest of the country. Moreover, an estimated 200,000 hectares (500,000 acres) of land was inundated by the Germans for defensive purposes. As one survivor described, "viable crops, livestock, farms and roads [were] completely destroyed ... This flooding [had] no strategic value at all, but it [made the] food position still more difficult."[86]

Sadly, liberation did not provide immediate relief. For a short period of time during the initial Allied occupation, the daily caloric intake in Area A actually dropped below that of the levels during German occupation. This was brief, however, as a report in mid-November 1944 pointed out that "the assistance given by the Allies to the Netherlands Administration did in fact provide a sufficiency of all commodities with effect ... to raise the Netherlands ration to the standard maintained in Belgium (1600 calories)."[87] The cold Dutch winter exacerbated supply problems particularly because foodstuffs froze before they could be distributed.[88] As survivor Elly Dull recalls, "It was incredibly cold that winter, the moisture just dripped off the inside of the walls. We all went to bed at seven o'clock with everything that we had that we could wear."[89]

For those 3.5 million Dutch civilians living in the German-occupied zones, the winter of 1944–45 would be one they would never forget. Food was scarce, people were starving, and fuel was nonexistent. The Allies knew that if they could not provide relief soon, civilians would begin dying in large numbers. One Dutch woman wrote, "Soon there was no more food and we starved ... Fortunately, the Swedish Red Cross sent each citizen one loaf of white bread. Some people gobbled it up right away, but we rationed ourselves, to one half slice a day, so that it would last. And we drank water so as to have something in our stomachs."[90] Henri van der Zee, a Dutch survivor, points out how children suffered the worst during that winter: "The average schoolboy of fourteen ... whose weight in 1940 was generally around 41 kilograms, weighed 37 kilograms ... Girls suffered more; they were 7 kilograms lighter and 6 centimetres shorter than those in 1940."[91]

Areas B-1 and C

By early 1945, reports of food shortages had become even more concerning. Richard Sanburn, correspondent for the *Hamilton Spectator*, commented on the conditions in the country:

> There have been no potatoes since December ... There is no feed for the cattle, so there is no milk for anybody. The meat ration is one-half ounce daily. There is no sugar, not even for children. There has been no margarine since last September and no butter since December. The civil affairs office where this information was obtained was in the spare room of a Dutch home in Wehl. For a check on the spot the officer went down the hall to the family dining room to inspect the midday meal of a Dutch family. He returned and reported, "they are eating crumbling potatoes mixed with corn meal."[92]

Operations to liberate Areas B and C commenced in the early spring of 1945. It became imperative that First Canadian Army Civil Affairs prepare to help civilians as quickly as possible after liberation. Staff officers of First Canadian Army and 21st Army Group, SHAEF Mission (Netherlands), and NMA officials were all involved in planning the relief efforts. Areas B-1 and C were liberated in April 1945, and both areas were found to have relatively strong, self-sustaining food supplies. Area B-1, south of the IJsselmeer, a fresh water lake in central Netherlands fed by the Ijssel River, was an agricultural region. Here, daily rations were quite limited, but because local civilians were used to a simple diet and had access to other food, there were no severe cases of malnutrition. The prewar population levels in B-1 were relatively low, and an estimated 90,000 refugees had migrated west, into Area B-2, in search of food. Conditions in Area B-1 rapidly improved after liberation. In Area C, the largely agricultural northeastern section of the Netherlands along the German border, the daily caloric intake was low, though not at emergency levels, at 900 calories per day. This region was still producing food, raising livestock, and growing crops. Malnutrition was rare and conditions continued to improve quickly after liberation. In an April report, G-5 commander Lt General Arthur Grasett wrote, "The general condition of people in the newly liberated areas is, so far, better than had been anticipated."[93]

At this point First Canadian Army Civil Affairs began to receive much needed reinforcements. Civil Affairs officers of I Canadian Corps, having just completed a transfer from the Italian theatre, first took part in the Dutch relief effort in Area B-1. In early April 1944, I Canadian Corps, under Lt General Charles Foulkes, established a bridgehead across the Neder River west of Arnhem, in coordination with II Canadian Corps's crossing of the IJssel River. Following this, I Canadian Corps captured Arnhem and carried out active offensive operations designed to strike hard into the western Netherlands while II Canadian Corps struck north. The western offensive of Foulkes's corps aimed at freeing the vast majority of the Dutch population, now inhabiting the major urban centres of Amsterdam, Rotterdam, and The Hague. Yet with every village, town, and city liberated I Canadian Corps faced significant food shortages.

Relief distribution problems in urban areas were in stark contrast to the situation in rural Netherlands. In rural areas, large tracts of agricultural land and easier access to food made the smaller population centres relatively self-sufficient in terms of producing and distributing food. CA officers of I Canadian Corps found that the issue in the larger cities was not a shortage of supplies but inconsistent distribution methods. Civilians in places like Apeldoorn, Arnhem, and Amersfoort were receiving certain foodstuffs in large quantities while other rations were almost nonexistent. After consulting with local civil officials and the NMA, the officers of the various Civil Affairs detachments under Colonel J.S. Adam, senior civil affairs officer of I Canadian Corps, implemented a plan, whereby the required rations were collected and stored in local food depots (called "dumps" by the military).

These local food depots were located at strategic points throughout the liberated areas; for instance, primary ones were located in Apeldoorn, Zutphen, Deventer, Zwolle, and Groningen. The rations delivered to these food dumps were often drawn from larger stores located south of the Maas River. These larger stores were supplied by a combination of 21st Army Group, First Canadian Army, and the NMA. It was First Canadian Army's responsibility to collect food supplies from these larger stores and move them to the local food depots in the required area. Generally, Canadian CA officers were in charge of collecting, protecting, and distributing these supplies for the first week the dump was open. Civilians had to direct any requests for further supplies to the local CA detachment supply officer, who in turn would forward the request to CA headquarters. The objective of this plan was to relieve CA officers of any long-term commitments while, for economical reasons, providing civilians with only the required rations for a balanced diet.[94] After this initial period, the NMA in conjunction with local officials took over the management of the food dumps.

Area B-2

Although all of the Dutch suffered as a result of the German occupation, no other area had such an acute humanitarian crisis as the western region of the Netherlands, identified by military planners at SHAEF as Area B-2 where "urgent attention [was] being paid to serious emergency which [was] almost certain to arise when Western Holland [fell] into Allied hands."[95] One Dutchman living in western Holland (comprising most of Area B-2) wrote in his diary, "The only thing I can do is stay in bed ... Today I got up at ten and was back in bed at seven ... to allay the hunger. I just eat sugarbeet cakes. Supper consisted of seven of those.

We bought one kilogram of rotting carrots for 2.50 guilders and are eating stew tomorrow ... I'm starving."[96] A message from Queen Wilhelmina to President Roosevelt pleaded for the speedy relief of this area: "I feel sure that you have been informed about the catastrophic situation in the Netherlands, especially the thickly populated western part ... May I also appeal to you to give orders in order that food and medical supplies be kept ready so that there is no delay in sending them into Holland once the country is freed."[97]

Men, women, and children were all feeling the brutal effects of slow starvation. A nutritional report for the city of Utrecht in Area B-2, published by I Canadian Corps CA headquarters, provides an insightful look into the hardships inflicted upon the civilian population during the German occupation. The estimated population in the city was 150,000 civilians. The average adult had lost 15 kilograms (33 pounds) during the German occupation, most of the weight being lost in the first year of occupation and the last six months before liberation. The report also noted that the infant mortality rate continued to rise and children under twelve were reported to be underdeveloped because of so many years of undernourishment.[98]

By February 1945 food shortages in Area B-2 were the worst in the entire country and were reaching near emergency levels. The director of the Netherlands Government Information Bureau (and future prominent Dutch historian), Dr J.J. Poelhekke, gave a speech to the Toronto Rotary Club in which he stated that the situation in Rotterdam "is so desperate that it is virtually impossible to keep a baby alive. The only food available for children is a weak beet-root soup."[99] A I Canadian Corps CA nutritional report on Utrecht reported that although the bread ration was supposed to be 600 grams per week, in fact only 200–400 grams were being supplied because no more bread was available. The milk ration was also drastically reduced from seven litres per week to three and a half litres per week for children up to fourteen years of age.[100] Utrecht was starving; 1,500 cases of famine oedema had been reported and "[c]onditions in Utrecht [were] considerably worse than in any other town ... There [were] more cases of oedema per capita."[101] Several church and civilian organizations attempted to alleviate some of the worst cases of acute starvation, but the lack of resources greatly hampered their attempts. A soup kitchen in the centre of town attempted to provide some relief but the "1/2 litre per day of rather poor soup made of bean-meal, some potatoes and a little meat and water" was hardly enough.[102] In *The Occupied Garden*, Tracy Kasaboski and Kristen Den Hartog write how in The Hague, "corpses were left above ground for days on end, because there was no wood for coffins, and no way to transport the bodies – the horses that pulled the hearses were dead themselves."[103] It was so bad that "the most basic food – potatoes – had become a rarity. When word spread that a gardener still had some, the droves came straight for him – not just from The Hague ... but from as far away as Amsterdam."[104]

The problem in Area B-2 was so severe that 21st Army Group would take direct action. In January of 1945 Gen. Montgomery established a special headquarters with the sole task of dealing directly with the B-2 relief problem, Netherlands District. Major General Alexander Galloway, a veteran of the First World War as well as the North African and Italian campaigns, was appointed commander of Netherlands District. Along with Gerald Templer, 21st Army Group's director of Civil Affairs and Military Government (the successor to Brigadier Robbins), and George Clark, SHAEF representative to the Dutch government, Galloway set about organizing a massive relief effort. First Canadian Army held operational responsibility for the western Netherlands and thus Netherlands District was placed under the command of General Harry Crerar's First Canadian Army headquarters, and CA liaisons from both I Canadian Corps and First Canadian Army headquarters were included in the planning staff. These men and their staff were responsible for organizing the immense relief effort that totalled more than 130,000 tons of supplies designed to provide food to more than three and a half million people for seventy-four days at a daily intake between 1,600 and 1,700 calories.

The relief plan was divided into four "plackets" labelled A, B, C, and D. These were essentially the four primary methods of delivering supplies to the western Netherlands. Placket A introduced supplies across the River Waal from the south. Placket B landed relief supplies on the west coast of Holland after the area had been cleared of the enemy. Placket C supplied drops from the air force. Placket D, operationally led by I Canadian Corps CA, delivered supplies from the east. General Templar's Netherlands District would be involved in all four plackets, to ensure operational continuity, while working closely with both FCA and I Canadian Corps.[105]

The issue of the western Netherlands's relief was serious enough to warrant the involvement of General Eisenhower himself. In a dispatch sent as early as November 1944, Eisenhower stated the following: "21 Army Group in process of establishing stock pile of relief supplies for thickly populated areas of Western Holland ... Main route for relief supplies should be direct from UK to Dutch coast with possible initial token delivery by air."[106] These stockpiles not only included food but also fuel, medical supplies, vehicles, and miscellaneous items such as shoes, blankets, and soap. The Allies primarily accumulated supplies at Oss and transported them via road and rail to liberated areas (the largest supply shipments came directly from the UK into Rotterdam once the city was liberated on 5 May). All of these supplies were located in massive depots along the French, Belgian, and Dutch coast and in ships protected by various CA detachments, regular units of the Canadian and British armies, navies, and air forces, as well as Dutch police and NMA representatives.

Reichkommissar Arthur Seyss-Inquart, the German-appointed head of the occupied Netherlands, feared for his postwar safety were mass starvation to become an acute issue and thus naïvely hoped to gain favour after the war by negotiating and eventually allowing the Allies to carry out air drops of civilian supplies. Though recalcitrant at first, General Eisenhower eventually came around to the idea of a massive air lift, after pleas from the Dutch royal family and the Dutch government-in-exile found favour with Churchill and President Roosevelt, who would die eighteen days before the operation commenced. So it was that between 30 April and 8 May 1945, RAF's Operation Manna and USAAF's Operation Chowhound dropped an estimated 9,890 tons throughout the B-2 area, utilizing nearly 900 bombers to do so. "I remember very vividly this most moving moment of the war," writes Henri van der Zee, "when forty heavily loaded planes flew low over the town and dropped their goods on the heath at Crailo. Our lane, so sad since the oak trees had disappeared that winter, and so shabby with its neglected houses, was full of waving and shouting people, while the green and brown coloured food-bombs, standing out sharply against the pale blue sky, came hurtling down. It gave me goose-pimples, and nobody cared about the tears that were running down all our faces."[107] Vicki Tassie, another Dutch survivor, vividly recalls these "flying grocers" and tells of how she and her sister "ran up to the roof and everywhere people appeared ... It was a jubilating crowd, some people with the tears streaming down their cheeks, trying to speak and not able to articulate sounds because of strong emotions."[108]

Supplies not only came through the air but also on the ground. On 2 May 1945, I Canadian Corps began Operation Faust, transporting goods via lorries through enemy lines. More than 300 lorries, divided into a dozen convoys, began a nearly continuous series of deliveries from Nijmegen into German occupied territory. Once through German lines, the Canadians turned over the supplies to Dutch officials at the town of Rhenen for further distribution. One witness wrote, "How the first convoys were greeted is not difficult to guess. When the first trucks rolled into Utrecht with three hundred tons of food, the whole city was in uproar. Women embraced the drivers, who, after unloading, turned back in a hurry to collect a new load."[109] Farley Mowat, a member of the Hastings and Prince Edward regiment, recalled how "[i]n towns and villages across the flooded land the convoy found itself engulfed and almost washed over the dykes by a wave of humanity. Flowers crushed wetly, underneath the tires. Women, fat or bony, young or aged, clambered aboard the vehicles until some trucks disappeared from view entirely."[110] Just more than 5,500 tons of desperately needed food, medicine and supplies were delivered to the Dutch this way.

Not all civilians were able to benefit from these epic supply operations, so plans were also in place for relief efforts to commence immediately after the German surrender. On 5 May 1945, the German-occupied Netherlands capitulated, and the Allies rushed to bring supplies to those still in desperate need of food. After entering Area B-2 with the 49th British Division, I Canadian Corps Civil Affairs established its headquarters in Utrecht and was fully operational by 8 May. Every detachment of I Canadian Corps, and more from First Canadian Army and 21st Army Group CA, had become operational in

Area B-2 by 9 May. Within four days of liberation more than twenty-one Civil Affairs detachments were scattered throughout B-2 bringing much-needed relief to a starving population. Henri van der Zee recalls the following:

> For five long years I had only been able to sniff longingly at a pot which had once contained peanut butter, but had never lost the smell of it – now I would taste it again. I would eat bananas, oranges, chocolate – but no more rye cakes, sugarbeet or skimmed milk. For eight long months I had tried to read and do my homework by the light of the candle or a little wick in a bowl filled with oil – soon we would be able to switch on the lights again. No more fear of the sound of jackboots; of the Landwacht who might confiscate my load of collected wood; of bombs. Real shoes, instead of crude wooden pattens. Perhaps even a bike, and certainly train rides again.[111]

Following the liberation, Netherlands District, in cooperation with the NMA, oversaw the movement of the resources made available by I Canadian Corps. This meant bringing food to starving Dutch men, women, and children. Dutch survivor Alida Monkman recalls her first experience being given food by a Canadian soldier: "We had gone too long without food, so we started with crackers and tea, which tasted unbelievable [sic] delicious."[112] Maria Haayen, another survivor, remembers the food as well: "We got these beautiful little biscuits; they were dry but they contained whale oil and were made especially for people who had vitamin deficiencies. They tasted fabulous. Every person got a whole tin of the biscuits and could eat as much as he or she wanted."[113] Actress Audrey Hepburn had just turned sixteen years old when Canadian troops liberated her and her family living in Velp. Hepburn was suffering from anaemia, jaundice, and asthma as a result of her malnutrition. She recalled her first real meal after liberation being oatmeal coated in sugar, prepared for her by Canadian soldiers. Though it was delicious, the food was so rich that she became violently ill, her body long unaccustomed to such culinary delights.[114] Major Charles Goodman of the South Saskatchewan Regiment was presented with a stark reminder of how difficult conditions were for the Dutch people when he saw a horse killed by shellfire in the streets of Groningen, "As soon as the firing died down, the Dutch rushed out of their houses and they butchered that horse, I was quite amazed ... that's when I realized these people are starving."[115] Even though the fighting had stopped, the humanitarian task facing Canadian CA had only just started.

Feeding the starving population was obviously a key priority for the men of Civil Affairs. By mid-May a series of kitchen centres had been set up in villages, towns, and cities throughout the region to dispense soup and stew. In Amsterdam, kitchen centres could feed up to 450,000 civilians. In Zaandem, kitchen centres were feeding 25,000 people and in Alkmar 20,000 civilians were being fed.[116] Even with these food distribution centres thousands of Dutch were simply unable physically to get to these "pop-up" kitchens. Captain George Eckenfelder recalls this problem: "I remember going into Amsterdam one day and there had been food kitchens established throughout the city and people would walk down to these ... some people were so weak from lack of food they didn't have the strength to get there. They just sat on the sidewalk waiting for help."[117] In more severe cases, the food had to be brought directly to where these starving civilians lived, as they had not the strength to get out of bed. In order to do this I Canadian Corps in conjunction with Netherlands District created an ad hoc organization to find, evaluate, and deploy feeding units to areas of acute starvation. Managed by an eight-person multinational advisory committee this "strike force" became an integral element of the relief effort in the Netherlands. The organization included two spearhead survey teams containing five people each, and fifty medical feeding teams, each with an average of twelve members. The survey teams were responsible for locating the worst cases or the hardest hit areas and report back to the advisory committee, which would then assign a medical feeding team to that area. The organization also had a mobile treatment and evaluation hospital as well as a mobile laboratory. The organization focused solely on "moribund starvation cases (invalid category). This [did] NOT include hungry people who [could] swallow, and walk without assistance."[118] The work of this "strike force" was emblematic of the overall effort by Civil Affairs to bring food to the Dutch in Area B-2, facilitating the delivery of an estimated 126,000 tons of food and successfully staving off what could have been another terrible calamity faced by civilians in Nazi occupied Europe.[119]

By the end of May the starvation crisis had abated and authority for Civil Affairs in Area B-2 passed from I Canadian Corps headquarters to Netherlands District, the joint administrative command of SHAEF Mission (Netherlands) and the NMA. I Corps headquarters remained in charge of Area B-1 and was required to make available corps resources to help in continuing efforts in Area B-2. In June 1945, all responsibility for Civil Affairs passed from First Canadian Army to SHAEF Mission (Netherlands) and the NMA. Finally, much to Brig. Wedd's relief and satisfaction, the Dutch had assumed full administrative responsibility for reconstruction and rehabilitation of their homeland.

A HUMANITARIAN VICTORY

The Dutch relief effort was one of the most complicated and significant tasks Civil Affairs undertook during the war and was nothing short of an immense accomplishment for Canadian Civil Affairs officers. This relief did not just involve bringing supplies to the Dutch people. Civil Affairs officers were challenged by multiple variables that made even the simplest tasks onerous. They had to delicately balance civil administration and diplomacy and make authoritative decisions to save civilian lives. Civil Affairs maintained order and cohesion in liberated areas while balancing demands on military resources and manpower. Once local authorities reestablished their civil administrations and were deemed to be running smoothly, military resources moved on to support the next most-pressing operation. The development of Canadian Civil Affairs reached its pinnacle in the Netherlands, military operations continued unimpeded even in the face of unprecedented supply and relief issues.

Before the liberation of the Netherlands, the Civil Affairs officers of First Canadian Army and the planners at SHAEF and 21st Army Group believed the situation to be much like that in Belgium. The Dutch were suffering relief supply shortages, but the Allies hoped that after the expected German withdrawal, it would be relatively simple to reestablish civil administration in the form of the NMA and to provide for the needs of the Dutch people. The initial planning was based heavily on the situations in France and Belgium, where large swathes of territory were liberated after some hard fighting. Instead, the Germans did not withdraw, and it took much longer to liberate the country. With military operations stalled on the River Waal, the Allies faced new and unique challenges while planning and executing relief efforts. Existing Civil Affairs doctrine would help, but innovation and creativity was needed for the operation in the Netherlands to succeed.

Efforts at relief and rehabilitation were hindered by the effects of four years of strict German rule on the administrative machinery. The roles of the NMA and SHAEF District (Netherlands) were limited because these organizations were located outside the main area of operations. Civil Affairs headquarters continually had to prod these administrative bodies to take responsibility of liberated regions. The piecemeal implementation of NMA authority along with the associated administrative issues seriously undermined efforts to rally Dutch civilian support and created serious concern amongst senior Canadian Civil Affairs officers. These challenges resulted in a slow and at times painstaking process of establishing an independent civilian administration. It is clear that the Dutch population never truly accepted their new administrators. As General Templer at 21st Army Group wrote, "The Dutch do not like the NMA, they want to see their military government go and get a new normal government as soon as they can."[120]

Charles Perry (C.P.) Stacey once described the Netherlands relief effort operation as "a difficult problem in the reconciliation of military and political objects."[121] Simply put, senior planners had to decide how important the Netherlands relief effort was in terms of resource allocation versus military effort to end the war. In terms of military significance, the surrounded German forces in the Netherlands were not a significant threat to the Allied military while many believed the fastest way to help the Dutch people was to focus all Allied efforts on defeating German resistance in Germany and bringing an end to the entire war. Liberating the Netherlands by force would involve heavy fighting in Dutch towns and cities, no doubt causing collateral damage. The Allies also feared the Germans would breach the dykes and flood the lowlands. It seemed Allied efforts would only further add to the suffering of the Dutch.

However, SHAEF could not ignore the serious threat of mass starvation of the Dutch people by the early spring of 1945. One SHAEF report noted that "if these large numbers were not to starve, immediate action would have to be taken after the Germans had withdrawn, which must be at the expense of operations."[122] Fortunately, negotiations with the German-appointed Dutch leader, Dr Seyss-Inquart, gave the Allies some hope in finding a solution to this problem.

Civil Affairs staff of First Canadian Army and the men of I and II Canadian Corps occupied themselves with solving this problem. From evacuating civilians and livestock, to transporting foodstuffs behind enemy lines, establishing and coordinating a working civil administration, and providing medicine, food, and supplies, Canadian CA detachments continuously worked in some of the most difficult circumstances of the entire war to bring aid to the Dutch people. The success of these efforts can truly be measured by the respect and adoration the Dutch people have for Canadians nearly three-quarters of a century later.

CHAPTER FIVE

From Civil Affairs to Military Government

"We are no longer a liberating army now we are in Germany,
we come as conquerors."[1]
– Canadian soldier with 11 Field Royal Canadian Engineers

The moment First Canadian Army crossed into German territory Civil Affairs personnel became members of Allied Military Government. Instead of liberators, they were now occupiers. Instead of assisting with the rehabilitation of a country so that it could support the war effort, they were now imposing their ultimate authority on a conquered people. As one officer wrote, "The velvet gloves have been removed."[2] This meant a changing mandate for the men of First Canadian Army Civil Affairs, and specifically II Canadian Corps Civil Affairs, who would be responsible for military government in the Canadian occupied section of Germany. Certainly, the fundamental attitude of MG was different than that of Civil Affairs; they were no longer helping to rehabilitate or rebuild an Allied nation so that it could regain its administrative autonomy. Though they were still helping to rebuild and rehabilitate Germany, just in a way that would ensure the supremacy of the Allies and Allied policy. The fundamental objective of the Allied occupation policy was ultimately to restore a de-Nazified German state that could administer itself while overseen by a United Nations (Allied) authority. With this in mind, the responsibilities of Canadian MG were fundamentally similar to CA operations in previous countries and the challenges that the Canadians faced were an extension of recognizable problems already encountered: population control, food, and maintenance of law and order.

STRATEGIC SITUATION

First Canadian Army entered Germany on 8 February 1945 with the launching of Operation Veritable. Veritable was the northern arm of a two-pronged assault against German forces positioned between the Maas and the Rhine rivers. The southern arm of this two-pronged assault was the US Ninth Army, temporarily under the command of Montgomery's 21st Army Group, which sat stalled for two weeks due to extensive flooding in the region. First Canadian Army thus faced a concentrated German defence in inhospitable terrain and ground its way forward against this stout defence. US Ninth Army was finally able to launch its assault on 23 February and with most of the German defenders facing First Canadian Army the Americans were able to break through. This American breakthrough triggered an entire collapse of German defence in the region. By 3 March the northern and southern Allied pincers were closing in on the west bank of the Rhine and the Germans began to retreat across the river. By 10 March the last of the German forces slipped across. On 13 March First Canadian Army was redirected northwards, and out of German territory, to focus on the liberation of the Netherlands. The Canadians would eventually reenter the hostile country via Netherlands's northeast border.

Though First Canadian Army would have little to do with the initial operations to cross the Rhine (Operations Plunder and Varsity March 23 to 24) Canadian soldiers from the 9th Canadian Infantry Brigade, temporarily attached to the 51st Highland Division, crossed the Rhine at Rees and 1st Canadian Parachute Battalion dropped east of the river near Wesel as part of Operation Plunder. Several days later, 3rd Canadian Infantry Division, temporarily attached to 30th British Corps of Second British Army, crossed the Rhine and fought its way to Emmerich.

First Canadian Army officially reentered Germany in early April when advance units of 4th Canadian Armoured Division crossed the border from the Netherlands into northwestern Germany, near the town of Nordhorn. At this point, First Canadian Army straddled the border between the Netherlands and Germany, with II Canadian Corps operationally responsible for northeastern Netherlands and northwestern Germany, while I Canadian Corps remained focused on the immense challenges within western Holland. By late April, I Canadian Corps would be given full operational responsibility for all of the Netherlands while II Canadian Corps would be given operational responsibility for Canadian occupied Germany, a strip of territory in Germany's northwest corner running from Emden along the north coast to Wilhelmsaven and down to Osnabruck. II Canadian Corps would remain operationally responsible for this territory until 15 June.

Though the war in Europe ended on 7 May the job for Canadian MG personnel was only just beginning. As war diarist for I Canadian Corps wrote, "It deserves mention in passing that word arrived today of the surrender of the German armies. Work continued much as usual, everybody happy enough about it, but restrained by knowledge of the enormous difficulties ahead. There was the odd bottle finished; the camp was strangely quiet."[3] The 8th of May 1945 was "A" Day, the official start of Operation Eclipse. Eclipse was the name given to Allied operations after the surrender of Germany, of which a significant portion was focused on military government "in Germany until control there is taken over from the Supreme Commander by the tripartite Military Government or by US and British commanders."[4] Eclipse planners accurately predicted a Germany that was utterly demoralized by total defeat and generally too exhausted physically and morally to continue resistance. Planners rightly anticipated some localized resistance (from Nazi fanatics and perhaps some senior SS leaders) but generally expected that the Allies would be encountering civilians and soldiers prepared to submit to Allied authority. Though First Canadian Army's role in Operation Eclipse technically began on 8 May, the implementation of Canadian Military Government began weeks before, the moment Canadian soldiers stepped onto German soil.

Organizational Change

The occupation and military government of Germany began the moment Allied soldiers set foot on German soil (credited to American soldiers on 11 September) and would continue long after hostilities had ended. The primary difference between Military Government and Civil Affairs was in doctrinal philosophy. Whereas the mandate of Civil Affairs had always been to help reestablish and rehabilitate liberated countries so they could effectively and eventually autonomously help in the war effort, the primary mandate of Military Government was to impose the will of the Allies upon an occupied Germany and "ensure that once and for all no possible shadow of a doubt shall be left in the mind of a single German that the military might of the Third Reich has been shattered."[5] Civil Affairs policy focused on limiting the amount of time and military resources spent in directly administering liberated countries while Military Government policy emphasized the direct control and administration of the conquered German nation. This direct imposition of Allied will included a number of long-term objectives:

A. The disarmament, control and ultimate disbandment of all German military forces, including para-military and police formations, thereby preventing a renewal of hostilities.
B. To assist the Royal Navy and Royal Air Force, upon request by either, to take similar action in respect of the German Navy and Air Force (and their auxiliaries), respectively.
C. The enforcement of the terms of surrender by the occupation of strategic areas within the British zone.
D. The elimination of Nazism and German Militarism and the arrest of War Criminals and Security Suspects.
E. The establishment of law and order, through the medium of Military Government, within the Army Group Zone in Germany. This implies the perseveration or re-establishment, of a suitable German civil administration, to the extent required to accomplish objectives.
F. The early relief and repatriation of Allied Prisoners of War and displaced Allied Nationals found in the British zone, and the min-

imum necessary control of enemy refugees and displaced persons. G. Protection of Allied property, control of certain properties and conservation of German foreign exchange assets.[6]

However, within these objectives 21st Army Group set out a series of short-term priority tasks that Canadian MG would have to deal with the moment they set foot on German soil: the organization and repatriation of displaced persons (DPS) and refugees (though Canadian MG made no more distinction between the two, officially labelling everybody they encountered DPS); the organization and enforcement of strict food rationing; the organization of agricultural labour to help with the anticipated food crisis; the establishment of a reliable police force and the de-Nazification of the public services.[7] Both the long-term and short-term objectives were designed with one result in mind, that an occupied and defeated Germany could help in administering its own people while strictly watched and controlled by the Allied authority. Military Government was the total and absolute imposition of Allied authority on the defeated German nation.

In terms of organizational structure, Canadian MG evolved over two phases. Phase one, from mid-February to 7 May 1945 (the formal capitulation of Nazi Germany), saw Military Government operate as part of the same administrative and command structure as Civil Affairs. During this phase both Military Government and Civil Affairs were subject to the same channels of command. CA detachments became MG detachments the moment they entered Germany, but the command structure that oversaw First Canadian Army Military Government in Germany was the same as that which oversaw First Canadian Army Civil Affairs elsewhere. This meant that the organizational foundations of Civil Affairs, detachment-based units, the use of specialized officers, and the existing chain of command, were consistent between Civil Affairs and Military Government. The most notable change during this phase was actually at 21st Army Group HQ where Brigadier Robbins stepped down and was succeeded by Major General Gerald Templer with the new designation of directorate of Civil Affairs and Military Government

(DCA/MG). Templer would now be the man directing Military Government for 21st Army Group.

Limited organizational restructuring occurred within First Canadian Army during what can be identified as the second phase, lasting from 8 May 1945 to the end of active Canadian Military Government on 15 June 1945 (at which point II Canadian Corps was swapped out for XXX British Corps and the Canadian Army Occupation Force took over the region as part of XXX British Corps). During this second phase, now officially part of Operation Eclipse, Wedd ordered II Canadian Corps to officially take over MG in Germany on behalf of First Canadian Army. All CA staff within II Canadian Corps immediately became MG staff. For instance, Col Hurley, once SCAO II Canadian Corps, now became deputy director Military Government (DDMG) for II Canadian Corps. In light of the monumental task ahead for Military Government the II Canadian Corps MG organization was expanded significantly receiving a fairly sizeable contingent of MG reinforcements, "cleaning out the pool" as Brigadier Wedd phrased it.[8] II Canadian Corps MG went from commanding sixteen detachments in early May to a total of thirty-three by the end of that month. Detachments were also reorganized in terms of responsibility. "K" Detachments would control either a rural country (Landkreis) or a larger town (Standtkreis) both being equivalent in terms of detachment responsibility. A grouping of rural counties or towns (called a Regierungsbezirk) would be under the operational responsibility of "L/R" Detachments. A group of Regierungsbezirk was called a province and would be administered by "P" detachments (a classification consistent with the Civil Affairs designation). Detachment reorganization also included "R" detachments to deal with displaced persons and refugees and court detachments to deal with courts, prisons, and tribunals.

First Canadian Army headquarters also received reinforcements in the form of forty-two new officers. These new additions became part of an MG reorganization at headquarters. MG staff were divided into an executive and administrative branch and each branch contained a series of subsections responsible for specific functions, similar to how the CA staff was organized at both FCA HQ and II Canadian Corps HQ. Under the executive branch there were three subsections: executive, finance, and legal. Under the administrative branch there were five subsections: administrative, civil maintenance, displaced persons, public health, and essential services. Brigadier Wedd was given command of this staff with the title of deputy-director Military Government and commanded both First Canadian Army Civil Affairs and Military Government through May and into the first half of June (in military documents his title is written as deputy director Civil Affairs/Military Government or DDCA/MG). This meant that from February to mid-June First Canadian Army HQ, stationed in Apeldoorn, Holland, oversaw Civil Affairs in the Netherlands while at the same time was also responsible for Military Government in Germany. (First Canadian Army would carry limited responsibility for Civil Affairs in the Netherlands until the end of June, two weeks after it relinquished responsibility for MG in Germany.)

The Challenges of Military Government

One of the most pressing tasks for Canadian MG personnel was to deal with the German population; at first this meant mostly local civilians and a small number of German soldiers but eventually turned into a torrent of thousands of surrendered soldiers. During the first phase of Military Government no serious problems with the German population were encountered. The Canadians easily handled the number of German soldiers surrendering and the minimal amount of territory occupied by First Canadian Army meant fairly limited numbers of civilians. Most of the interaction with Germans was in the form of evacuation, generally removing them away from the battle space. For instance, II Canadian Corps MG executed a sizeable evacuation of 27,000 German civilians living on the west bank of the Rhine in mid-March. This was done to ensure secrecy in regards to the impending attack across the great river. For the most part the mood of the German population during this early phase was one of acceptance and even some indifference towards Allied soldiers. As Wedd wrote, "In all places the German population continues to be relatively orderly and obedient. It is noticeable however that there is a great tendency to place the blame on the Nazi

Party, and not, in fact, acknowledge any part of the blame themselves ... and in some cases, the attitude tends to border on arrogance."[9]

In terms of German soldiers, most Canadians reported fairly amicable relations with the defeated enemy. Many German soldiers were conscripted into labour battalions to help rebuild destroyed infrastructure. Col Robert Carson, commanding a section of Canadian Royal Engineers, recalled being responsible for German POWs helping to rebuild a destroyed airfield; he commented, "we had a very good relationship with the German troops" even though there were nearly 170,000 of them in his immediate area.[10] Lawrence Henderson, a colonel with the Canadian Scottish Regiment, recalled that between Canadian and German soldiers "there was no animosity that I noticed" and generally speaking the job of the Canadians was to "guard German POW camps followed by sorting them out to repatriate them back to their own homes."[11]

The most serious issue in regards to the German population now under Canadian control was feeding them. Initially the area occupied by FCA had no pressing food shortages but the sudden influx of tens of thousands of surrendered German soldiers, plus the liberation of tens of thousands of displaced non-German civilians and soldiers, added to the already two million German civilians under Canadian control. This placed a great strain on the ability for MG to ensure that everybody in the Canadian occupation zone had access to food. As one newspaper reporter summarized, "Trouble may come to Germany this winter, but authorities are hopeful that the north-western zone under Canadian control will come through without incidents. They say that as long as adequate food supplies are available for the civilian population, trouble should be avoided ... Rationing so far has been unable to maintain the 1,550 calories daily prescribed by military government as the minimum for civilians."[12] If food could not be delivered to these people then serious threats to law and order would most likely arise.

II Canadian Corps MG created a regional food detachment headquartered at Oldenburg that would oversee this growing problem. The detachment built a census of all available food stocks and crops in the region and followed this by developing a ration scale for all the persons under Canadian jurisdiction, this included categories such as displaced persons, children of different age categories, nursing and expectant mothers, German POWs, labourers, heavy and very heavy workers.¹³ A pressing issue facing the detachment was the sudden decrease in available farm labour to help bring in the spring harvest. This work had been performed by slave labour, non-Germans who had been moved into the region to provide support for Nazi Germany's war machine. Now that these people were free, a new source of labour needed to be found. II Canadian Corps found this source amongst the German prisoners of war (POWs). German officers were ordered to find amongst their men soldiers who had previously worked on farms. Promptly, a large and experienced group of German POWs was found and put to work on the land bringing in the spring harvest.¹⁴

As well, in order to ensure maximum food production II Canadian Corps MG ordered extensive cultivation to take place. All available grassland was to be ploughed and used for growing crops. Livestock were to be slaughtered in sufficient numbers so that pastures could also be ploughed. Farmers were told to increase their grain and potato crops and to eliminate flowerbeds and luxury crops such as asparagus and strawberries in order to make room. MG authorities even carried out a propaganda campaign directed at town and urban dwellers to begin growing their own vegetable gardens. Everybody within the Canadian area was expected to contribute to food stocks and through this effort a food crisis was averted. When XXX British Corps took over in mid-June they found a region fully mobilized to producing food for the coming winter.¹⁵

Displaced Persons

As mentioned, tens of thousands of people from all over Europe were liberated in the Canadian occupation zone, loosely categorized by MG authorities as displaced persons. This category included thousands of civilians who had either voluntarily or forcibly been moved into Germany for work on German farms or in the German war industry. This category also included prisoners of war. There was also a multifarious mix of political prisoners uncovered in death camps, concentration camps, labour camps, and punishment camps. The organization, control, and eventual repatriation of this large group posed a significant challenge for First Canadian Army Military Government. At the end of May, for instance, the Cameron Highlanders reported to have liberated 1,554 displaced persons of whom 524 were Dutch, 510 Russian, 306 Polish, 132 French, 69 Italian, and a small number of Belgians, Finns, and Norwegians.[16] All these people now had to go home. It was the responsibility of Canadian MG to facilitate this incredible return migration.

There is no doubt that earlier operations to control and guide refugee movement operations informed much of the planning for the handling of DPs. DPs were first classified into "westbounders" or "eastbounders" depending on which nation they originally came from (the largest numbers of westbounders being French, Belgians, Dutch, and the largest number of eastbounders being Russians and Poles). Based on this initial distinction, DPs were then guided to either westbound or eastbound transit centres set up and operated by Canadian MG. For westbounders, most of these transit centres were actually established in the eastern Netherlands, at Enschede, Hengelo, Ondeznaal, Almelo, and Hardenbergh.[17] The Netherlands Military Administration in cooperation with I Canadian Corps established Frontier Control Posts along the border between the Netherlands and Germany to ensure that any "stragglers," as Col Hurley put it, were directed to the appropriate centre depending on their nationality. As well, this "frontier line" prevented any Wehrmacht deserters from escaping the Canadian zone. Any Germans caught trying to cross the frontier line were immediately imprisoned.

If eastbounders were encountered they were sent to transit centres along the eastern frontier of the Canadian zone of occupation in Germany. Specific regions of the Canadian occupation zone were organized into "static national areas" with camps constructed to accommodate the DPs and run by specific Canadian MG detachments. All Russians were directed to camps in the Wilhelmshaven region, Poles to Leer and the surrounding countryside, Italians and other miscellaneous eastbounder nationalities were directed to Oldenburg. Often the camps chosen for these static national areas were previously occupied and controlled by the Germans. In most cases the camps were punishment camps, where a wide range of German and non-German military personnel and civilians had been previously incarcerated. Though these camps were in fairly dilapidated condition, Canadian MG was able to quickly get most of them functioning to serve their new inhabitants. In a few more morbid situations some of the camps chosen had previously functioned as death camps; significant upgrading was needed for those.[18]

Captain Labrosse was given the job of setting up Camp B3 near the village of Buldern, on the outskirts of the city of Munster, located 130 kilometres south of the Canadian area of occupation. The camp was a former training camp for Hitler Youth, and on 5 April 1945 Labrosse was dropped off at the camp by himself to begin preparing it to receive refugees and displaced persons. That afternoon Labrosse encountered two French refugees searching for food and quickly hired them as his support staff (one actually remained his batman for the remainder of Labrosse's time in charge of the camp). The next day Labrosse received a party of one hundred Germans from Buldern who set about cleaning the entire camp. While the cleaning was taking place, Labrosse received his operations staff, consisting of two officers (one Canadian and one British captain) as well as a Canadian sergeant (Sergeant Brown of the Royal Canadian Army Service Corps from Vancouver, British Columbia).[19] Together they would make up the leadership for the camp under Labrosse's supervision. Labrosse then secured provisions from the local village and posted guards on the roads to begin collecting refugees and displaced persons. That evening, 6 April, 150 were collected, by 7 April 300 were living in the camp. Labrosse then put together an administrative staff, recruited from the refugees, which would be responsible for the day-to-day operations of the camp. He then created a central refugee committee, which represented all the nationalities within the camp (French, Belgian, Dutch, Italian, Polish, and Russian) and would meet with Labrosse regularly every morning to discuss camp issues. Each nationality was represented on this committee by a "chief" who was responsible for his countrymen's actions and ensuring that the people in his "tribe" obeyed Allied rules and regulations while helping to maintain cleanliness and order within the camp. Under this system the camp effectively cared for upwards of 1,000 refugees (women and children as well as men) civilians, and former prisoners of war.[20]

The camp was run with military-like discipline. Regardless of whether one was a civilian or soldier each group of nationals was subdivided into companies, platoons, and sections. This allowed for assignment of sleeping quarters, efficient roll call and inspection, camp duties to be distributed fairly, as well as the process of feeding the camp inhabitants to be carried out in an organized and timely manner. Reveille and roll call were at 0700 every morning. Everyone was expected on the parade ground at this time for inspection. After inspection, breakfast was served; "It usually consisted of ersatz coffee or, when possible, good Allied coffee, two slices of German bread, two pieces of sausage (when we were able to get them) or oatmeal with powdered milk."[21] Mornings were usually filled with a variety of camp duties assigned to different groups including custodial duties, kitchen work, sanitation duties, "there were carpenters and their helpers who built new huts; lawn-makers and the gardeners who worked in the flower garden," there was even an auto-mechanics team tending to the mechanical needs of the camp's fleet of requisitioned German vehicles.[22] As there were limited shower facilities, a schedule was meticulously kept designating when specific groups could utilize the showers. Everybody was required by camp rules to shower at least once a week. Other than the showers, a makeshift bathing facility was erected consisting of six large water tubs and two salamander stoves.

Lunch was served at 1200 hours followed by an afternoon of leisure activity. Sports were often organized during these hours, "Our object was to keep their minds busy so they would not get into mischief."[23] One of the more popular activities were the soccer matches pitting teams of military personnel against the camp refugees. One of the highlights for Labrosse, however, was when several American soldiers taught the refugees how to play baseball.

Dinner parade then began at 1700 hours. During the evenings, loudspeakers in the camp played music, as well as the BBC news at 2100. Often during the evenings, entertainment came in the form of concerts, each nationality taking turns putting on a production for the camp. (Labrosse was known to lead the sing along when the Canadians took their turn.) The night would come to an end with the British, American, and other Allied nations' anthems being played over the loud speakers prior to curfew being imposed. Curfew was at 2130 sharp and was rigorously enforced; in fact, each evening a burst of machine gun fire indicated curfew was in effect, a not-so-subtle reminder that a war was still going on.[24]

These camps were crucial in carrying out one of MG's key objectives: to organize and control all aspects of a massive migration of peoples. Brigadier Wedd and his staff recognized the threat to law and order that roving groups of soldiers and civilians could pose to both the German people and to the ability for the Allied occupation to operate effectively. During the first weeks of April the flow of DPs into these transit centres was handled fairly easily. First Canadian Army was not making any serious territorial advances into Germany and thus could easily cope with the steady yet small stream of displaced persons encountered. By the end of April, 4,000 westbounders had been processed by transit centres in the Netherlands. More than 11,000 Poles, Russians, and Italians had been processed as eastbounders and were being held in a number of transit centres, organized by nationality, in II Canadian Corps' occupation zone.

In early May, with First Canadian Army's thrust into northwestern Germany, the flood of displaced persons almost overwhelmed the system. Nearly 12,000 new DPs were encountered within the first few days of May. Transportation available was simply not enough for this deluge of DPs now being encountered by the Canadians. As well, the number of MG detachments dealing with DPs became wholly inadequate for the sudden problem. Simply put, if resources were not directed towards the DP effort, thousands of people would be roaming the German countryside with little support or supervision.

Unlike earlier similar situations faced by Civil Affairs, the movement of people was now a high priority for both FCA and 21st Army Group, and thus with very little prodding, Wedd was able to secure significant logistical support. The keys to a large number of trucks and lorries were handed over to the nearly overwhelmed MG detachments. To support II Canadian Corps specifically, all available CA/MG detachments were brought forward, including many detachments already operating in the Netherlands. Eighteen detachments under II Canadian Corps MG were now increased to thirty-five while MG planners at II Canadian Corps HQ worked closely with the Royal Canadian Army Service Corps to establish an effective transportation and maintenance plan. This allocation of resources certainly helped in solving what could have easily become a crisis of movement and control. By 17 May all westbounders encountered by II Canadian Corps had been evacuated from Germany and were on their way home.

The eastbounders, however, were going to pose a longer-term problem. By 17 May nearly 70,000 were living in twenty-two Canadian controlled camps, and more were on the way.[25] These camps had essentially become holding centres while Canadian officials waited on the appropriate national authorities to come and get their people. In one example a Polish camp had reached capacity, in which case local German villages were evacuated to make room for Polish DPs, creating, as one report stated, temporary "Polish villages."[26] In another instance near Papenburg, 815 Detachment commanded by Major Robert T. Colquhoun from Vancouver, British Columbia, and formerly an officer in the Canadian Forestry Corps, ordered all houses on one side of the highway evacuated to make room for Polish DPs. The Germans living on the opposite side of the highway were ordered to accommodate their now homeless neighbours.[27]

Most DPs were accommodated in camps. Usually one MG detachment would be placed in charge of a single camp. Camps were initially organized by nationality and then once again by sex, with other camps put aside for the sick and wounded. For instance, a camp near the village of Neusustrum, thirty kilometres north of Meppen, held nearly 1,500 Polish women. Another camp near the town of Wietmarschen, approximately thirty kilometres south of Meppen, contained 1,700 Russian POWs of whom 710 had tuberculosis. The largest camp was at Adelheide, thirty-two kilometres east of Oldenburg, which contained nearly 18,000 Russians and was overseen by 201 Detachment under Lt Col R.A. Lindsay. By early June, thirty-eight camps were operational within II Canadian Corps MG's jurisdiction with an estimated total of 115,000 DPs in those camps. By the time responsibility for the area was handed over to XXX British Corps on 15 June, the movement of all eastbounders to their holding camps was complete. At this point nearly 81,000 eastbounders had been encountered and moved by II Canadian Corps, though it would be the responsibility of XXX British Corps to ensure these east-bounders eventually returned home.

Law and Order

The personnel of II Canadian Corps Military Government were responsible for law and order in the Canadian occupied territory. All Germans and any First Canadian Army personnel were subject to MG law. In order to maintain law and order the Public Safety (PS) branch of MG was given several weapons. It became responsible for the military court system, overseen by Detachments 821, 630, and 613. MG was also given command of Field Security (FS) for II Canadian Corps as well as Counter-Intelligence (CI), both FS and CI became a special branch of MG. Helping MG was a local German police force overseen by Canadian MG.[28] This force was unarmed and relatively small in terms of personnel. It was not intended to act as any authority for non-Germans, that would still be the role of Canadian provost and field security, but it was generally quite successful in helping to maintain law and order amongst the German population. With these organizational weapons in hand, MG set about enforcing the law of the occupying forces.

This included hunting and arresting Nazis. Most times arrests of high-ranking Nazi personnel were achieved through standard investigation techniques. Charles Goodman described his company's method of tracking down suspected Nazis: "the company would go out and surround a town during the wee small hours of the morning and then we would go through the town house by house asking people for identity cards and checking them out."[29] Sometimes the capture of a Nazi was achieved through local collaboration; in the town of Haren the local police chief, Lt Blum, helped arrest two high-ranking Nazi officials and provided information on the whereabouts of several more. Other times arrests were carried out with a bit of trickery. In Emden, the commanding officer of 818 Detachment, Major Newroth, sent out an invitation to local Nazi officials-in-hiding to attend a conference. The Nazis, twenty-four in all including the mayor of Emden and his chief of police, assumed they were going to discuss possible terms of surrender. Instead,

Newroth had them arrested the minute they all sat down. The same tactic was also successfully used in Wilhelmshaven. Canadian MG personnel arrested nearly 400 Nazi officials during their time in Germany.

In general, the German civilian population was obedient, though a number of arrests and prosecutions of German civilians occurred. Charges ranged widely from being in possession of Allied material, not carrying identification, ignoring curfew to far more serious ones such as carrying or owning a firearm, looting, disrespect to an Allied soldier or failure to comply with Allied orders, and on rare occasions violence against displaced persons (there were no recorded incidences of violence committed against Canadian soldiers by German civilians). Some of the heaviest sentences handed down to German civilians included a one-year sentence for assaulting a Russian and a five-year sentence for two German civilians found guilty of six counts of false assumption of authority and acts prejudice to the interests of the Allied forces.

Unlike the German population, the tens of thousands of displaced persons, a diverse group of civilians and prisoners of war (Canadian reports rarely distinguished between civilian DPs and POW DPs), posed a considerable challenge to the maintenance of law and order. Captain Horace Beach recalled his time in Oldenburg stating, "We had almost as much problems from the refugees as we did with the Germans."[30] Canadian MG authorities struggled to impose any sort of law and order on a large number of these men. As one MG report put it, "The main threat to law and order came from the Displaced Persons, who, once they had been liberated, roamed the countryside committing every conceivable crime, including murder."[31] Another report stated that, "no householder can consider himself safe from the DPs, mainly Russians and Poles. They appear to have complete freedom to murder, loot and rape as and when they please."[32] In Wismar a Canadian paratrooper recalled subduing a recently liberated Soviet soldier whom he had found attempting to shoot a naked German woman.[33] Captain Labrosse wrote that, "The refugees and Displaced Persons with whom we had the greatest trouble were the Poles and the Russians. They were disliked by every other nationality."[34] The threat from this group was so great that many German citizens saw the Canadians as their only protectors. As one First Canadian Army MG report stated, "complaints of looting and rape are quickly reported to detachments, with the plea for protection against roving bands of displaced persons, prisoners of war, etc. They particularly show an obvious fear of Russians and Poles."[35] MG authorities seemed to have been particularly concerned with Russian gangs of soldiers and civilians who were reported to be arming themselves and at night heading out into the countryside to loot, pillage, and rape.[36] No statistics were kept but based on a variety of reports from Canadian units, MG headquarters, field security detachments and censorship reports, crimes against the German population by DPs were a constant concern for the Canadians. One of the more horrific cases is recorded here:

> One night about 2300 hrs, one of the farmers from whom we obtained milk for the camp hospital, came and told us that Russians were looting a neighbour. At once the squad jumped in the jeep. A few other G.I.s, who were not on duty, followed them with another vehicle. When they reached the farm and entered his house, they found out the farmer had been killed; his throat cut open with a razor, his wife raped and disembowelled with a knife. His daughter had also been raped and one of her breasts cut and the baby's hands cut. Finally the culprits were found in the barn, three of them slaughtering the livestock. One of the G.I.s, who spoke German, asked them what they were doing. They answered it was none of our business. They assumed a threatening attitude as they had knives and one had a revolver. The soldiers ordered them to surrender, but they paid no attention, pretending not to understand. The G.I.s then opened fire killing three of them; two others, who were hidden, fired on the soldiers but were wounded. They were taken at once to the hospital at the Chateau. We learned later that they had been hanged. This was not an act of vengeance on their part, it was an atrocity.[37]

II Canadian Corps MG struggled to prevent these attacks. MG authorities allowed for a German police force to remain functioning (after a vetting of any Nazis), but the police were banned from carrying firearms and proved near useless against armed bands of recently liberated civilians and soldiers committing crime throughout the German countryside. Canadian soldiers were in fact ordered to patrol at night to help prevent crimes against the German civilians. On numerous occasions these Canadian patrols encountered roving bands of men, armed with weapons and often carrying looted food and goods. On one such night a Canadian patrol arrested thirty Russians who were looting farmsteads.[38] Other Canadians simply refused to intervene on behalf of German civilians. In one case a Canadian sergeant was asked by an elderly German woman to stop some Polish soldiers from looting her home but he writes that, "she didn't get any sympathy from us."[39] On rare occasions there is evidence that some Canadians even supported the actions of DPs against the German population, "Parties go out at night and raid these Germans houses and farms – of course the Jerries come and complain here ... And the Russians carry on the good work – it will give these Jerries a bit of their own medicine."[40]

Even if arrested by Canadian patrols most of the DPs, especially liberated POWs, were rarely tried or convicted by Canadian MG courts. Any Canadian military court trying, for example, a Russian soldier or civilian committed of a crime in Canadian-occupied Germany faced both a potential political and legal firestorm. In most cases, DPs would simply be returned to the camp they came from. Lt Col Paxton's 601 Detachment, responsible for the prosecution of criminal offenses in Oldenburg, had only one case throughout April, May, and June where any non-Canadian or non-German was brought up on charges.[41] On 31 May three Polish DPs were found guilty on the charge of looting, though the charge that they carried firearms was dropped. The accused were remanded into the custody of the officer commanding the local Polish DP camp and the matter ended there.[42] Brig. Wedd pressured senior officers within eastbounder camps and liaison officers working with MG to take strong disciplinary action against men suspected of crimes against German civilians but this produced very little success. On 4 June the head of the USSR mission in Germany actually visited II Canadian Corps headquarters to discuss the issue of discipline and agreed that no Russian soldiers would be allowed to leave their camps carrying weapons and that any DPs found with weapons in and around Russian camps would be disarmed.[43] It seemed for a time that the issue of discipline had been solved, as Canadian MG diaries reported no further problems for the final week and a half of their control over the area. However, as soon as XXX British Corps replaced II Canadian Corps' operational responsibility for the region XXX British Corps reported renewed and escalating problems with eastbounder DPs.[44]

Canadian soldiers were also posing a problem for Canadian MG officials seeking to maintain law and order. Like in Belgium, problems arose with Canadians selling military goods on the black market. This was a particular issue throughout most of Germany as many regions had been almost totally emptied in support of the German war effort. Lt Col James Baird recalled that the Germans in the Canadian occupation zone had "stripped themselves clean of anything ... all we found were weapons ... even the rats had left."[45] This created a golden opportunity for those soldiers wishing to capitalize on their access to war material. Charles Goodman recalls that "we were all engaged in black market activities because the Germans were desperate" and goes on to say that the only thing a private was interested in was "bartering for liquor and sex ... it was just the question of going and trading what you had for what you wanted, and that was that."[46]

Protecting German civilians from Canadian soldiers also became a concern for MG officials. Looting and pillaging (or "liberating" as many Canadian soldiers called the taking of German goods) was quite commonplace. The censorship reports are full of evidence that Canadian soldiers looted while in Germany. One Canadian soldier wrote home stating, "The first thing we do is go looting in the houses. Of course we don't call it looting here, its booty" while another soldier wrote, "Tomorrow morning I'm going looting (and I do mean looting) like nothing you have ever seen. So I'll see if I can get something to send home."[47] One soldier recalled breaking open a safe full of watches and sending four back home to his mother while another soldier became part of an old-fashioned bank heist, "Some of us blew a bank in the last town we were in, and my split was little over 1000 of them. I sent you some of the marks I looted in the last parcel I sent you."[48]

Interactions between Canadian soldiers and German civilians were also a concern for MG authorities. For most of the period that II Canadian Corps occupied Germany a "non-fraternization" order was in effect for all of 21st Army Group, making it a military offense for Canadians to interact with German civilians outside of their official duties. As Charles Goodman recalls, "It was directed at us and German women of course."[49] This certainly did not stop Canadians from interacting with German women as Goodman bluntly put it, "the no fraternization policy really never worked from the start."[50]

Fifty-eight Canadian soldiers were accused of rape in Germany and it was this disturbing trend that truly concerned Canadian MG.[51] Charges of rape against Canadian soldiers dramatically increased upon First Canadian Army's entry into Germany, peaking at fifty in the months of April and May (compared, for instance, with twenty-two in the entire seventeen months of Canadian operations in Italy).[52] During that same period one case was reported to Canadian authorities in France, one in Belgium, and six in the Netherlands. A censorship report from April 1945 captured this disturbing trend in a soldiers letter, "One of the guys I joined up with ... got himself into a hell of a jam here just the other day. He and another fellow hurded [sic] a couple of German Frauleins 'up them stairs' ahead of a Sten gun. While one held the Sten gun the other gave them a painless meat injection, now they are both up on a charge of RAPE, which isn't so good."[53] Private Albert Pollard and a fellow soldier descended upon a German farmhouse in the middle of the night, waking a German family. They proceeded to get drunk on liquor found in the kitchen at which point Pollard attempted to rape a Russian girl working on the farm and then, after realizing she was not German, he sexually assaulted the German mother. Him and his accomplice then looted the house making off with wedding rings, watches, and cash. Pollard received eight years for the crime of attempted rape and robbery. General Crerar later reduced Pollard's sentence to five years.[54] This event speaks to several trends when discussing rape in Germany. Often charges of robbery coincided with charges of rape, Canadian soldiers taking advantage of vulnerable German civilians to line their pockets. As well, many of the sentences were reduced or commuted by senior officers, sometimes even by General Crerar himself. Of the fifty-eight charges of rape brought against Canadian soldiers in Germany, nineteen soldiers were convicted of the act by a military trial, nineteen more were convicted of fraternization, four of indecent assault, and three of attempted rape, while the rest were acquitted. In every case where the sentence handed out was more than a year, it was eventually reduced. One soldier, Gunner Stanley Jones, received a life sentence for a particularly violent sexual assault on a German woman but had his sentence commuted by Crerar to ten years, later a board of inquiry shortened this sentence to five. Only two soldiers served anything longer than a two-year sentence.[55]

When II Canadian Corps handed over control of northwest Germany to XXX British Corps they relinquished the last of First Canadian Army's Military Government responsibilities.[56] There is no doubt that they left the region in far better shape than when they entered it. Tens of thousands of displaced persons had either been returned to the west or remained in suitable camps waiting to be repatriated eastwards. Hundreds of thousands of German civilians and surrendered soldiers remained law abiding and accepting of their new masters. Most of the major Nazi officials in the region had been arrested while a small German police force was set to grow into the cornerstone of a nascent German administrative apparatus beholden unto Allied occupational policy. The region was pacified. No serious crises had erupted, no starvation had occurred, while law and order had been just barely maintained. The illegal activities of displaced persons had been temporarily neutralized, while some, though not all, Canadians who had been caught committing crimes had been punished. This was not perfect by any means, but it was enough. A brief but important period of occupation that became absolutely crucial to the transition from wartime to peacetime as part of a larger Allied effort to ensure its authority was absolute while overseeing the rebuilding of a de-Nazified Germany. First Canadian Army had helped win the war and now its Civil Affairs/Military Government branch had taken an important early step in helping to win the peace.

Conclusion

"We must concentrate not merely on the negative expulsion of war but on the positive affirmation of peace."
— Martin Luther King Jr

In the ultimate goal of the defeat of Nazi Germany, the Allies were faced with the challenge of large civilian populations that could very well impede active military operations or threaten the postwar peace if they were not properly managed. A strange limbo existed in areas that were no longer the site of active military operations but had yet to see a fully functioning civilian administration. Civil Affairs officers became the "front line troops" executing Allied policy during these transition periods, building relationships with civilian populations in order to ensure the success of military operations. Every new region Civil Affairs entered promised a variety of intriguing challenges and complicated tasks. The Civil Affairs officer could never rest on his laurels nor enact any inflexible doctrinal solution to problems because the social, economic, and political realities of his whereabouts forced him to manoeuvre within a complicated and uncertain environment.

The achievements of Canadian Civil Affairs in France, Belgium, and the Netherlands are linked by common themes: control of movement, maintenance of morale, reconstruction and rehabilitation, all to serve the ultimate purpose of ensuring civilian populations did not impede ongoing military operations while effectively mobilizing their support for the ongoing war effort. Canadian Civil Affairs developed and refined operational practices within these countries, providing support for civilian populations while also facilitating the transition to a civilian authority. Civil Affairs played out in different ways in each country, yet these operations highlighted the evolving CA mandate and operational practices of CA work in northwest Europe.

In northern France, Canadian Civil Affairs established an operational template that would guide them for much of First Canadian Army's advance through northwest Europe. It was in northern France that many gained their first practical experience in how to control and direct refugee movement, provide relief, medical aid and shelter, impose law and order, gain the cooperation of resistance groups and help reestablish and support a local political administration that would aid in the continued fight against Nazi Germany (though this was complicated at first by Charles de Gaulle's thorny relationship with the Anglo-American leadership). The Canadian CA experience in northern France resulted in greater clarification in the procedure by which Canadian CA would hand over administrative control to Allied-approved civilian bodies. At the sharp end, the city of Caen proved to be a critical battlefield classroom for many Canadian CAOs, and while the work of Civil Affairs in Caen proved effective, a number of ineffectual practices were identified and discarded. As First Canadian Army continued advancing through northern France the operations of Civil Affairs became more and more efficient so that by the time the coastal cities of Calais, Boulogne, and Dunkirk were liberated the movement of civilians away from the battle space, the control of refugees in the country side, and the provision of relief for civilians no longer posed obstacles to the conduct of military operations. The operations in northern France created important doctrinal templates that could be built upon and added to in a flexible fashion in response to the various unique challenges posed by every new country entered by First Canadian Army.

The importance of flexibility in Civil Affairs doctrine was made all too real with the Canadian CA experience in Belgium. The practices developed in France coupled with the speed by which Belgium was liberated meant that CAOs proved effective in terms of providing relief for Belgian civilians, coordinating refugee control, and dealing with resistance groups (though the Belgian resistance proved to be far more fractious than in France). CA objectives were, however, hindered by a hesitant, unpopular and generally ineffective Belgian administration led by Hubert Pierlot. This led to Civil Affairs playing a far more direct and involved role in governing the country than they had in France. This was a source of continual frustration for the Canadian leadership as they saw what was supposed to be a short-term CA role dragged out into a longer-term commitment. Nothing highlighted this more than the decision by Canadian CA authorities to take complete control of the distribution of coal within the country. The distribution of this key source of fuel was disrupted by the machinations of a large black market that was running rampant throughout the country. If the Belgian government could not get coal to its own people – and in turn crack down on the black market – then First Canadian Army CA would have to. Once this happened, the coal distribution problem was solved.

The most critical challenge to Canadian Civil Affairs in Belgium was in the city of Antwerp and in ensuring the continued functionality of Antwerp's port facilities in the face of constant German V-1 and V-2 rocket attacks. The use of Antwerp's port would allow the rapid build up of supplies, which were to be absolutely essential to Gen. Montgomery's plan for a hard thrust into Germany. Suddenly Canadian CAOs found themselves coordinating Civil Defence, something they had little to no training for. Ultimately, they were successful in their CD mission as seen in the fact that despite the ongoing air attacks by German V-weapons, Antwerp's port remained functional and crucial supplies continued to arrive.

While the situation in Belgium had required Civil Affairs to become progressively more involved in the administration of the country it was in the Netherlands where Canadian Civil Affairs would face their most in-depth and complex task. The unique geography of the Netherlands, coupled with the slow process of liberation, and the almost complete stripping of the country's resources by German occupiers, meant that the Civil Affairs task in the Netherlands became a long, drawn out affair, something that was never part of the original plan. Nonetheless, CAOs carried out their standard responsibilities such as civilian movement control, provision of food and medicine, maintenance of law and order,

Conclusion

and ensuring the cooperation of resistance groups. Similar to Belgium, all of these responsibilities were performed within a larger administrative quagmire brought on by the failure of the Netherlands Military Administration. The NMA was intended to take over the nation's civilian administration fairly quickly after liberation; however, this did not occur. The administration was viewed generally with suspicion and at times outright hostility by many of the Dutch who had remained in the country during the war. This, coupled with its own inherent administrative weaknesses, hindered its ability to govern effectively. In many cases, particularly in regards to refugee control, coal distribution, and food provisioning, FCA CA took over near complete responsibility as the only organisation with the experience and know-how to effectively deal with these widespread issues. The prior experience gained by the men of FCA CA meant that while the tasks at hand were large in nature, the templates for success had already been created. Thus First Canadian Army Civil Affairs (now incorporating both I Corps CA and II Corps CA) propped up the ineffectual NMA, effectively took over the coal distribution networks of the Netherlands, as well as coordinated food relief for the hundreds of thousands of Dutch that were on the brink of starvation. This Dutch relief effort stands as one of the most enduring legacies of the Canadian Second World War experience.

While the CA mission in Belgium and the Netherlands was initially conceived of in terms of a limited role which was then discarded once realities within each country set in, the period of Civil Affairs/Military Government in Germany was always conceived of in terms of a direct and resource-intensive mission. Many of the tasks and challenges faced by Military Government in Germany were operationally consistent with previous CA operations. Newly titled MG personnel were tasked with de-Nazifying regional government and building and supporting a local administrative authority that would abide by broader Allied policy objectives. MG personnel were required to control population movements, this time in the form of tens of thousands of refugees and displaced persons liberated from German prisons and labour camps. Canadian MG became responsible for the housing and feeding of these people while they were being repatriated to their home countries. MG personnel were also responsible for the maintenance of law and order, which became a serious problem as revenge attacks against the German civilian population became more and more common. Canadian MG officers (MGOS) found themselves in the unusual position of having to protect the civilian population from the rampages of both Canadian soldiers but more commonly Russian and Polish DPS. FCA CA/MG responded effectively to these challenges, however, and by the time the handover to XXX British Corps was accomplished, the region was stabilized.

It is difficult to quantify the success of Civil Affairs. Whereas battle outcomes can be measured in casualties, objectives achieved, and material destroyed, it is harder to assess evacuation schemes, civil defence preparation and effectiveness, as well as the beneficial effects of working relationships between civilian administrators and military officers. The complex organizational structure of CA coupled with the fact that detachments and personnel were often moving from one headquarters to another makes it even more difficult to measure the organizations accomplishments.

Yet, we can see some indications of success. Throughout northwest Europe, CA successfully evacuated tens of thousands of refugees from the front line. In Antwerp, the port facilities continued to function with a full labour complement because of Civil Affair's success in creating an effective civil defence organization. In the Netherlands, Civil Affairs prevented acute starvation for hundreds of thousands of Dutch through quick thinking and preparation. In Germany population control was effectively rendered, hundreds of thousands of Germans as well as foreign displaced persons now under the care of II Canadian Corps were fed, and the region was de-Nazified and prepared for a long-term Allied occupation. Besides these obvious indicators, CA officers accomplished more subtle and quotidian successes in their day-to-day tasks in various unknown villages, small towns, and cities where they dealt with a number of complex issues such as the delivery and distribution of food, medicine, and water, controlling population movement, providing shelter for the homeless, transportation for the displaced, vetting of local officials, supporting local administration while dealing with a variety of resistance groups and political factions. Effectively handling these issues meant continued support for First Canadian Army combat operations that were for the most part unimpeded by the civilian populations on the ground.

Thus, Civil Affairs proved instrumental to the Allied war effort. Overall, the civilians of France, Belgium, and the Netherlands were regarded as friendly to the Allied war-effort and protecting the rights and well-being of these civilians became an important though secondary objective of Allied CA strategy. Weinberg and Coles perhaps put it best when they wrote, "Every politico-social objective undoubtedly coincided to a considerable extent with long-term military interests, but it also conflicted to a greater or lesser degree with immediate military expediency, in which case the civil affairs authority could only try, without sacrificing either competing interest too greatly, to bring the two into the best possible accommodation."[1] The continued doctrinal development of Civil Affairs emphasized a desire on behalf of its leadership to evolve in its functional capacity. This was made quite clear when it entered Germany. While the mandate and philosophy of CA in Germany changed to MG, operationally speaking there was considerable consistency with previous action along First Canadian Army's liberation route.

The legacy of this branch is obvious in the Canadian Armed Forces today, where the importance of civil-military cooperation (CIMIC) is recognized and plays a pivotal role in military doctrine. "Whenever a military force deploys somewhere, whether it is for a peace support operation, for humanitarian assistance or for warfighting, there is always a civilian dimension to consider. It may consist of refugees, a local population, local officials, even workers from international organizations. CIMIC constitutes a primary link between the military and these organizations. It works to coordinate and elicit cooperation from, and with, the civilian dimension, in order to help ensure the overall success of a mission."[2] NATO's CIMIC definition supports this strategic principle: "The co-ordination and co-operation, in support of the mission, between the NATO Commander and civil actors, including national population and local authorities, as well as international, national and non-governmental organisations and agencies."[3] CIMIC functions are thus "conducted in support of [the joint force commander's] mission and are related to implementing the overall strategy and achieving a stable and sustainable end-state."[4]

The role of CIMIC and Civil Affairs is more valuable than ever in current war zones. Provincial reconstruction teams (PRTs), American CA battalions, government agencies such as the United Kingdom's

Department for International Development (DFID), nongovernment agencies such as OXFAM and UNICEF, CIMIC groups, quick impact project (QIP) teams, and a myriad of other actors all participate in contemporary military campaigns. Newer doctrinal concepts, such as "Joint, Interagency, Multinational, Public" (JIMP) and "Whole of Government" (WOG), are further emphasizing close cooperation between civilian and military actors. Although these military forces and organizations have realized the importance of cooperation, they can continue to improve their policies and overcome obstacles on a constantly changing battlefield by understanding CA's history.

This book touches on a number of topics that could benefit from further exploration, including the experiences of Canadian Civil Affairs officers in Italy who operated as part of AMGOT and the experience of the Canadian Army Occupation Force as part of XXX British Corps. Further issues that played a significant part in the relationship between soldiers and civilians need to be examined, such as gender relations, creating and maintaining law and order, narcotic use, and racial and ethnic tensions. Finally, historians have yet to explore the social, economic, and political relationships between Canadian troops and the German civilian population.[5]

The work of Canadian Civil Affairs/Military Government provided a crucial link between Canadian soldiers and civilians. The continual redefining of the relationship between these two macro-actors speaks to the complicated and ever-changing realities of the modern battlefield, where civilian presence is a significant factor. First-hand civilian accounts from the Second World War rarely mention Civil Affairs by name, yet more often than not the soldiers these civilians encountered and the aid they received came from this branch. Beyond the study of the Canadian example, general Civil Affairs history offers insight into the complex relationship between civilian populations and militaries: how militaries supported or failed to support civilian administrative bodies, how they allocated resources to civilian populations, and how they interacted with vulnerable civilian populations. These issues are as important today as they were seventy-five years ago.

Notes

INTRODUCTION

1 Diamond, *Fleeing Hitler*, 67.
2 Bond, *Chief of Staff*, 324.
3 "21st Army Group: Letter from the War Office to the Commanders-in-Chief, Organization for Civil Affairs in the Field," 26 January 1944, WO 219/3729, TNA.
4 "21st Army Group: The Purpose of the Civil Affairs Organization," 1943, WO 33/1769, 5, TNA.
5 Such as the United Nations Relief and Rehabilitation Administration (UNRRA).
6 "21st Army Group: The Purpose of the Civil Affairs Organization," 1943, WO 33/1769, 5, TNA.
7 Ibid.
8 "Canadian Participation in Civil Affairs/Military Government: Part 1: Background and Beginning," Canadian Military Headquarters (CMHQ) Reports: Report 140, July 1945, 3, DHH.
9 "21st Army Group: The Purpose of the Civil Affairs Organization," 1943, WO 33/1769, 7, TNA.
10 Coles and Weinberg, *Civil Affairs: Soldiers Become Governors*.
11 Ziemke, *The US Army in the Occupation of Germany*.
12 Donnison, *Civil Affairs and Military Government*. The American CA/MG experience is covered in Ziemke's *The US Army in the Occupation of Germany*.
13 Brown, "To Bury the Dead," 35–48.
14 Muschamp, "Living under Allied Military Government."
15 Copp and Fowler, "Heavy Bombers and Civil Affairs."
16 Sean Kennedy's *The Shock of War* published in 2011 is a thoughtful examination of the civilian war experience from 1937 to 1945. It places civilians at the centre of military events during this period and compares their various

experiences, though has little mention of their interactions with Civil Affairs specifically.

17 Goodlet, "The Province of Zeeland, War and Reconstruction," 29–56.
18 Ibid., 51.
19 Ben Shephard points out that the term "displaced person" was first used by the Allies in Italy in the autumn of 1943 and referred to any civilian that had been displaced by the war. This vague definition evolved by the time the Allies entered northwest Europe in June 1944. "Displaced person" then referred to civilians who had been forcibly moved by the Germans to territories or countries outside their home region. As well, by the time the Allies entered Germany they further distinguished between Allied displaced persons and German refugees. This was further complicated by the large number of Allied soldiers (especially from the eastern front) who were also present in Germany and were classified as "displaced persons." Frankly, these distinctions and definitions were crude and the terms "refugee" and "displaced person" were often used interchangeably. Shephard, "Becoming Planning Minded," 416–17.

CHAPTER ONE

1 Donnison, *Civil Affairs and Military Government*, 7.
2 Ibid., 8.
3 Ibid., 11.
4 Glover, *The Velvet Glove*, 37.
5 Section III of the 1907 Hague Conventions deals with the responsibilities of a military authority governing a hostile population, while Section II chapter 1 establishes rules for attacking cities, towns, and villages where civilians are present. International Committee of the Red Cross, "Convention (IV) Respecting the Laws and Customs of War on Land and its Annex: Regulations Concerning the Laws and Customs of War on Land. The Hauge, 18 October 1907."
6 War Office, *Manual of Military Law*, 236.
7 Cohen, "Mesopotamia in British Strategy," 171–81.
8 Donnison, *Civil Affairs and Military Government*, 14.
9 Ibid., 16.
10 Ibid.
11 Ibid., 17.
12 Ibid., 19.
13 Ibid., 253.
14 *Extracts from Manual of Military Law 1929: Reprinted for Canadian Army*. Ottawa: His Majesty's Stationary Office, 1941.
15 French North Africa was jointly administered by CA representatives from both the United States and the United Kingdom.
16 Flint, "The Development of British Civil Affairs," 60.

17 Ibid., 62.
18 For further reading on the Italian situation see Harris's *Allied Military Administration of Italy* and G.W.L. Nicholson's *Official History of the Canadian Army in the Second World War Volume II: The Canadians in Italy*, Ottawa: Queens Printer and Controller of Stationary, 1956. As well, for recent discussions of the Italian state under Mussolini see Neville's *Mussolini* and Hoffman's *Fascist Effect*.
19 "Civil Affairs in the Mediterranean, June 1943–May 1945," November 1951, Army Headquarters (AHQ) Report #45, DHH.
20 Ziemke covers establishment of the school and the American CA/MG experience in North Africa in his official history *The US Army in the Occupation of Germany*, 10–55.
21 Emsley, *Exporting British Policing*, 117.
22 Coles and Weinberg, *Civil Affairs: Soldiers Become Governors*, 177.
23 "Civil Affairs in the Mediterranean, June 1943–May 1945," November 1951, Army Headquarters (AHQ) Report #45, 4, DHH.
24 "Toronto Man in Leading Role," *Hamilton Spectator*, 11 May 1944.
25 Harris, *Allied Military Administration of Italy*, 79–81.
26 Flint, "The Development of British Civil Affairs," 139.
27 Ibid.
28 Coles and Weinberg, *Civil Affairs: Soldiers Become Governors*, 60.
29 Ibid.
30 Flint, "The Development of British Civil Affairs," 139.
31 Harris, *Allied Military Administration of Italy*, 4.
32 See Nicholson's *Official History of the Canadian Army* for a detailed accounting of the invasion and Canada's role in it.
33 "Civil Affairs in the Mediterranean, June 1943–May 1945," November 1951, Army Headquarters (AHQ) Report #45, 2, DHH.
34 Major Reid also hinted at other factors responsible for the name, including the fact that AMGOT was rumoured to be an Arabic word for "horse manure" and an acronym for "Ancient Military Gentleman on Tour."
35 "Civil Affairs in the Mediterranean, June 1943–May 1945," November 1951, Army Headquarters (AHQ) Report #45, DHH.
36 Flint, "The Development of British Civil Affairs," 140.
37 Harris, *Allied Military Administration of Italy*, 43.
38 Ibid., 28.
39 Ibid., 43.
40 Field security officer Norman Lewis wrote that "most of the newly military government appointed mayors were members of the criminal group Camorra. They were assisted into position by the influence exercised by American gangster Vito Genovese [Mafia don of the powerful American Genovese crime family]." Flint, *Allied Military Administration of Italy*, 143.
41 Ibid.
42 "Canadian Participation in Civil Affairs/Military Government: Part 1:

Background and Beginning," Canadian Military Headquarters (CMHQ) Reports: Report 140, July 1945, 3, DHH.
43 Flint, "The Development of British Civil Affairs," 145.
44 Rennell, "Allied Military Government in Occupied Territory," 311.
45 Zach Cavasin in his MA dissertation "Hai visto I Canadesi?" gives a particularly detailed account of the living situation of the people of Ortona when Canadians first entered the battle-ravaged Italian town in December 1943.
46 Flint, "The Development of British Civil Affairs," 145.
47 Muschamp, "Living under Allied Military Government," 372. It is interesting to note that Muschamp is far more critical of Canadian interaction with Italian civilians than Cavasin though Muschamp is explicit in stating that she is looking at a region relatively untouched by war while Cavasin is looking at a region entirely destroyed by it.
48 Ibid., 372–3.
49 Harris, *Allied Military Administration of Italy*, 108.
50 Fisher, "Allied Military Government in Italy," 114–22.
51 Stein, "War, Politics, Law, and Love," 553–70; and Flint, "The Development of British Civil Affairs," 144.
52 Flint, "The Development of British Civil Affairs," 147.
53 Harris, *Allied Military Administration of Italy*, 113. With ACC coming into existence, Rennell's position was eliminated, and he was offered a position in the ACC as vice president of the Economic and Administrative Section. Rennell declined the offer and returned to England.
54 Fisher, "Allied Military Government in Italy," 121.
55 Fisher, Inglis, and Harris all make this quite clear in their work.
56 Major Mathew J. Inglis provides an excellent account of this in his dissertation "Civil Affairs and Military Government Operations," 62–8.
57 See Brown's "To Bury the Dead and Feed the Living," 45–6.
58 Flint, "The Development of British Civil Affairs," 143
59 Cavasin discusses how 1st Canadian Division's strategy to combat security threats was strict control of mobility. Civilians needing to travel throughout the countryside had to acquire a military pass. Any civilian caught wandering the countryside without a pass would be detained and interrogated. "Hai visto I Canadesi?" 72–5.
60 "Civil Affairs in the Mediterranean, June 1943–May 1945," November 1951, Army Headquarters (AHQ) Report #45, 5, DHH.
61 Rennell, "Allied Military Government in Occupied Territory," 315.
62 See discussions by D'Este in *Bitter Victory*, 622; and Benson and Neufeld's "American Government in Italy," 136. Cavasin also discusses this aspect of Canadian–Italian interaction showing clearly how reliant the hungry people of Ortona were on AMG food distribution, "Hai visto I Canadesi?" 81–5.
63 Cavasin, "Hai visto I Canadesi?" 61–3.
64 Flint, "The Development of British Civil Affairs," 153

65 Fisher, "Allied Military Government in Italy," 122.
66 Rennell, "Allied Military Government in Occupied Territory," 312.
67 "Tons" here and throughout refer to imperial tons.
68 Ibid., 312.
69 Ibid.
70 Harris, *Allied Military Administration of Italy*, 89.
71 Ibid., 86.
72 Cavasin shows how in Ortona Canadian medical personnel were concerned with both typhus and venereal disease, "Hai visto I Canadesi?" 67–9.
73 Fisher, "Allied Military Government in Italy," 120.
74 Flint, "The Development of British Civil Affairs," 137.
75 Ibid., 150.
76 "Report by Deputy Quartermaster General, CMHQ," 1943, RG 24, Vol 12, 744, LAC.
77 Flint, "The Development of British Civil Affairs," 244–6.
78 "21 Army Group CA/Mil Gov Branch Historical Survey: D-Day to Fall of Caen," 1944, WO 219/3727, 7, TNA.
79 Six CA officers and eleven other ranks landed on Mike beach several hours after the first wave had landed.

CHAPTER TWO

1 "Civil Affairs in Liberated Holland," 1945, FO 371/40411, TNA.
2 "Memorandum No 12 Digest of Civil Affairs Considerations in Liberated Territories (France, Belgium, the Netherlands, Denmark and Norway)," March 1944, WO 219/3729, TNA.
3 "Canadian Participation in Civil Affairs/Military Government: Part 1: Background and Beginning," CMHQ Reports: Report 140, July 1945, 8–10, DHH.
4 Fear of fifth column troops, the use of civilians as human shields, and the difficulty air crews encountered in distinguishing columns of refugees from columns of enemy troops were other reasons for preventing refugees from using the main road networks.
5 "Canadian Participation in Civil Affairs/Military Government: Part 1: Background and Beginning," CMHQ Reports: Report 140, July 1945, 8, DHH.
6 Ibid., 9.
7 Patterson, "Revisiting a School of Military Government," 8.
8 Harris, "Selection and Training of Civil Affairs Officers," 697.
9 Patterson, "Revisiting a School of Military Government," 9; and Harris, "Selection and Training of Civil Affairs Officers," 699.
10 "Canadian Participation in Civil Affairs/Military Government: Part 1: Background and Beginning," CMHQ Reports: Report 140, July 1945, 10, DHH.
11 Ibid., 9.

12 "Supplementary Report on Canadian Participation in Civil Affairs," AHQ Reports: Report No. 9. 13. DHH
13 Though as Edward Flint has shown, the British were by this time struggling to recruit able CA officers, having recently turned away a 78-year-old retired general, a British officer considered medically insane, and a suspected murderer. "The Development of British Civil Affairs," 183.
14 Ibid., 4.
15 "Train Canadians To Govern Lands Freed From Foe," *Hamilton Spectator*, 2 December 1943.
16 Mollie McGee, "Ontario Officers to Assist in Civil Affairs Program," *Globe and Mail*, 23 May 1944.
17 "Supplementary Report on Canadian Participation in Civil Affairs: Appendix C" AHQ Reports: Report No. 9. 2.
18 "Policy – Civil Affairs Organization," Nov 1942, RG 24-M30-E133 Vol 133. LAC.
19 "Civil Affairs Organization and Administration – CA Correspondence," May 1944, RG 24 Vol 10570, LAC.
20 Ibid.
21 "Civil Affairs Organization and Administration – CA Correspondence," June 1944, RG 24 Vol 10570, LAC.
22 As a result of the rapid breakout from the Normandy bridgehead and the creation of 12th US Army Group, the Allies actually deintegrated their Civil Affairs units in late August 1944 (swapping all American CA personnel in 21st Army Group with "British" CA personnel in 12th US Army Group). There were, however, never any serious ensuing discussions of further separating the British from the Canadians.
23 Flint, "The Development of British Civil Affairs," 7.
24 Ibid., 8.
25 "Civil Affairs Organization and Administration – CA Correspondence," May 1944, RG 24 Vol 10570, LAC.
26 "Canadian Participation in Civil Affairs – Military Government. Part II: Planning and Training, 31 Jan 44–30 Jul 44," January 1946, CMHQ Reports: Report No. 148, 3, DHH.
27 See Figure 5 for chart showing Civil Affairs command structure.
28 "Canadian Participation in Civil Affairs/Military Government: Part 1: Background and Beginning," CMHQ Reports: Report 140, July 1945, 16, DHH.
29 "Report by Captain E.G. Pury to 21st Army Group Headquarters: Front Line Villages," 1944, WO 219/3727, TNA.
30 "Canadian Participation in Civil Affairs/Military Government: Part 1: Background and Beginning," CMHQ Reports: Report 140, July 1945, 26, DHH.
31 "First Canadian Army CA Fortnightly Report No. 3," 1944, WO 371/42018, TNA.
32 See Figure 6 for organizational chart.

33 Williams, *Far from Home*, 74.
34 "Military Manual of Civil Affairs in the Field," February 1944, WO 219/3729, TNA.
35 "Civil Administration Instructions for Civil Affairs in France, March 1944, and Technical Instructions for Civil Affairs in France," May 1944. WO 219/3729, TNA.
36 J.E.G. Labrosse, "The Personal Experiences of a Canadian Civil Affairs Officer in France and Belgium June 1944–March 1945," December 1946, CMHQ Reports: Report No. 12, 8, DHH.
37 Ibid., 8.
38 Ibid., 9–10.
39 Flint, "The Development of British Civil Affairs," 199.
40 For a broader understanding of this policy debate, see Foottit and Simmonds. *France, 1943–1945*, 51–8.
41 "Directive to Supreme Commander Allied Expeditionary Force in Civil Affairs in France: Appendix 5," 1944–1945, WO 32/11153, TNA.
42 Edward Flint spends time exploring this political back and forth on pages 227–31 in his PhD dissertation "The Development of British Civil Affairs."
43 "Directive to Supreme Commander Allied Expeditionary Force in Civil Affairs in France: Appendix 5," 1944–1945, WO 32/11153, TNA.
44 See Harris's *Allied Military Administration of Italy*, for a discussion on the vetting of Italian officials in Italy. For a discussion on the vetting of French officials, see Wieviorka's *Normandy*.
45 Under the Vichy government, France had been divided into regions controlled by regional commissioners. These regions were further subdivided into several departments, each run by a prefect. Within each department, subprefects headed numerous arrondissements. The arrondissements were divided into cantons, which were then subdivided into communes, and each commune was overseen by a mayor.
46 Wieviorka, *Normandy*, 302.
47 "SHAEF Field Handbook of Civil Affairs: France," June 1944, WO 204/12317, TNA.
48 "Technical Instructions for Civil Affairs in France," May 1944, WO 219/3729, TNA.
49 "21 Army Group CA/Mil Gov Branch Historical Survey: D-Day to the Fall of Caen," 1945, WO 219/3727,
50 Wieviorka, *Normandy*, 333.
51 "Civil Affairs in Caen – First Phase," July 1944, RG 24 Vol 16632, LAC
52 J.E.G. Labrosse, "The Personal Experiences of a Canadian Civil Affairs Officer in France and Belgium June 1944–March 1945," December 1946, CMHQ Reports: Report No. 12, 12-15, DHH.
53 Interestingly, while Wedd prepared to go operational he commented on the large buildup of CA officers and the large staffs that seemed to be forming with every detachment and HQ that became operational; "Too many

cooks," as he put it. Wedd went about reducing the size of his own staff and all those under him before he even became operational.
54 "Canadian Participation in Civil Affairs/Military Government. Part III: France, General Historical Survey, July–October 1944," January 1946, CMHQ Reports: Report 149, 16, DHH.
55 "Civil Affairs in Caen: Appendix A to Part III Detailed Report 4. CA First Canadian Army," July 1944, RG 24, Vol 16632, 2, LAC.
56 Donnison. *Civil Affairs and Military Government*, 85.
57 "Civil Affairs in Caen – First Phase," July 1944, RG 24 Vol 16632, 2, LAC.
58 "Reconnaissance Report on Caen," 12 July 1944. WO 219/3727. 3, TNA.
59 "Canadian Participation in Civil Affairs/Military Government. Part III: France, General Historical Survey, July–October 1944," January 1946, CMHQ Reports: Report 149, 9, DHH.
60 A large red cross, made up of sheets covered in blood from the wounded, had been placed on the roof to show that it was a hospital and hopefully prevent Allied bombing. The church survived destruction, though this was probably more from pure luck then the symbol of the red cross averting any would-be bombers.
61 "Reconnaissance Report on Caen," 12 July 1944. WO 219/3727, 2, TNA.
62 "First Canadian Army Fortnightly Report No 1," July 1944, RG 24 Vol 16632, 3, LAC.
63 "Civil Affairs in Caen – First Phase," July 1944, RG 24 Vol 16632, 2, LAC. Several reports confirm that German snipers and artillery continued firing on Allied soldiers and civilians throughout the evacuation process. However, the night of 13/14 July appears to have been the worst such incident. No casualty numbers were reported in the documents, but many people were reported killed and wounded. "First Canadian Army Fortnightly Report No 1," July 1944. RG 24 Vol 16632, 3, LAC.
64 "First Canadian Army Fortnightly Report No 1," July 1944, RG 24 Vol 16632, 3, LAC.
65 Roberts, *D-Day Through French Eyes*, 140.
66 "Canadian Participation in Civil Affairs/Military Government. Part III: France, General Historical Survey, July–October 1944," January 1946, CMHQ Reports: Report 149, 9, DHH.
67 "Civil Affairs in Caen – First Phase," July 1944, RG 24 Vol 16632, 7, LAC.
68 "Canadian Participation in Civil Affairs/Military Government. Part III: France, General Historical Survey, July–October 1944," January 1946, CMHQ Reports: Report 149, 9, DHH.
69 Roberts, *D-Day Through French Eyes*, 158–9.
70 "Civil Affairs in Caen – First Phase," July 1944, RG 24 Vol 16632, 2, LAC.
71 "Canadian Army Overseas Field Censors: Special Report on Mail from Canadian Military Hospitals, 1st August to 15th August 1944," RG 24 Vol 12322, T-17924, File 4/Censor Reps/1/5, LAC.

72 "Reconnaissance Report on Caen," 12 July 1944, WO 219/3727, 1, TNA.
73 Ibid.
74 Roberts, *D-Day Through French Eyes*, 80.
75 "Canadian Participation in Civil Affairs/Military Government. Part III: France, General Historical Survey, July–October 1944," January 1946, CMHQ Reports: Report 149, 8, DHH.
76 Donnison, *Civil Affairs and Military Government*, 85. Recent scholarship by Andrew Knapp as well as Terry Copp and Michelle Fowler have provided clear arguments that the bombing of Caen provided no tactical benefit for the Allies, delivering only destruction to those living in the city.
77 "Reconnaissance Report on Caen," 12 July 1944, WO 219/3727, 1, TNA.
78 "First Canadian Army Fortnightly Report No 3," August 1944, RG 24 Vol 16632, 3, LAC.
79 "Civil Affairs in Caen – First Phase," July 1944, RG 24 Vol 16632, 4, LAC.
80 "Civil Affairs in Caen – First Phase," July 1944, RG 24 Vol 16632, 3, LAC.
81 "Civil Affairs in Caen – First Phase," July 1944, RG 24 Vol 16632, 4, LAC.
82 "First Canadian Army Fortnightly Report No 3," August 1944, RG 24 Vol 16632, 6, LAC.
83 "Canadian Army Overseas Field Censors: Special Report on Mail from Canadian Military Hospitals, 16th August to 31st August 1944," RG 24 Vol 12322, T-17924, File 4/Censor Reps/1/5, LAC.
84 Martin. "Un Officier Canadien avec la 3 Armée Américaine en 1944," 63–72.
85 J.E.G. Labrosse, "The Personal Experiences of a Canadian Civil Affairs Officer in France and Belgium June 1944–March 1945," December 1946, CMHQ Reports: Report No. 12, 6, DHH. In fact, there was a "sniper mania" throughout northern France as American, British, and Canadian soldiers all reported cases of French civilian women shooting at Allied soldiers. One Canadian soldier wrote, "The pin and knife was taken off a sniper that shot at me. She got five before we got her. It was a woman, 19 years old and married to a German, there are a lot like that" in "Special Report on Mail from Canadian Military Hospitals," 16th July to 31st July 1944, RG 24, T-17924, Vol 12322, LAC.
86 "15th Cdn Field Security Section (FSS) War Diary," July 1944, RG 24 Vol 16396, LAC.
87 Ibid.
88 Ibid.
89 "First Canadian Army Fortnightly Report No 3," August 1944, RG 24 Vol 16632, 5, LAC.
90 Ibid.
91 Ibid.
92 Ibid., 6.
93 Ibid., 3.
94 Ibid., 5.

95 "Canadian Army Overseas Field Censors: Special Report on Mail from Canadian Military Hospitals, 16th July to 31st July 1944," RG 24, Vol 12322, T-17924, 4/Censor Reps/1/5, LAC.
96 "Louise Tremblay," The Memory Project: Veterans Stories of the Second World War. Accessed 2018, www.thememoryproject.com.
97 "15th Cdn Field Security Section (FSS) War Diary." July 1944, RG 24 Vol 16396, LAC.
98 "First Canadian Army Fortnightly Report No 3," August 1944, RG 24 Vol 16632, 10, LAC.
99 Ibid., 10.
100 "No. 1 Canadian Town Major Unit: Part 1 Orders," 22 August 1944, RG 24, Vol 16511, Serial 2349, LAC.
101 Ibid.
102 "Civil Affairs in Caen – First Phase," July 1944, RG 24 Vol 16632, 10, LAC.
103 "First Canadian Army Fortnightly Report No 3," August 1944, RG 24 Vol 16632, 10, LAC.
104 Ibid., 11.
105 Flint, "The Development of British Civil Affairs," 73.
106 "225 Civil Affairs Detachment Copies of Reports from Files," 2 July 44–10 May 45, RG 24, Vol 10567, LAC.
107 "Canadian Participation in Civil Affairs/Military Government. Part III: France, General Historical Survey, July–October 1944," January 1946, CMHQ Reports: Report 149, 18, DHH.
108 "William Hallett 'Bill' Heron," The Memory Project: Veterans Stories of the Second World War. Accessed 2018, www.thememoryproject.com.
109 "Canadian Participation in Civil Affairs/Military Government. Part III: France, General Historical Survey, July–October 1944," January 1946, CMHQ Reports: Report 149, 13, DHH.
110 "War Diary, Civil Affairs HQ First Canadian Army," August 1944, RG 24 Vol 16632, LAC.
111 Stacey. *The Victory Campaign*, 329.
112 Ibid., 307.
113 Ibid.
114 Coakley and Leighton. *Global Logistics and Strategy*, 182.
115 Ibid., 374.
116 Excerpt from Gen. Crerar's diary reprinted in Stacey's *The Victory Campaign*, 330.
117 One of the channel ports not mentioned in the ensuing discussion is the infamous town of Dieppe. It was evacuated by the Germans prior to the Canadian arrival and liberated on 2 September.
118 "Notes on the Movements of 213 Civil Affairs Detachment: From Landing on 14 June 44 to Dec 44," February 1945, WO 219/3974, 3–4, TNA.
119 "First Canadian Army CA Fortnightly Report No 4," September 1944, FO 371/42020, 1, TNA.

120 Knapp. "The Destruction of Le Havre," 476.
121 "Memorandum: Conditions at Havre," 17 October 1944, FO 371/42020, TNA.
122 Andrew Knapp clearly shows that it was the bombing run on 5 September, aimed at the city centre's core, which is the least explicable tactically and caused the most damage and civilian casualties. In contrast the bombings of 6 September to 11 September were aimed at the city's peripheral defences where there were few civilians and significantly more enemy targets. *The Destruction of Le Havre*, 483.
123 Copp, *Cinderella Army*, 61.
124 Ibid.
125 Ibid., 292.
126 "Civil Affairs Weekly Summary No. 16," September 1944, WO 219/3530, 2, TNA.
127 Ibid.
128 "Memorandum: Conditions at Havre," 17 October 1944, FO 371/42020, TNA.
129 "Report on Le Havre," 19 October 1944, WO 219/3974, TNA.
130 "Civil Affairs Weekly Summary No. 16," September 1944, WO 219/3530, 4, TNA.
131 "Report on Le Havre," 19 October 1944, WO 219/3974, TNA.
132 The presence of Americans in Le Havre resulted in the city being nicknamed "Lucky Strike City" because all the billet camps located in and around the city were named after famous American cigarette brands. Furthermore, Le Havre acted as one of the major ports for Americans entering and leaving Europe, thus acquiring the title of "Gateway to America." Knapp, "The Destruction of Le Havre," 479.
133 Although SHAEF was concerned about civilian casualties at Caen, it was after Le Havre that concerns about civilian casualties actually affected operational doctrine in the urban space. Stacey writes about how the use of indirect artillery was limited in the assault on Boulogne due to concerns about civilians in the battle space. Stacey, *The Victory Campaign*, 326.
134 Not only was Le Havre denied to 21st Army Group but the port of Antwerp, liberated by the British 11th Armoured Division on 4 September 1944, was inoperative. Although the capture of Antwerp boosted morale, its port facilities could not be used until the Allies cleared the Scheldt Estuary and the aquatic approaches to the city. Thus, with Antwerp unusable and 12th American Army Group controlling Le Havre, 21st Army Group needed the coastal cities along the channel in order to support Montgomery's northern advance.
135 "War Diary, II Canadian Corps," September 1944, RG 24, Vol 13713, Reel T-1866, LAC.
136 Ibid.
137 "War Diary, Civil Affairs II Canadian Corps," September 1944. RG 24, Vol 16633, LAC.
138 "War Diary, Stormont, Dundas and Glengarry Highlanders," September 1944. RG 130, Vol 15128, LAC.

139 "War Diary, Civil Affairs II Canadian Corps," September 1944. RG 24, Vol 16633, LAC.
140 "War Diary, 3rd Canadian Infantry Division Headquarters," July 1944, RG 24 C 3, Vol 13786. LAC.
141 "War Diary, II Canadian Corps," September 1944, RG 24, Vol 13713, Reel T-1866, LAC.
142 Copp, *Cinderella Army*, 63.
143 "Appendix 4: Scheme for Evacuation of Boulogne – Security Belt," September 1944, RG 24, Vol 16633, 1, LAC.
144 "Appendix 5: Report on Scheme for Evacuation of Boulogne – Security Belt," September 1944. RG 24, Vol 16633, 1.
145 Ibid., 2.
146 Ibid.
147 "Civil Affairs Weekly Summary No. 16," September 1944, WO 219/3530, 6, TNA.
148 Ibid., 4.
149 "First Canadian Army CA Fortnightly Report No. 3," 1944, WO 371/42018, TNA.
150 "Report on Supply System, France," 20 September 1944, WO 171/722, TNA.
151 "War Diary, The Highland Light Infantry of Canada," September 1944, RG 24, Vol 15076, LAC.
152 Ibid.
153 "War Diary, Stormont, Dundas and Glengarry Highlanders," September 1944. RG 130, Vol 15128, LAC.
154 Ibid.
155 Ibid.
156 "War Diary, The North Nova Scotia Highlanders," September 1944, RG 24, Vol 15122, LAC.
157 "War Diary, Royal Winnipeg Rifles," September 1944, RG 24, Vol 15234, LAC.
158 "War Diary, 7th Canadian Infantry Brigade," September 1944, RG 24, Vol 14131, LAC.
159 "War Diary, Stormont, Dundas and Glengarry Highlanders," September 1944. RG 130, Vol 15128, LAC.
160 "War Diary, Canadian Scottish Rifles," September 1944, RG 24, Vol 15038, LAC.
161 "War Diary, Royal Winnipeg Rifles," September 1944, RG 24, Vol 15234, LAC.
162 "War Diary, 1st Battalion Canadian Scottish," September 1944, RG 24, Vol 15038, LAC.
163 Ibid.
164 "War Diary, 7th Canadian Infantry Brigade," September 1944, RG 24, Vol 14131, LAC.
165 "George Heron," The Memory Project: Veterans Stories of the Second World War, Accessed 2018, www.thememoryproject.com. Mr Heron also

relates an incredible tale of 200 German soldiers who surrendered during the truce. Mr Heron was in fact ordered to guard this group and comments on the friendliness between the Canadian guards and their German "captives." This mass surrender, however, was contrary to the terms of the truce and the German soldiers had to return to the German lines. A senior German officer arrived, gave them a stern lecture, then marched them back to the German lines.

166 "War Diary, 7th Canadian Infantry Brigade," September 1944, RG 24, Vol 14131, LAC.
167 "War Diary, HQ II Canadian Corps Civil Affairs," September 1944. RG 24 Vol 12760, LAC.
168 "War Diary, 7th Canadian Infantry Brigade," September 1944, RG 24, Vol 14131, LAC.
169 "225 Civil Affairs Det Copies of Reports from Files 2 July 44/10 May 45," May 1945, RG 24, Vol 10567, LAC.
170 "Proposed Evacuation of the Civilian Population – Dunkirk," 21 September 1944, WO 219/3728, LAC.
171 Ibid.
172 "Evacuation of Civs – Dunkirk," 5 October 1944, WO 219/3728, 3, TNA.
173 By late September, Foulkes's 2nd Division had already moved away from Dunkirk and into Belgium to support II Canadian Corps as they cleared the Scheldt Estuary and the approaches to Antwerp. Thus, the masking of Dunkirk was carried out by several successive formations of First Canadian Army: the 4th Special Service Brigade (British Commandos), the 154th British Infantry Brigade, and the 1st Czechoslovakian Armoured Brigade.
174 "Evacuation of Civs – Dunkirk," 5 October 1944, WO 219/3728, 2, TNA.
175 Ibid., 3.
176 Ibid.
177 "First Canadian Army CA Fortnightly Report No 4," September 1944, FO 371/42020, 7, TNA.
178 Ibid., 10.
179 This was first reported in "War Diary, Civil Affairs First Canadian Army Headquarters," September 1944, RG 24, Vol 16632 and later reiterated in "Canadian Participation in Civil Affairs/Military Government. Part III: France, General Historical Survey, July–October 1944," January 1946, CMHQ Reports: Report 149, 13, DHH.
180 For an excellent study on French Resistance groups see Kedward's *In Search of the Maquis*.
181 Jackson, *France: The Dark Years*, 484
182 Foottit and Simmonds, *France, 1943–1945*, 33.
183 Kedward, *In Search of the Maquis*, 50–60.
184 "War Diary, Civil Affairs II Canadian Corps," September 1944. RG 24, Vol 16633, LAC.

185 Ibid.
186 "First Canadian Army CA Fortnightly Report No 4," September 1944, FO 371/42020, 1, TNA.
187 "War Diary North Nova Scotia Regiment," September 1944. RG 24, Vol 15122, LAC.
188 "Civil Affairs Weekly Summary No. 16," September 1944, WO 219/3530, 3, TNA.
189 "First Canadian Army Fortnightly Report No. 3," September 1944, WO 371/42018, TNA.
190 "First Canadian Army CA Fortnightly Report No 4," September 1944, FO 371/42020, 5, TNA.
191 "First Canadian Army Fortnightly Report No. 3," September 1944, WO 371/42018, TNA.
192 "Org and Admin Civil Affairs Correspondence 22 April 44/June 45, Apr/May 45, Jan/July 45, Turnover from Military to Civilian Authority," 11 August 1944, RG 24, Vol 10570, LAC.
193 Ibid., 1.
194 Ibid., 2.
195 Ibid.
196 A reference both to general disease and to venereal disease, the most commonly shared health issue amongst Canadian soldiers. Ibid.
197 Ibid., 3.
198 Ibid.
199 "Civil Affairs Weekly Summary No. 16," September 1944, WO 219/3530, 7, TNA.

CHAPTER THREE

1 "Canadian Participation in Civil Affairs/Military Government. Part IV: Belgium and the Netherlands, General Historical Survey," March 1947, CMHQ Reports: Report 172, 15, DHH.
2 An excellent account of the battle is given by Terry Copp in *Cinderella Army*.
3 Conway, *Collaboration in Belgium*, 4.
4 Ibid., 6.
5 Jay Howard Geller argues that Himmler forced Reeder into accepting membership into the SS in "The Role of Military Administration in German-Occupied Belgium," 102
6 Warmbrunn, *The German Occupation of Belgium*, 29.
7 Geller, "The Role of Military Administration in German-Occupied Belgium," 108.
8 "Army Service Forces Manual. Civil Affairs Handbook on Belgium," April 1944, WO 168/3497, 4, TNA.
9 Ibid., 3.

10 Ibid., 31.
11 Schrijvers, *Liberators*, 9.
12 "SHAEF Memorandum to Headquarters, Northern Group of Armies: Civil Affairs – Belgium," 1 September 1944, WO 321/1158, TNA.
13 "Report on Civil Affairs in Belgium," November 1944, WO 219/3738, 12, TNA.
14 Ibid.
15 Ibid.
16 "War Diary, Civil Affairs First Canadian Army Headquarters," December 1944, RG 24, Vol 16632, LAC.
17 "Report on Civil Affairs in Belgium," November 1944, WO 219/3738, 13, TNA.
18 "Second Army CA Report No. 6," September 1944, WO 171/252, 2, TNA.
19 "Canadian Participation in Civil Affairs/Military Government. Part IV: Belgium and the Netherlands, General Historical Survey," March 1947, CMHQ Reports: Report 172, 10, DHH.
20 "21 Army Group CA/Mil Gov Branch: Historical Survey," Autumn 1944, WO 219/3727, 16, TNA
21 "Second Army CA Report No. 6," September 1944, WO 171/252, 2, TNA.
22 "Canadian Participation in Civil Affairs/Military Government. Part IV: Belgium and the Netherlands, General Historical Survey," March 1947, CMHQ Reports: Report 172, 11, DHH.
23 Ralph Allen, "Pierlot Hard Pressed Between Past, Future," *Globe and Mail*, 19 October 1944.
24 Warner, "Allies, Government, and Resistance," 48–60.
25 Robert Eunson, "Leadership of Pierlot Challenged in Belgium by Chief of 'Resistance,'" *Globe and Mail*, 11 December 1944.
26 "CA First Canadian Army Fortnightly Report No. 4," September 1944, FO 371/42020, 5, TNA.
27 This argument was first forwarded CMHQ Report 172 and echoed again by Warner in his article "Allies, Government, and Resistance."
28 Warner, "Allies, Government, and Resistance," 28.
29 "CA First Canadian Army Fortnightly Report No. 4," September 1944, FO 371/42020, 5, TNA.
30 "War Diary, Civil Affairs II Canadian Corps," October 1944. RG 24, Vol 16633, LAC.
31 "War Diary, Civil Affairs First Canadian Army Headquarters," October 1944, RG 24, Vol 16632, LAC.
32 "Report on Civil Affairs in Belgium," November 1944, WO 219/3738, 15, TNA.
33 "War Diary, Civil Affairs II Canadian Corps," October 1944. RG 24, Vol 16633, LAC.
34 Ibid.
35 "War Diary, Civil Affairs II Canadian Corps," September 1944. RG 24, Vol 16633, LAC.
36 Ibid.

37 "War Diary, Civil Affairs First Canadian Army Headquarters," September 1944, RG 24, Vol 16632, LAC.
38 Ibid.
39 "War Diary, Civil Affairs II Canadian Corps," October 1944. RG 24, Vol 16633, LAC.
40 This was told to Lt Col Walker of II Canadian Corps CA by Lt Col F.L. Price, S.O. 1 (Staff), of FCA HQ and was recorded in the II Canadian Corps CA War Diary on 1 October 1944. "War Diary, Civil Affairs II Canadian Corps," October 1944. RG 24, Vol 16633, LAC.
41 "War Diary, Civil Affairs II Canadian Corps," September 1944. RG 24, Vol 16633, LAC.
42 Conway, *The Sorrows of Belgium*, 93.
43 Ibid.
44 "War Diary, Civil Affairs First Canadian Army Headquarters," September 1944, RG 24, Vol 16632, LAC.
45 "CA First Canadian Army Semi-Monthly Report No. 7," November 1944, RG 24, Vol 16632, 1, LAC.
46 "Canadian Participation in Civil Affairs/Military Government. Part IV: Belgium and the Netherlands, General Historical Survey," March 1947, CMHQ Reports: Report 172, 18, DHH.
47 J.E.G. Labrosse, "The Personal Experiences of a Canadian Civil Affairs Officer in France and Belgium June 1944 – March 1945," December 1946, CMHQ Reports: Report No. 12, 43–5, DHH.
48 Ibid.
49 Charles Goodman, "Goodman, Charles: My Army Recollections," interview, Canadian Military Oral History Collection University of Victoria, 1 December 1979, SC104_GCE_172.
50 Robert F. Gallagher, "World War Two Story. United States Army, 815th Anti-Aircraft Artillery Battalion, Third Army," Accessed 2019, https://gallagherstory.com/ww2/index.html.
51 Schrijvers, *Liberators*, 230.
52 Harold Bertrand Gonder, "Gonder, Harold Bertrand: My Army Recollections," interview, Canadian Military Oral History Collection University of Victoria, June 10 1986, SC104_FRF_054.
53 Ronald Fraser Ferrie, "Ferrie, Ronald Fraser: My Army Recollections," interview, Canadian Military Oral History Collection University of Victoria, 23 July 1985, SC104_GHB_171.
54 "War Diary, Civil Affairs First Canadian Army Headquarters," October 1944, RG 24, Vol 16632, LAC.
55 "War Diary, Civil Affairs II Canadian Corps," October 1944. RG 24, Vol 16633, LAC.
56 "L of C (Civil Affairs) Fortnightly Report No. 6," October 1944, WO 171/722, TNA.
57 Ibid.

58 Schrijvers, *Liberators*, 161.
59 Conway, *Sorrows*, 77.
60 J.E.G. Labrosse, "The Personal Experiences of a Canadian Civil Affairs Officer in France and Belgium June 1944 – March 1945," December 1946, CMHQ Reports: Report No. 12, 51, DHH.
61 "L of C (Civil Affairs) Fortnightly Report No. 8," December 1944, WO 202/682, TNA.
62 J.E.G. Labrosse, "The Personal Experiences of a Canadian Civil Affairs Officer in France and Belgium June 1944 – March 1945," December 1946, CMHQ Reports: Report No. 12, 51, DHH.
63 Ibid.
64 Ibid.
65 Ibid.
66 "War Diary, Civil Affairs First Canadian Army Headquarters," November 1944, RG 24, Vol 16632, LAC.
67 Conway, *Sorrows*, 89.
68 Schrijvers, *Liberators*, 161.
69 "Antwerp Civilians go to War Front by Tram," *Globe and Mail*, 3 October 1944.
70 "Civil Defence in Antwerp," May 1945, WO 171/7982, 3, TNA. Martin Conway supports this contention in *Sorrows*, 59.
71 Antwerp and the rest of northern Belgium passed from First Canadian Army HQ control to L of C HQ control in October 1944, yet almost all of the First Canadian CA detachment remained on duty within the city. First Canadian Army headquarters also remained in the city, and thus the rocket attacks and the ensuing civil defence operation held a special significance for First Canadian Army's senior officers. It is important to note here the difference between First Canadian Army HQ command and L of C HQ command. In the initial phases of an army's advance, the headquarters of the combat units occupying that area would command the forward operational zones or military zones. For instance, by early September 1944, First Canadian Army had full operational control over the northern half of Belgium, which was designated a military zone. The southern half of Belgium and the French coastal region, which the Canadian army recently advanced through, passed to the command of L of C HQ. Essentially, L of C HQ was in charge of maintaining supply and transportation routes, road networks, and the forward combat units' miscellaneous logistical requirements, as well as maintaining a relationship with the civilian administration. Within L of C, CA officers, usually from static detachments, continued in their traditional roles, although it was not uncommon for CA detachments and officers to move from L of C to military zones and vice versa. This was able to occur because at its very essence L of C was still part of First Canadian Army organization; it was the subformation responsible for ensuring FCA stayed supplied.

72 Moulton, *Battle for Antwerp*, 185.
73 Collier, *The Battle of the V-Weapons*, 2.
74 Ibid., 125.
75 "Civil Defence in Antwerp," May 1945, WO 171/7982, 2, TNA. The seminal work on V-weapons is Collier's *The Battle of the V-Weapons* while a more recent and equally fascinating study is John Cornwell's *Hitler's Scientists*.
76 "Civil Defence in Antwerp," May 1945, WO 171/7982, 2, TNA.
77 Ibid., 4.
78 Ibid.
79 Ibid., 3.
80 Ibid., 6.
81 Ibid., 7.
82 This twenty-four-storey building is considered Europe's first skyscraper and was the tallest building in Antwerp until 1964.
83 "Civil Defence in Antwerp," May 1945, WO 171/7982, 9, TNA
84 By February 1945 all movement of labour had to be authorized by the Ministry of Labour under the new Civilian Mobilization Legislation. "SHAEF Report" February 1945, CAB 121/408, 2, TNA.
85 "War Diary, Civil Affairs II Canadian Corps," October 1944, RG 24, Vol 16633, LAC.
86 "Civil Defence in Antwerp," May 1945, WO 171/7982, 14, TNA.
87 Ibid., 16.
88 Ibid.
89 Ibid., 17.
90 "Canadian Participation in Civil Affairs/Military Government. Part IV: Belgium and the Netherlands, General Historical Survey," March 1947, CMHQ Reports: Report 172, 22, DHH.
91 "CA First Canadian Army Semi-Monthly Report No. 7," November 1944, RG 24, Vol 16632, 7, LAC.
92 "Civil Defence in Antwerp," May 1945, WO 171/7982, 18, TNA.
93 Ibid., 22.
94 Neufeld. *The Rocket and the Reich*, 274.
95 "Civil Defence in Antwerp," May 1945, WO 171/7982, 23, TNA.
96 Ibid., 25.
97 Ibid., 25.
98 Collier, *The Battle of the V-Weapons*, 243.
99 Irons, *The Price of Vengeance*, 147.
100 Ibid., 148.
101 "Civil Defence in Antwerp," May 1945, WO 171/7982, 25, TNA.
102 Ibid., 27.
103 Ibid.
104 Ibid.
105 Ibid., 28.

106 Ibid.
107 Ibid., 29.
108 Ibid., 30.
109 Ibid.
110 Ibid.
111 Ibid., 31.
112 "War Diary, Civil Affairs II Canadian Corps," October 1944, RG 24, Vol 16633, LAC.
113 "Civil Defence in Antwerp," May 1945, WO 171/7982, 32, TNA.
114 Ibid., 33
115 Ibid.
116 Ibid., 34.
117 Ibid.
118 "Letter to Major Foreshew from Major E. Van Cappellen," June 1945, WO 171/7982, TNA.
119 "Civil Defence in Antwerp," May 1945, WO 171/7982, 35, TNA.
120 "Civil Affairs Responsibility in France, Belgium and the Netherlands, 21 Army Group/5911/CA," November 1944, RG 24, Vol 10570, LAC.
121 Ibid.
122 Ibid.
123 "Civil Affairs Responsibility in France, Belgium and the Netherlands, SHAEF/G5/OPS/3509," 16 November 1944, RG 24, Vol 10570, LAC.
124 "Responsibility for Civil Affairs in Belgium and the Netherlands, SHAEF/G5/OPS/701," 26 Nov 1944, RG 24, Vol 10570, LAC.
125 Ibid.

CHAPTER FOUR

1 "Canadian Participation in Civil Affairs/Military Government. Part IV: Belgium and the Netherlands, General Historical Survey," March 1947, CMHQ Reports: Report 172, 29–33, DHH.
2 Stacey covers this period in great detail, as does Copp in *Cinderella Army*.
3 Today there are twelve provinces in the Netherlands, the twelfth being the province of Flevoland, added in 1989 and made up almost entirely of reclaimed land.
4 Many books cover the tale of the Dutch resistance, excellent ones include Jeroen Dewulf's *Dutch Clandestine Literature During the Nazi Occupation* and the earlier yet still well written text by Herman Friedhoff *Requiem for the Resistance*.
5 Warmbrunn, *The Dutch Under German Occupation*, 36.
6 "The Netherlands Responsibilities and Arrangements for Command and Control within First Canadian Army," 22 April 1945, WO 205/1052, TNA.
7 "SHAEF European Allied Contact Section: Minutes of Meeting between Dutch and SHAEF Representatives," 16 May 1944, FO 371/40411, 2, TNA.

8 "The Netherlands Responsibilities and Arrangements for Command and Control within First Canadian Army," 22 April 1945, WO 205/1052, TNA.
9 "Canadian Participation in Civil Affairs/Military Government. Part IV: Belgium and the Netherlands, General Historical Survey," March 1947, CMHQ Reports: Report 172, 21, DHH.
10 Ibid., 27.
11 "Weekly CA Report Hague Province," 16 May 1945, WO 219/3979, TNA.
12 II Canadian Corps took over responsibility of Area A from XXX British Corps in early November 1944.
13 "Report on Civil Affairs," April 1945, WO 219/3738, 17, TNA.
14 "War Diary, Civil Affairs II Canadian Corps," October 1944. RG 24, Vol 16633, LAC.
15 Ibid.
16 "Canadian Participation in Civil Affairs/Military Government. Part IV: Belgium and the Netherlands, General Historical Survey," March 1947, CMHQ Reports: Report 172, 29, DHH.
17 "War Diary, Civil Affairs II Canadian Corps," October 1944, RG 24, Vol 16633, LAC.
18 "Public Safety in the Netherlands," May 1945, FO 371/42021, TNA.
19 "Canadian Participation in Civil Affairs/Military Government. Part IV: Belgium and the Netherlands, General Historical Survey," March 1947, CMHQ Reports: Report 172, 53, DHH.
20 "War Diary, Civil Affairs First Canadian Army Headquarters," October 1944, RG 24, Vol 16632, LAC.
21 Ibid., 53.
22 "Canadian Participation in Civil Affairs/Military Government. Part IV: Belgium and the Netherlands, General Historical Survey," March 1947, CMHQ Reports: Report 172, 56, DHH.
23 Ibid.
24 "CA HQ First Canadian Army Weekly Report No 11," 30 January 1945, RG 24 Vol 16632, LAC.
25 Ibid.
26 "Canadian Participation in Civil Affairs/Military Government. Part IV: Belgium and the Netherlands, General Historical Survey," March 1947, CMHQ Reports: Report 172, 56, DHH.
27 "Brig. Wedd to Brig. Robbins," January 1945, RG 24 Vol 16632, LAC.
28 "CA HQ First Canadian Army Weekly Report No 5," 19 December 1944, RG 24 Vol 16632, LAC.
29 Ibid.
30 Warmbrunn, *The Dutch Under German Occupation*, 197.
31 "First Canadian Army Civil Affairs Monthly Report," November 1944, WO 171/252, TNA.
32 Ibid.

33 "War Diary, Civil Affairs II Canadian Corps," October 1944, RG 24, Vol 16633, LAC.
34 "War Diary, Civil Affairs First Canadian Army Headquarters," December 1944, RG 24, Vol 16632, LAC.
35 "War Diary, Civil Affairs First Canadian Army Headquarters," January 1945, RG 24, Vol 16632, LAC.
36 "Canadian Participation in Civil Affairs/Military Government. Part IV: Belgium and the Netherlands, General Historical Survey," March 1947, CMHQ Reports: Report 172, 55–8, DHH.
37 Ibid.
38 Ibid.
39 Ibid., 71.
40 Ibid., 74.
41 Donnison, *Civil Affairs and Military Government*, 402 and "Civil Affairs Report on Holland," November 1944, WO 219/3532, 20, TNA.
42 "Civil Affairs First Canadian Army Fortnightly Report," 13 November 1944, WO 219/3976A, TNA.
43 "Canadian Participation in Civil Affairs/Military Government. Part IV: Belgium and the Netherlands, General Historical Survey," March 1947, CMHQ Reports: Report 172, 73, DHH.
44 This is corroborated by "Report on Civil Affairs," April 1945, WO 219/3738, 17, TNA; as well as "Canadian Participation in Civil Affairs/Military Government. Part IV: Belgium and the Netherlands, General Historical Survey," March 1947, CMHQ Reports: Report 172, 37, DHH; and Donnison, *Civil Affairs and Military Government*, 402.
45 "Canadian Participation in Civil Affairs/Military Government. Part IV: Belgium and the Netherlands, General Historical Survey," March 1947, CMHQ Reports: Report 172, 74, DHH.
46 "CA HQ First Canadian Army Weekly Report No 6," 27 December 1944, RG 24 Vol 16632, LAC.
47 "War Diary, Civil Affairs II Canadian Corps," October 1944, RG 24, Vol 16633, LAC.
48 "CA HQ First Canadian Army Weekly Report No 7," 5 January 1945, RG 24 Vol 16632, LAC.
49 "CA HQ First Canadian Army Weekly Report No 12," 6 February 1945, RG 24 Vol 16632 LAC.
50 "Canadian Participation in Civil Affairs/Military Government. Part IV: Belgium and the Netherlands, General Historical Survey," March 1947, CMHQ Reports: Report 172, 75, DHH.
51 Ibid., 38.
52 "DP Org in the Netherlands," 12 January 1945, RG 24 Vol 16632, LAC.
53 "CA HQ First Canadian Army Weekly Report No 12," 6 February 1945, RG 24 Vol 16632 LAC.

54 "Canadian Participation in Civil Affairs/Military Government. Part IV: Belgium and the Netherlands, General Historical Survey," March 1947, CMHQ Reports: Report 172, 77, DHH.
55 Ibid., 78.
56 "Extract from 8 Corps Report," April 1945, WO 171/252, TNA.
57 "225 Civil Affairs Detachment Copies of Reports from Files 2 July 44/10 May 45: First Report – Meppel," 15 April 1945, RG 24 Vol 10567, LAC.
58 J.E.G. Labrosse, "The Personal Experiences of a Canadian Civil Affairs Officer in France and Belgium June 1944 – March 1945," December 1946, CMHQ Reports: Report No. 12, 38, DHH.
59 "Civil Affairs Report on Holland," November 1944, WO 219/3532. 20, TNA.
60 "War Diary, Civil Affairs II Canadian Corps," 11 October 1944. RG 24, Vol 16633, LAC.
61 Collection centres for the various evacuations of Zeeland province were also established in Antwerp and Carpelien with approval from Belgian officials. "War Diary, Civil Affairs II Canadian Corps," 24 October 1944, RG 24, Vol 16633, LAC.
62 "War Diary, Civil Affairs II Canadian Corps," 10 October 1944, RG 24, Vol 16633, LAC.
63 "Appendices to WD First Canadian Army Civil Affairs: Dispositions Taken to Cope With Refugees," 27 October 1944, RG 24 Vol 16632, LAC.
64 "War Diary, Civil Affairs II Canadian Corps," 26 October 1944, RG 24, Vol 16633, LAC.
65 J.E.G. Labrosse, "The Personal Experiences of a Canadian Civil Affairs Officer in France and Belgium June 1944 – March 1945," December 1946, CMHQ Reports: Report No. 12, 41, DHH.
66 "War Diary, Civil Affairs First Canadian Army Headquarters," 28 October 1944, RG 24, Vol 16632, LAC.
67 J.E.G. Labrosse, "The Personal Experiences of a Canadian Civil Affairs Officer in France and Belgium June 1944 – March 1945," December 1946, CMHQ Reports: Report No. 12, 39, DHH.
68 Ibid., 37.
69 "Report on Evacuation of Venraij," November 1944, WO 171/252, TNA.
70 "Canadian Participation in Civil Affairs/Military Government. Part IV: Belgium and the Netherlands, General Historical Survey," March 1947, CMHQ Reports: Report 172, 77, DHH.
71 Ibid., 88.
72 "War Diary, Civil Affairs II Canadian Corps," November 1944, RG 24, Vol 16633, LAC.
73 "Canadian Participation in Civil Affairs/Military Government. Part IV: Belgium and the Netherlands, General Historical Survey," March 1947, CMHQ Reports: Report 172, 79, DHH.
74 Ibid., 86.
75 "Appendix A to Weekly Report," 27 April 1945, WO 171/8022, TNA.

76. "War Diary CA Rear HQ I Canadian Corps," 1 May 1945, RG 24 Vol 16633, LAC.
77. "Civil Affairs I Canadian Corps Weekly Report," 5 May 1945, RG 24 Vol 16633, LAC.
78. "Civil Affairs I Canadian Corps Weekly Report," 30 May 1945, RG 24 Vol 16633, LAC
79. "Canadian Participation in Civil Affairs/Military Government. Part IV: Belgium and the Netherlands, General Historical Survey," March 1947, CMHQ Reports: Report 172, 30, DHH.
80. Ibid., 30–1.
81. "Civil Affairs I Canadian Corps Weekly Report," 30 May 1945, RG 24 Vol 16633, LAC
82. "Civil Affairs/Military Government – Planning Memorandum," 14 April 1945, RG 24 Vol 16633, 3, LAC.
83. Fuykschot, *Hunger in Holland*, 124.
84. Hibbert, *Fragments of War*, 178.
85. Horn and Kaufman, *A Liberation Album*, 66.
86. Quoted by Dr Mees in Van der Zee's *The Hunger Winter*, 226.
87. "Report on Civil Affairs," April 1945, WO 219/3738, 18, TNA.
88. Ibid.
89. Goddard. *Canada and the Liberation of the Netherlands*, 140.
90. Alida Monkman nee Sikkink, "Letter to her granddaughter Victoria Monkman recalling her experience under German occupation" 19 April 1993.
91. Van der Zee, *The Hunger Winter*, 151.
92. Richard Sanburn, "Holland People Cannot Obtain Food Supplies," *Hamilton Spectator*, 4 April 1945.
93. "Report by Lt-Gen. A.E. Grasett, A C of S, G-5, on Civil Affairs work by 21st Army Group," April 1945, WO 219/3537, 18, TNA.
94. "Civil Affairs First Canadian Army Administrative Instruction No 2: Maintenance Plan – Netherlands Areas B1 and C," 4 April 1945, RG 24 Vol 16632, LAC.
95. "Summary of Civil Affairs/Military Government Operation for period ending 11 November 1944," 14 November 1944, CAB 121/408, 3, TNA.
96. Van der Zee, *The Hunger Winter*, 224.
97. "SHAEF Message: Reproduction of message cabled to President Roosevelt from Queen Wilhelmina," 26 October 1944, WO 219/16, TNA.
98. "War Diary for Civ Affairs Branch – Rear HQ 1 CDN Corps, 1 May 45 – 31 May 45: Nutritional Report of Utrecht Town," 11 May 1945, RG 24 Vol 16633, LAC. The statistics were compiled by a series of Dutch medical teams working for I Canadian Corps CA.
99. "Near Starvation, Says Poelhekke," *Globe and Mail*, 28 April 1945.
100. "War Diary for Civ Affairs Branch – Rear HQ 1 CDN Corps, 1 May 45 – 31 May 45: Nutritional Report of Utrecht Town," 11 May 1945, RG 24 Vol 16633, 1, LAC.

101 Ibid., 1.
102 Ibid., 3.
103 Kasaboski and Hartog. *The Occupied Garden*, 193.
104 Ibid., 199.
105 "The Netherlands Responsibilities and Arrangements for Command and Control within First Canadian Army," 22 April 1945, WO 205/1052, 4, TNA.
106 "SHAEF Message: Eisenhower to SHAEF Mission (Netherlands) 21 Army Group Civil Affairs," November 1944, WO 219/16, TNA.
107 Van der Zee, *The Hunger Winter*, 254.
108 Horn and Kaufman, *A Liberation Album*, 106.
109 Van der Zee, *The Hunger Winter*, 270.
110 Mowat, *The Regiment*, 308.
111 Van der Zee, *The Hunger Winter*, 277.
112 Monkman nee Sikknk, *Letter*, 19 April 1993.
113 Horn and Kaufman, *A Liberation Album*, 118.
114 Dando-Collins, *Operation Chowhound*, 184–5.
115 Charles Goodman, "Goodman, Charles: My Army Recollections," interview, Canadian Military Oral History Collection University of Victoria, 1 December 1979, SC104_GCE_172.
116 "Report by 720 (P) Detachment Civil Affairs for period ending 16 May 1945," 16 May 1945, WO 171/8062, TNA.
117 George V Eckenfelder, "Eckenfelder, George V: My Army Recollections," interview, Canadian Military Oral History Collection University of Victoria, 7 August 1987, SC104_EGV_066.
118 "Civil Affairs/Military Government – Planning Memorandum," 14 April 1945, RG 24 Vol 16633, 2, LAC.
119 "Canadian Participation in Civil Affairs/Military Government. Part IV: Belgium and the Netherlands, General Historical Survey," March 1947, CMHQ Reports: Report 172, 46, DHH.
120 Templer finished his thoughts by saying, "But that no longer concerns us." "Org and Admin – Civil Affairs – Correspondence: 22 April 44/ 30 Jan 45," January 1945, RG 24 Vol 10570, File 9/ORG/I-O Vol 1, LAC.
121 Stacey, *The Victory Campaign*, 581.
122 "Notes on CAO's Meeting at HQ SHAEF," 20 October 1944, WO 106/4426, TNA.

CHAPTER FIVE

1 "Censorship Reports for 21st Army Group: Censorship Report for period 16–28 Feb 45," RG 24 Vol 12322 ,T-17925, File 4/Censor Reps/2/3, LAC.
2 "Canadian Participation in Civil Affairs/Military Government: Part 1: Background and Beginning," Canadian Military Headquarters Reports: Report 140, July 1945, 4, DHH.

NOTES TO PAGES 185–95

3   "War Diary Civ Affairs Branch – Rear HQ I Canadian Corps," May 1945, RG 24 Vol 16633, File BR/16 MIL GOV, LAC.
4   "Operation Eclipse: Appreciation and Outline Plan," World War Two Operational Documents, 1, Combined Arms Research Library (CARL), http://cgsc.contentdm.oclc.org/cdm/ref/collection/p4013coll8/id/2948.
5   "The Canadian Army Occupation Force in Germany May 1945-June 1946," CMHQ Reports: Report 174, March 1947, 2, DHH.
6   Ibid., 3.
7   "Priority of Tasks, DCA/MG Templer 21 AG to First Canadian Army (Mil Gov)," June 1945, RG 24 Vol. 10570, File 9/Org/1-0, LAC.
8   "CA/MG Org and Admin Jan to Jun 45: Letter to General Templar," June 1945, RG 24 Vol. 10570, File 9/Org/1-0 Vol 3, LAC.
9   "Canadian Participation in Civil Affairs/Military Government Part V: Germany, General Historical Survey," June 1947, CMHQ Reports: Report 176, 5, DHH.
10 Robert John Carson. "Carson, Robert John: My Army Recollections" interview, Canadian Military Oral History Collection University of Victoria, 24 May 1980, SC104_CRJ_026.
11 Lawrence S. Henderson. "Henderson, Lawrence S.: My Army Recollections," interview, Canadian Military Oral History Collection University of Victoria, 14 January 1982, SC104_HLS_064.
12 "Difficult Winter Facing Germans," *Hamilton Spectator*, 15 December 1945.
13 These two categories referred to the miners and industrial workers in the Ruhr and Westphalia regions. "Canadian Participation in Civil Affairs/Military Government Part V: Germany, General Historical Survey," June 1947, CMHQ Reports: Report 176, 12, DHH.
14 Ibid., 14.
15 Ibid., 15–16.
16 "War Diary Queen's Own Cameron Highlanders of Canada Active Service Force," May 1945, RG 24-C-3 Vol 15165, LAC.
17 "First Canadian Army HQ Mil Gov Branch Weekly Report Ending 16 May 45," RG 24-G-3-1-a, Vol 10619, LAC.
18 "HQ 2 CDN Corps Mil Gov Branch Weekly Report Ending 6 Jun 45," RG 24, Vol 10569, File 8/CORPS/WEEKLY/4-2-4-4, LAC.
19 J.E.G. Labrosse, "The Personal Experiences of a Canadian Civil Affairs Officer in France and Belgium June 1944 – March 1945," December 1946, CMHQ Reports: Report No. 12, 23, DHH.
20 Ibid., 5–9.
21 Ibid., 11.
22 Ibid.
23 Ibid., 13.
24 Ibid., 14.

25 "HQ 2 CDN Corps Mil Gov Branch Weekly Report Ending 6 Jun 45," RG 24, Vol 10569, File 8//CORPS/WEEKLY/4-2-4-4, LAC.
26 "Canadian Participation in Civil Affairs/Military Government Part V: Germany, General Historical Survey," June 1947, CMHQ Reports: Report 176, 10, DHH.
27 "Priority of Tasks, DCA/MG Templer 21 AG to First Canadian Army (Mil Gov)," June 1945, RG 24 Vol. 10570, File 9/Org/1-0, LAC.
28 The intention within the areas occupied by 21st Army Group was to rebuild the German police force along a British "Bobby" model, unarmed and nonpolitical. Training for this police force began in the Netherlands in February 1945. The British policing experience is covered in Emsley's *Exporting British Policing During the Second World War*.
29 Charles Goodman, "Goodman, Charles: My Army Recollections," interview, Canadian Military Oral History Collection University of Victoria, 1 December 1979, SC104_GCE_172.
30 Horace Dougald Beach. "Beach, Horace Dougald: My Army Recollections," interview, Canadian Military Oral History Collection University of Victoria, 15 May 1978, SC104_BHD_017.
31 "Canadian Participation in Civil Affairs/Military Government Part V: Germany, General Historical Survey," June 1947, CMHQ Reports: Report 176, 6, DHH.
32 "Public Safety 821 Detachment Military Government Oldenburg," 8 May 1945, WO171/8084, TNA.
33 Gordon, "Cheers and Tears," 152.
34 J.E.G. Labrosse, "The Personal Experiences of a Canadian Civil Affairs Officer in France and Belgium June 1944 – March 1945," December 1946, CMHQ Reports: Report No. 12, 10, DHH.
35 "Weekly Report No. 25 Military Government Branch, Main HQ First Canadian Army," 8 May 1945, RG 24, Vol 9768, File 2/Civ Offers//S/2, LAC.
36 "Canadian Participation in Civil Affairs/Military Government Part V: Germany, General Historical Survey," June 1947, CMHQ Reports: Report 176, 7, DHH.
37 J.E.G. Labrosse, "The Personal Experiences of a Canadian Civil Affairs Officer in France and Belgium June 1944 – March 1945," December 1946, CMHQ Reports: Report No. 12, 17, DHH.
38 "Canadian Participation in Civil Affairs/Military Government Part V: Germany, General Historical Survey," June 1947, CMHQ Reports: Report 176, 7, DHH.
39 "Censorship Report for 21st Army Group: Censorship report for period 16–30 April 1945," RG 24 Vol 12322, T-17925, LAC.
40 Gordon, "Cheers and Tears," 310.
41 This was a Polish POW. The charges were dropped and the soldier returned to a Polish camp for supposed punishment from his superiors.

42 "HQ 2 CDN Corps Mil Gov Branch Weekly Report Ending 6 Jun 45," RG 24, Vol 10569, File 8//CORPS/WEEKLY/4-2-4-4, LAC.
43 Ibid.
44 "Canadian Participation in Civil Affairs/Military Government Part V: Germany, General Historical Survey," June 1947, CMHQ Reports: Report 176, 8, DHH.
45 James Douglas Baird, "Baird, James Douglas: My Army Recollections," interview, Canadian Military Oral History Collection University of Victoria, 17 June 1980, SC104_BJD_003.
46 Charles Goodman, "Goodman, Charles: My Army Recollections," interview, Canadian Military Oral History Collection University of Victoria, 1 December 1979, SC104_GCE_172.
47 "Censorship Report for 21st Army Group: Censorship Report for period 1–15 March 45," RG 24 Vol 12322, T-17925, File 4/Censor Reps//2/3, LAC and "Censorship Report for 21st Army Group: Censorship Report for period 16–31 March 45," RG 24 Vol 12322, T-17925, File 4/Censor Reps//2/3, LAC.
48 Ibid.
49 Ibid.
50 Ibid.
51 This is written about in Claire Cookson-Hills' work, "Sexual Violence as Combat Motivation."
52 Ibid., 19.
53 Gordon, "Cheers and Tears," 224.
54 Ibid., 215–16. Pollard actually received and served the longest sentence. Interestingly, Albert Pollard was described as "black" by some of the witnesses. This also fits a disturbing racial trend amongst the western Allies where "black" soldiers received harsher penalties than their "white" counterparts for similar crimes. Gordon, "Cheers and Tears," 210–24.
55 Gordon, "Cheers and Tears," 220–3.
56 XXX British Corps would certainly face its own issues. It would also rely on a new Canadian formation, the Canadian Army Occupation Force (CAOF), to help keep the peace and enforce Allied authority.

CONCLUSION

1 Coles and Weinberg. *Civil Affairs: Soldiers Become Governors*, 287.
2 Longhurst, "The Evolution of Canadian Civil–Military Cooperation," 57.
3 NATO Civil–Military Cooperation (CIMIC) Doctrine: AJP-9. June 2003. www.nato.int/ims/docu/ajp-9.pdf.
4 Ibid., 2.
5 Though Robert Engen's recent book *Strangers in Arms* certainly starts some dialogue in regards to this.

Bibliography

ARCHIVAL SOURCES
Army Headquarters (AHQ) Reports, 1948–59.
CAB 121/408, War Cabinet Files
Canadian Military Headquarters (CMHQ) Reports, 1940–49
Canadian Military Oral History Collection, University of Victoria
Directorate of History and Heritage (DHH)
FO 371/40411, Foreign Office Files
FO 371/42020, Foreign Office Files
FO 371/42021, Foreign Office Files
Library Archives Canada (LAC)
The Memory Project. www.thememoryproject.com
The National Archives UK (TNA)
RG 24, Department of National Defence fonds
WO 106/4426, War Office Files
WO 168/3497, War Office Files
WO 171/252-8062, War Office Files
WO 202/682-767, War Office Files
WO 204/12317, War Office Files
WO 205/1052, War Office Files
WO 219/16 – 3979, War Office Files
WO 371/42018, War Office Files

OTHER SOURCES
Ashworth, G.J. *The City as Battlefield: The Liberation of Groningen, April 1945.* The Netherlands: University of Groningen Press, 1995.
Barnett, Michael. *Empire of Humanity: A History of Humanitarianism.* New York: Cornell University Press, 2011.
Benson, George, and Maurice Neufeld. "American Military Government in Italy." In *American Experiences in Military Government in World War II* edited by Carl J. Friedrich, 111–48. New York: Rinehart, 1948.
Best, Geoffrey. *War and Law Since 1945.* Toronto: Clarendon Press. 1994.

Bond, Brian, ed. *Chief of Staff: The Diaries of Lieutenant General Sir Henry Pownall.* London: Leo Cooper, 1972.

Brown, Cindy. "To Bury the Dead and Feed the Living: Allied Military Government in Sicily, 1943." *Canadian Military History* 22, no. 3, (summer 2013): 35–48.

Cavasin, Zachary, "Hai Visto I Canadesi? A study of the Social Interactions between Canadian Soldiers and Italian Civilians before, during and after the Battle of Ortona." MA diss., University of Ottawa, 2010.

Coakley, Robert W., and Richard M Leighton. *Global Logistics and Strategy, 1943–1945.* Washington: Officer of the Chief of Military History United States Army, 1968.

Coates, Ken, and W.R. Morrison. "The American Rampant: Reflections on the impact of US Troops in Allied Countries during World War Two." *Journal of World History* 2, no. 2 (1991): 201–21

Cohen, Stuart. "Mesopotamia in British Strategy, 1903–1914." *International Journal of Middle Eastern Studies* 9, no. 2, (April 1978): 171–81.

Coles, Harry L., and Albert K. Weinberg. *Civil Affairs: Soldiers become Governors.* Washington, DC: Office of the Chief of Military History, 1964.

Collier, Basil. *The Battle of the V-Weapons: 1944–1945.* London: Hodder and Stoughton, 1964.

Conway, Martin. *Collaboration in Belgium: Leon Degrelle and the Rexist Movement, 1940–1944.* New Haven: Yale University Press, 1993.

– "The Liberation of Belgium, 1944–1945." In *The End of the War in Europe, 1945,* edited by Gill Bennett, 117–38. London: HMSO, 1996.

– *The Sorrows of Belgium: Liberation and Political Reconstruction, 1944–1947.* New York: Oxford University Press, 2012.

Conway-Lanz, Sahr. *Collateral Damage: Americans, Noncombatant Immunity, and Atrocity after World War II.* New York: Routledge, 2006.

Cook, Tim. *The Necessary War.* Vol. 1: *Canadians Fighting the Second World War, 1939–1943.* Allen Lane: Toronto, 2014.

Cookson-Hills, Claire. "Sexual Violence as Combat Motivation." In *Why We Fight: the Modern History of Combat Motivation,* edited by Allan English, Hans Christian Brede, and Robert Engen. Montreal & Kingston: McGill-Queen's University Press, forthcoming 2020.

Copp, Terry. *Cinderella Army: The Canadians in North-West Europe, 1944–1945.* Toronto: University of Toronto Press, 2006.

– *Fields of Fire: The Canadians in Normandy.* Toronto: University of Toronto Press, 2003.

Copp, Terry, and Mark Osborne Humphries. *Combat Stress in the 20th Century: The Commonwealth Perspective.* Kingston: Canadian Defence Academy Press, 2010.

Cornwell, John. *Hitler's Scientists: Science, War and the Devil's Pact.* New York: Penguin Press, 2004.

Court, W.H.B. *Coal.* London: Her Majesty's Stationary Office, 1951.

D'Este, Carlo. *Bitter Victory: The Battle for Sicily, 1943.* London: Collins, 1988.

Dewulf, Jeroen. *Spirit of Resistance: Dutch Clandestine Literature during the Nazi Occupation*. Rochester, New York: Camden House, 2010.
Diamond, Hanna. *Fleeing Hitler: France 1940*. Toronto: Oxford University Press, 2007.
Donnison, F.S.V. *Civil Affairs and Military Government: Central Organization and Planning*. London: Her Majesty's Stationary Office, 1966.
Emsley, Clive. *Exporting British Policing During the Second World War: Policing Soldiers and Civilians*. New York: Bloomsberg, 2017.
Engen, Robert. *Strangers in Arms: Combat Motivation in the Canadian Army, 1943–1945*. Montreal & Kingston: McGill-Queen's University Press, 2016.
Finer, S.E. *The Man on Horseback: The Role of the Military in Politics*. London: F. Pinter, 1988.
Fisher, Thomas R. "Allied Military Government in Italy." *Annals of the American Academy of Political and Social Science* 267 (January 1950): 114–22.
Flint, Edward. "The Development of British Civil Affairs and its Employment in the British Sector of Allied Military Operations During the Battle of Normandy, June to August 1944." Phd diss., Cranfield University. 2008.
Footitt, Hilary, and John Simmonds. *France, 1943–1945*. New York: Holmes and Meier, 1988.
Friedhoff, Herman. *Requiem for the Resistance: The Civilian Struggle Against Nazism in Holland and Germany*. London: Bloomsbury Press, 1988.
Futselaar, Ralf. *Lard, Lice and Longevity: The Standard of Living in Occupied Denmark and the Netherlands, 1940–1945*. Amsterdam: Aksant, 2008.
Fuykschot, Cornelia. *Hunger in Holland: Life During Nazi Occupation*. Amherst: Prometheus Books, 1995.
Gallagher, Robert F. "World War Two Story. United States Army, 815th Anti-Aircraft Artillery Battalion, Third Army." Accessed 2019. https://gallagherstory.com/ww2/index.html.
Glover, Michael. *The Velvet Glove: The Decline and Fall of Moderation in War*. Toronto: Hodder and Stoughton, 1982.
Goddard, Lance. *Canada and the Liberation of the Netherlands, May 1945*. Toronto: Dundern Press, 2005.
Gordon, Hugh Avi. "Cheers and Tears: Relations between Canadian Soldiers and German Civilians, 1944–1946." PhD diss., University of Victoria, 2010.
Great Britain War Office. *Manual of Military Law*. London: Her Majesty's Stationary Office, 1914.
Grimsley, Mark, and Clifford J. Rogers, eds. *Civilians in the Path of War*. London: University of Nebraska Press, 2002.
Hammond, R.J. *Food: Volume II, Studies in Administration and Control*. London: Her Majesty's Stationary Office, 1962.
Harris, C.R.S. *Allied Military Administration of Italy, 1943–1945*. London: Her Majesty's Stationary Office, 1957.
Harris, Joseph P. "Selection and Training of Civil Affairs Officers." *The Public Opinion Quarterly* (winter 1943): 699.

Henshall, Philip. *Hitler's Rocket Sites*. New York: St Martin's Press, 1985.
Hibbert, Joyce. *Fragments of War: Stories from Survivors of World War II*. Toronto: Dundern Press, 1985.
Hirschfeld, Gerhard. *Nazi Rule and Dutch Collaboration: The Netherlands under German Occupation, 1940–1945*. New York: St Martin's Press, 1988.
Hitchcock, William I. *The Bitter Road to Freedom: A New History of the Liberation of Europe*. Toronto: Free Press, 2008.
Hoffman, Reto. *Fascist Effect: Japan and Italy 1915–1952*. Ithaca: Cornell University Press, 2015.
Horn, Michiel. "More than Cigarettes, Sex, and Chocolate: the Canadian Army in the Netherlands, 1944–1945." *Journal of Canada Studies* 16, no. 3–4 (1981): 156–73.
Horne, John, and Alan Kramer. *German Atrocities, 1914: A History of Denial*. New Haven: Yale University Press, 2001.
Inglis, Mathew J. "Civil Affairs and Military Government Operations in Post-Fascist Italy." MA diss., Fort Leavenworth, Kansas: School of Advanced Military Studies, United States Army Command and General Staff College, 2014.
International Committee of the Red Cross: Treaties, States Parties and Commentaries. "Convention (IV) Respecting the Laws and Customs of War on Land and its Annex: Regulations Concerning the Laws and Customs of War on Land. The Hauge, 18 October 1907." https://ihl-databases.icrc.org/ihl/INTRO/195.
Irons, Roy. *Hitler's Terror Weapons: The Price of Vengeance*. London: Harpers Collins, 2002.
Jackson, Julian. *France: The Dark Years, 1940–1944*. New York: Oxford University Press, 2001.
de Jong, Louis. *The Netherlands and Nazi Germany*. Cambridge, MA: Harvard University Press, 1990.
Kasaboski, Tracy, and Kristen Den Hartog. *The Occupied Garden: Recovering the Story of a Family in the War-Torn Netherlands*. Toronto: McClelland and Stewart, 2008.
Kaufman, David, and Michiel Horn. *A Liberation Album: Canadians in the Netherlands 1944–45*. Toronto: McGraw-Hill Ryerson, 1980.
Kedward, H.R. *In Search of the Maquis: Rural Resistance in Southern France, 1942–1944*. Oxford: Clarendon Press, 1993.
Kennedy, Sean. *The Shock of War: Civilian Experiences 1937–1945*. Toronto: University of Toronto Press, 2013.
Knapp, Andrew. "The Destruction and Liberation of Le Havre in Modern Memory." *War in History* 14, no. 4 (2007): 476–98.
Lagrou, Pieter. *The Legacy of Nazi Occupation: Patriotic Memory and National Recovery in Western Europe, 1945–1965*. Cambridge: Cambridge University Press, 2000.
Lamb, Richard. *War in Italy: 1943–1945, A Brutal Story*. London: John Murray, 1993.
Laub, Thomas J. *After the Fall: German Policy in Occupied France, 1940–1944*. London: Oxford University Press, 2012.

Lieber, Francis, and Richard Shelley Hartigan. *Lieber's Code and the Law of War.* Chicago: Precedent, 1983.
Longhurst, Graham M. "The Evolution of Canadian Civil–Military Cooperation (CIMIC)." *Canadian Military Journal* (Winter 2006–07): 55–64.
Martin, Jean. "Un officier canadien avec la 3 armée américaine en 1944, de la Normandie à la Lorraine en passant par l'Anjou." *Revue historique des armées* 266 (15 mars 2012): 63–72.
Milner, Marc. *Stopping the Panzers: The Untold Story of D-Day.* Kansas: University Press of Kansas, 2014.
Moulton, General J.L. *Battle for Antwerp: The Liberation of the City and the Opening of the Scheldt, 1944.* London: Ian Allan, 1978.
Mowat, Farley. *The Regiment.* Toronto: McClelland and Stewart, 1973.
Muschamp, Amy. "Living under Allied Military Government in Southern Italy during the Second world War: A Case Study of the Region of Molise." *Journal of Military History* 79 (April 2015): 372.
NATO. NATO Civil–Military Cooperation (CIMIC) Doctrine: AJP-9. June 2003. www.nato.int/ims/docu/ajp-9.pdf.
Neufeld, Michael J. *The Rocket and the Reich: Peenemunde and the Coming of the Ballistic Missile Era.* Toronto: The Free Press, 1995.
Neville, Peter. *Mussolini.* New York: Routledge, 2015.
O'Brien, Terence H. *Civil Defence.* London: Her Majesty's Stationary Office, 1953.
Patterson, Rebecca. "Revisiting a School of Military Government: How Reanimating a World War II-Era Institution Could Professionalize Military Nation Building." *Kauffman Foundation Research Series: Expeditionary Economics*, June 2011.
Proctor, Tammy M. *Civilians in a World At War, 1914–1918.* New York: New York University Press, 2010.
Rennell, Lord. "Allied Military Government in Occupied Territory." *Royal Institute of International Affairs* 20, no. 3, (July 1944): 307–16.
Roberts, Mary Louise. *D-Day Through French Eyes: Normandy, 1944.* Chicago: University of Chicago Press, 2014.
Schrijvers, Peter. *Liberators: The Allies and Belgian Society, 1944–1945.* London: Cambridge University Press. 2009.
– *The Unknown Dead: Civilians in the Battle of the Bulge.* Kentucky: University Press of Kentucky, 2005.
Schulten, C.M. "Commentary on the Liberation of the Netherlands." In *World War II in Europe: The Final Year*, edited by Charles F. Brower, 209–17. New York: St Martin's Press. 1998.
Semelin, Jacques. *Unarmed against Hitler: Civilian Resistance in Europe, 1939–1943.* London: Praeger, 1993.
Shephard, Ben. "Becoming Planning Minded: The Theory and Practice of Relief 1940-1945." *Journal of Contemporary History* 43, no. 3 (July 2008): 416–17.
Simms, Brendan, and D.J.B. Trim, eds. *Humanitarian Intervention: A History.* London: Cambridge University Press, 2011.

Stacey, C.P. *The Victory Campaign: The Operations in North-West Europe, 1944–1945*. Ottawa: Queen's Printer, 1960.

Stein, Eric. "War, Politics, Law, and Love." *Michigan Journal of International Law* 32 (Spring 2011): 553–70.

Stortz, Paul, and E. Lisa Panayotidis, eds. *Cultures, Communities and Conflict: Histories of Canadian Universities and War*. Toronto: University of Toronto Press, 2012.

Taylor, Lynne. *Between Resistance and Collaboration: Popular Protest in Northern France, 1940–1945*. London: Macmillan Press, 2000.

The Central Statistical Office. *Statistical Digest of the War*. London: Her Majesty's Stationary Office and Longmans, Greens and Co., 1951.

Torrie, Julia S. *For Their Own Good: Civilian Evacuations in Germany and France, 1939–1945*. New York: Berghahn Books, 2010.

United Kingdom Ministry of Defence. *Civil Military Cooperation (CIMIC): Joint Doctrine Publication 3–90*. April 2006. www.mod.uk/NR/rdonlyres/1265DF1B-739A-4CE0-A04D.../jdp3_90.pdf.

United States Army. *Stability Operations: Field Manual 3–07*. October 2008. http://usacac.army.mil/cac2/repository/FM307/FM3-07.pdf.

Van Der Zee, Henri A. *The Hunger Winter: Occupied Holland 1944–1945*. London: Jill Norman and Hobhouse, 1982.

Warmbrunn, Werner. *The Dutch under German Occupation: 1940–1945*. California: Stanford University Press, 1963.

– *The German Occupation of Belgium: 1940–1944*. New York: Peter Lang, 1993.

Warner, Geoffrey. "Allies, Government, and Resistance: The Belgian Political Crisis of November 1944." *Transactions of the Royal Historical Society: Fifth Series* 28 (1978): 48–60.

Werth, Alexander. *France, 1940–1955*. London: Readers Union, 1957.

White Peter. *With the Jocks: A Soldier's Struggle for Europe 1944–1945*. Gloucestershire: Sutton Publishing, 2001.

Wieviorka, Olivier. *Normandy: The Landings to the Liberation of Paris*. Cambridge, MA: Harvard University Press, 2008.

Williams, Jefferey. *Far From Home: A Memoir of a 20th Century Soldier*. Calgary: University of Calgary Press, 2003.

Ziemke, Earl F. *Army Historical Series: The US Army in the Occupation of Germany 1944–1946*. Washington: Center of Military History, United States Army, 1975.

Zuelkhe, Mark. *Forgotten Victory: First Canadian Army and the Cruel Winter of 1944–1945*. Toronto: Douglas & McIntyre, 2014.

– *On to Victory: The Canadian Liberation of the Netherlands, March 23–May 5 1945*. Toronto: Douglas & McIntyre, 2010.

Index

I Canadian Corps Civil Affairs: in Area B-2, 173–80; in the Netherlands, 172–3, 176; relief operations. *See* Operation Faust

II Canadian Corps Civil Affairs: in Boulogne (*see* Boulogne); in Caen (*see* Caen); in Calais (*see* Calais); in Dunkirk (*see* Dunkirk); formation, 64; objectives in northwest Europe, 45–6

II Canadian Corps Military Government, 185–203; dealing with Canadian crimes against German population, 201–20; dealing with the German population, 189–91, 198; hunting Nazi's, 197; MG objectives in Germany, 186; as part of Operation Eclipse, 188–9; responsibility for displaced persons (*see* displaced persons)

ACC (Allied Control Commission): cooperation with AMG, 30; jurisdictional issues, 31–4, 40; formation, 29; in Italy, 25

Adam, Col J.S., 173

Alexander, General Harold, 23; decision to employ a regional approach in Italy, 25–7

Allenby, General Edmund 16

AMG (Allied Military Government), 26–37, 40; administrative issues, 26–7; defascistisation, 32; in Naples (*see* Naples); partisans (*see* resistance groups); problems dealing with the military chain of command, 27–9; problems with ACC, 30–2; reaction by Allied military, 40–1

AMGOT (Allied Military Government of Occupied Territories): debate over indirect vs. direct approach, 24–5; educating soldiers on AMGOT's role, 23–4; in Italy, 20–5; name change to Civil Affairs, 45; objectives in Italy, 22

Antwerp, 123–40; civil defence (*see* civil defence in Antwerp); civil defence in the suburbs, 137–9; first responder services, 130–1; strategic importance, 104; temporary shelters, 134–5

Badoglio, Marshal Pietro, 20, 29; issues with the Allies, 32–3

Barnes, Lt Col Henry: dealing with staff shortages, 127–8; organizing Antwerp's civil defence, 125–6; organizing debris removal teams, 136; re-establishing PLB headquarters, 127; reflecting on CD efforts, 139

Belgium: adapting to a long-term mission, 112; CA objectives, 109; handover to FCA CA, 109–10; liberation, 108; occupation, 106–7; pre-war, 105–6

black market: in Belgium, 118; Canadian complicity in the Belgian black mar-

ket, 119–20; coal (*see* coal shortages); effect on Pierlot's popularity, 122–3; in Germany 201; in Italy, 36–7
Boer War, 14
Bonomi, Ivanoe, 33
Boulogne, 85–92; civilian evacuation, 86–8; relief supplies, 88–90
British Military Administration, 19–20
Byatt, Horace Archer, 16

Caen: civilian evacuation, 66–71; destruction, 65; establishing law and order, 75–7; establishing spearhead detachments, 7; morale of civilians, 69; problems with decentralized command structure, 71; problems with returning refugees, 71–4
Calais, 92–5; civilian evacuations, 93–4
Casablanca Conference, 20–1
Cazanove, Gen Franck, 148, 150
Charlottesville School of Military Government, 48
Civil Affairs Training Schools (CATS), 48
civil defence in Antwerp, 124–40; German efforts at CD, 124–5
civilian evacuations: in Boulogne, 86–8
Clayton, General Sir Gilbert, 16
coal shortages: in Belgium, 121–2; in the Netherlands, 155–7
Comité Français de Libération Nationale (CFLN), 61; as the GPRF, 62
Coté, Lt Col Ernest, 88–90, 99
Coulet, Francois, 41
Cox, Sir Percy, 15
Crerar, Gen Harry, 145

DCA (Directorate, Civil Affairs), 52–3
de Gaulle, Charles: concerns over French sovereignty, 58; reaction to AMG, 41–2; relationship with Allied military leadership, 62–3
displaced persons, 191–6; classifying DPs, 192; dealing with increasing numbers, 195; liberated POWs, 200; threat to law and order, 198–201

Dunkirk, 95–7; civilian evacuations, 96–7

Eisenhower, General Dwight D., 23, 30, 32

Falaise Pocket, 78–80; First Canadian Army logistical issues, 79–80
Fergusson, Lt General Sir Charles, 17–18
First Canadian Army Civil Affairs: becomes operational, 68; transitions to MG, 186
food shortages: in Belgium, 112; fears of Dutch starvation, 170–1; in Germany 190–1; in Italy, 35–7; in the Netherlands, 167; relief operations in liberated Netherlands, 171–5; relief operations in occupied Netherlands, 175–80; supply procedures in the Netherlands, 168–9
Foulkes, Gen. Charles, 96, 172
French Forces of the Interior (FFI). *See* resistance groups

G-5, 23, 141, 147
Galloway, Major General Alexander, 175
Grasett, Lt General Alexander, 23, 53

Le Havre, 83–5
Henderson, Col. George P., 64
historiography, 7–9
Holmes, Colonel Julius C. Holmes, 23
Hurley, Col. J.J., 79; at Boulogne, 86; commenting on the coal crisis in the Netherlands, 156; dealing with logistical issues, 80; dealing with the Belgian resistance, 115; meeting with Col Schroeder at Calais, 95; promoted to DDMG II Can Corps CA, 188

internationalization of CA personnel, 51

Kirby, Major General Stanley, 52

Labrosse, Captain J.E.G, 72; in Belgium 119, 121–2; setting up a transit camp in

INDEX

Germany, 193–5; on Walcheren Island, 163
laws of war regarding civilians and soldiers, 18–19
Lee, Brigadier Swinton, 52
looting: in Caen, 74–7; in Germany, 201–2

Maude, Lt General Stanley, 16
Maxwell, Major General John, 14
Military Government; II Canadian Corps in Germany (*see* II Canadian Corps Military Government); in German East Africa, 16; in Mesopotamia, 15; in Palestine, 16–17; in the Rhineland, 17–18; in South Africa, 14
Milner, Sir Alfred, 14
Montgomery, General Bernard, 25; attempt to shed responsibility for CA, 140–2; establishing Netherlands District, 175; importance of Antwerp, 104; strategy for the channel ports, 80–1
Morgan, General Sir Frederick, 81
Mussolini, Benito, 20–1

Naples, 37–42; food crisis 38–9; typhus 40
the Netherlands: Allied strategy, 147; under German occupation, 145–6
Netherlands District, 175–80
Netherlands Military Administration, 148; dealing with the refugee problem, 159; difficulty finding accommodation for refugees, 165; distributing food, 173; early difficulties, 149–54; issues with coal distribution, 156; problems with the resistance, 153–5; taking command of relief supplies, 169
northern France: CA objectives, 57–8, under German occupation 60–1; indirect vs. direct approach, 58; logistical issues after Falaise, 81; refugee policy, 58–9

OETA (Occupied Enemy Territory Administration): East Africa as BMA, 19; in Palestine, 16–17
Operation Eclipse, 185
Operation Faust, 177
Operation Husky, 25
Operation Veritable, 184

partisans. *See* resistance groups
Pierlot, Hubert, 111; black market problems, 118, 120–3; dealing with resistance groups, 113, 117; poor leadership, 112
PLB (Passieve Lucht-Bescherming), 125–8; equipment and vehicle shortages, 128–9; training, 129–30, 135–8
Pretyman, Major General George T., 14

refugees: in Caen 66–8, 70–4; in Calais, 94; in Dunkirk, 96; evacuations from the Breskens Pocket, 161; evacuations from Walcheren Island, 162; in Italy, 34–5; in the Netherlands, 158–66; in northern France 58–60, 101
Reid, Major A.K., 7
Rennell, Lord Major General Francis Rodd: on ACC-AMG tension, 31; on food shortages in Italy, 36; leading AMGOT, 22; as lecturer at CA school, 24; in Naples, 38
resistance groups: in Belgium, 113–18; in France, 98–100; in Italy, 33–4; in the Netherlands, 153–5
Robbins, Brigadier Thomas, 53; stepping down as DCA, 187
Royal Military College Civil Affairs School, 47; curriculum, 50; discussions to create all-Canadian civil affairs group, 50–2; recruits, 49

Seyss-Inquart, Arthur, 146; agreement to allow relief to western Netherlands, 176
SHAEF Mission (Netherlands), 148; controlling supply depots, 168
Simonds, Gen. Guy, 96, 145
Smith, Professor G.M., 50

spearhead detachments, 55
static detachments, 56–7
structure of CA organization, 53–4

Templer Major General Gerald, 187–8
training, 46–7; debates over opening a Canadian training program, 48–9

Usher, Col. Charles, 65, 71
Utrecht, 174

V-weapons, 123–4; attacks on Antwerp, 132–3, 137

Wedd, Brigadier-General W.B., 48, 51, 53, 64, 70; asserting FCA CA authority, 154, 157; in Belgium, 111; as DDCA/MG, 189, 195; dealing with attacks against German civilians, 200; frustrations with NMA, 151–2; on handover to civilian authorities, 100–2; on looting, 76; in the Netherlands, 149
Wimbledon Civil Affairs Staff Centre, 47